Students Library

Mary in Our Life

MARY IN OUR LIFE

BY

WILLIAM G. MOST

Associate Professor of Classical Languages
Loras College

New York
P. J. KENEDY & SONS

NIHIL OBSTAT: Ernestus P. Ament
   Censor Deputatus
IMPRIMATUR: ✠ Henricus P. Rohlman
   Archiepiscopus Dubuquensis
Die 6 ianuarii 1954
Die 15 augusti 1954

First Edition, May 1954
Second Edition, January 1955

To the Sacred Heart of Jesus

THROUGH THE IMMACULATE HEART OF MARY
THAT THEIR KINGDOM MAY COME
IN THE HEARTS OF ALL MEN

PRAYER OF POPE PIUS XII
Composed for the Marian Year, 1954

ENRAPTURED by the splendor of your heavenly beauty, and impelled by the anxieties of the world, we cast ourselves into your arms, O Immaculate Mother of Jesus and our Mother, Mary, confident of finding in your most loving heart appeasement of our ardent desires, and a safe harbor from the tempests which beset us on every side.

THOUGH degraded by our faults and overwhelmed by infinite misery, we admire and praise the peerless richness of sublime gifts with which God has filled you, above every other mere creature, from the first moment of your Conception until the day on which, after your Assumption into heaven, He crowned you Queen of the Universe.

O CRYSTAL Fountain of faith, bathe our minds with the eternal truths! O fragrant Lily of all holiness, captivate our hearts with your heavenly perfume! O Conqueress of evil and death, inspire in us a deep horror of sin which makes the soul detestable to God and a slave of hell!

O WELL-BELOVED of God, hear the ardent cry which rises up from every heart in this year dedicated to you. Bend tenderly over our aching wounds. Convert the wicked, dry the tears of the afflicted and oppressed, comfort the poor and humble, quench hatreds, sweeten harshness, safeguard the flower of purity in youth, protect the holy Church, make all men feel the attraction of Christian goodness. In your name, resounding harmoniously in heaven, may they recognize that they are brothers, and that the nations are members of one family, upon which may there shine forth the sun of a universal and sincere peace.

RECEIVE, O Most Sweet Mother, our humble supplications, and above all obtain for us that, one day, happy with you, we may repeat before your throne that hymn which today is sung on earth around your altars: You are all beautiful, O Mary! You are the glory, you are the joy, you are the honor of our people! Amen.

Preface

THE THEME of this book can be summed up in one sentence: God has given to Mary an all-pervading place in the work of the Redemption; therefore, if we wish to imitate the ways of God as perfectly as possible, we should give her a corresponding place in our spiritual lives.

We are going to study both aspects of that theme: the dogmas that show Mary's place in the plans of God, and the means by which we can make our lives harmonize with God's plans. For doctrine and devotion are closely interrelated. Our devotion must be solidly grounded on the firm rock of dogma; otherwise devotion will be shallow. But knowledge of dogma should deepen devotion; otherwise we may become hard. In our Introduction we present the deeper reasons why devotion should flow from doctrine, so that the reader may gain the maximum profit from this book.

The two aspects of our theme indicate the twofold division of the book. The first part (chapters I–VIII) analyzes Mary's place in the Redemption, from the first promise of the Redeemer in paradise, to her role in the second coming of Christ at the end of the world. This dogmatic section rests chiefly on a careful analysis of the most recent papal statements on Mary's place in the entire scheme of the Redemption. The major emphasis and attention are given to those truths that are most intimately related to the development of a *sound Marian spirituality*.

Now, if Mary is to pervade all our spiritual life, we should not be satisfied merely with certain prayers or particular devotional exercises in her honor: we should bring her influence into the most basic structure of our spiritual life. For this reason, the second section opens with a group of seven chapters on the general principles of the spiritual life, explained in such a way as to show how Mary is our model and constant companion and helper. These chapters draw chiefly on the works of St. Thomas Aquinas, St. Francis de Sales, St. John of the Cross, St. Teresa of Avila, St. Thérèse of Lisieux, and St. Louis de Montfort; the best works of modern theologians are also utilized. In these chapters we discover the very essence of spiritual growth — growth in love of God and neighbor. We study the principal virtues that make room for love: humility and mortification. We examine the nature and the normal stages in the development of mental prayer, from the meditation of beginners up to the first forms of mystical infused prayer. After this we discuss the great means of grace — the Mass and the Sacraments, and Mary's relation to them (XVI–XVII). We then study total consecration to Mary, a great means that in itself is a synthesis of all other means (XVIII): if a soul lives out its consecration perfectly, it will be more and more guided and moved by the Holy Spirit, whose Spouse Mary is (XIX). But devotion to Mary is meant to lead us through her Immaculate Heart to the Sacred Heart of her Son; therefore chapter XX treats the relation between these two Hearts in our devotion. We then consider certain outward aspects of devotion to Mary: her recent apparitions, and the classic Marian devotions of the Rosary and the Scapular (XXI–XXII). The final chapter (XXIII) completes the program with some specific suggestions for forming a private Marian rule of life.

Readers in France, Germany, Spain, and Italy today are able to obtain precise and thorough information about Mariology from many works in their native languages. Now, while there are many excellent books about Mary in English, few of them set out to give the reader a precise, documented study. While the pronouncements emanating from the Holy See over the past century have been numerous and rich, most American readers have heard of little more than the definition of the Assumption. Hence this book aims in a very modest way to help make more readily available to American readers some part of what readers in many other nations already possess. It is designed, therefore, for anyone who desires to have theologically exact, documented information presented in language that he can understand even though he has not had the advantage of formal courses in philosophy and theology.

Again, many writers, *after* offering a detailed presentation of basic spiritual principles and their applications, urge us to give Mary a large place in our personal spiritual lives. But it is not too easy to find works that actually show in detail and in a practical fashion how this can be done, how to bring Mary's influence into the basic structure of our spiritual lives. The second part attempts to fill that need to some extent. In the course of that part, many difficult but practical problems are faced and a solution is attempted. Therefore it is hoped that the book will be helpful to the many good people today who sincerely want to grow spiritually, but who do not know precisely how to go about it.

The book was first written as a series of chapters for Mariology study clubs at Loras College. The actual experience and the suggestions of these groups have shown the way to many revisions and improvements. The questions have been retained at the end of the book, for the benefit of other such study groups, or for classes in Mariology using this book as a text. The material should be sufficient for a semester's course in college.

Sincere thanks and appreciation are due to many friends who have helped in this work. A large number of Mariologists and other theologians have kindly answered personal letters of consultation. But thanks are especially due to those who read various portions of the manuscript, and made valuable suggestions: Juniper Carol, O.F.M., founder and at this writing president of the Mariological Society of America; Eamon Carroll, O. Carm., of the Carmelite College of St. Albert, Rome; John A. Driscoll, O.P., Joseph B. Malvey, O.P., and Augustine Rock, O.P., of the Dominican House of Studies, Dubuque, Iowa; Sebastian Carlson, O.P., of the Dominican House of Studies, River Forest, Ill.; Charles T. Hunter, S.J., of St. Stanislaus Seminary, Florissant, Mo.; Christian Ceroke, O. Carm., of Whitefriars Hall at the Catholic University of America, Washington, D.C.; Roger M.

Charest, S.M.M., of the De Montfort Fathers, Bay Shore, L.I.; and Richard L. Rooney, S.J., of the Queen's Work staff, St. Louis, Mo.

My thanks are extended also to the publishers mentioned below, for their kind permission to quote from certain of their publications:

B. Herder Book Co. (*Christian Perfection and Contemplation, The Mother of the Saviour,* and *The Three Ages of the Interior Life,* all by R. Garrigou-Lagrange);

The Newman Press (*St. Irenaeus: Proof of the Apostolic Preaching; The Complete Works of St. John of the Cross; Treatise on the Love of God, Spiritual Conferences,* and *Introduction to the Devout Life,* all by St. Francis de Sales; *The Practice of Mental Prayer,* by G. Bélorgey; *St. John of the Cross,* by Gabriel of St. Mary Magdalen; *Exhortations, Conferences, and Instructions,* by St. Jane Frances Frémyot de Chantal; *Prayer,* by T. V. Moore; and *Your Brown Scapular,* by E. K. Lynch);

Sheed & Ward, Inc. (*The Complete Works of St. Teresa of Jesus;* and *The Collected Letters of St. Thérèse of Lisieux*).

Finally, I wish to express very sincere appreciation to the editorial staff of P. J. Kenedy & Sons for many excellent suggestions that have resulted in substantial improvement in this book.

WILLIAM G. MOST

Loras College, Dubuque, Iowa
Feast of the Immaculate Conception,
First Day of the First Marian Year, December 8, 1953

Bibliographical Note

ALL quotations from St. John of the Cross are taken from *The Complete Works of St. John of the Cross,* translated by E. Allison Peers (Westminster, Newman Press, 1946). All quotations from St. Teresa of Avila are taken from *The Complete Works of St. Teresa of Jesus,* translated by E. Allison Peers (New York, Sheed and Ward, 1949). In citing references to these works in the Notes, the first notation refers to the individual title (e.g., *The Dark Night of the Soul),* and the numerals following in parentheses refer to the position of this title in the collected works.

In references to other spiritual classics (e.g., *The City of God, The Introduction to the Devout Life),* the numerals refer to the standard divisions of these works, common to all editions.

For the sake of uniformity, the Douay-Rheims translation is used almost entirely in quotations from Sacred Scripture. With the exception of these scriptural passages and certain quotations from other texts as indicated in the Notes, the translations are original with the author.

The following abbreviations are used in the Notes to indicate frequently cited sources:

> AER — *American Ecclesiastical Review*
> AAS — *Acta Apostolicae Sedis*
> ASS — *Acta Sanctae Sedis*
> PL — J. P. Migne, *Patrologia Latina*
> ST — St. Thomas Aquinas, *Summa Theologica*

W. G. M.

Contents

xiii

Introduction ...

Knowledge and Love

MANY an eloquent speaker has told his hearers: "To know God is to love Him." The statement is true but is easily misunderstood. It certainly does not mean that a mere increase in information about God automatically increases love. If such were the case, every good theologian would inevitably be on fire with love of God; whereas it is all too true that some persons with but little instruction in the faith may show more love than many a theologian. What the statement does mean is this: The more one knows, the more he *ought* to love God, the more *motives* he has at his disposal which should urge him on to love.

There are various ways in which we may know the truths about God. In heaven there is direct, face-to-face knowledge of God; in that vision it is impossible not to love. But in this life our knowledge is indirect, in a mirror, in a dim manner — to paraphrase St. Paul.[1] Now, there are two kinds of knowledge in this life. Suppose I read in the news that there is a famine in India. I know that fact and accept it without question, yet it probably does not impress me deeply. Were I to go to India, and perhaps even feel hunger myself, I would not merely add new facts and details to my knowledge; what is more important, I would *realize* my knowledge. We might call my first knowledge "notional knowledge." The second kind would be "realized knowledge." The first has little if any effect on our lives; the second is vital.

Our knowledge of the truths of faith tends to remain to a large extent in the class of notional knowledge. Of course we accept these truths. With the help of grace, we would stand ready to die rather than deny them. But at present our knowledge is apt to remain mostly notional — we do not *realize* it sufficiently.

In the pages that follow we hope to learn a great many things about Mary. But if this knowledge is to remain merely notional, unrealized, it will do us little good. In fact, it might even be somewhat harmful to us. The reason is simple: in learning these things, we have at hand the motives for greater love of God (for love of Mary is a means to love of God). When God gives us better opportunities, He expects more of us. The greater the talents given us, the greater the return we should make. But if we learn much about God and about Mary and remain untouched by this new knowledge, we are apt to become calloused, hardened, blinded — for we do not respond to motives that ought to fire us with love.

Cardinal Manning gives us a forceful description of an extreme case of hardness, that of a sinful priest whose life does not correspond with his knowledge of God:

> Next to the immutable malice of Satan is the hardness of an impenitent priest. Priests who fall, if they do not return to God with greater facility and speed than other men, may become blinder and more hardened in heart than all other sinners.[2]

The Cardinal continues, explaining the reason for this extreme hardness:

> They have been so long familiar with all the eternal truths, they have preached them so often . . . they have had so great a profusion of lights . . . and all in vain, that their end is like the dying man, on whom all remedies, medicine, and skill have been exhausted, but death has fastened so firmly that the dying must surely die.

The fundamental reason underlying the development of hardness is this: there ought to be a harmony between our words and our acts,[3] between what we believe and what we do. If there is such a harmony, all is well. If not, a tension arises.[4] Our faith says: "Only the things of eternity are really worth while," but our actions say: "The things of eternity are of little or no importance." In time one of the conflicting sides must give in. Either a man will bring his actions into accord with his faith and his knowledge, or he will bring his beliefs into accord with his actions.

There are many degrees of hardness. In general, the further a man's conduct varies from what his faith and knowledge call for, the more hardness is likely to result. A layman who avoids mortal sin, but in other respects shows scant signs of any thought of eternity, develops a lesser callousness than the sinful priest. But Catholics who live for a long time in many habitual mortal sins may find that hardness can advance even to complete loss of faith.

There is a striking example of misused knowledge in the Gospels. When the Magi from the East came to Jerusalem to see the newborn Saviour, they appealed to King Herod for help in their quest. Herod, though not himself a Jew, knew perfectly well where this information could be obtained. Calling in the Jewish theologians, he asked them where the Christ was to be born. These learned men were easily able to give the right answer to Herod and the Magi: Christ was to be born in Bethlehem. They knew that answer; they knew all the prophecies about Him: yet they themselves did not find Him. Their knowledge was not a realized, a vital thing for them; instead, they were puffed up with pride. Far from being an asset to them, their learning was actually a liability, since it served not to increase their love of God, but to inflate their pride.

Hence it should be clear that in starting out to learn more about the things of God we are taking on a greater responsibility. Our sins, if we continue to commit them, will be more terrible from the very fact that we will know more of the goodness of God and the horror of sin. We must work and pray diligently for an increase of love to match our new knowledge lest we become mere windbags of pride.

There is, however, a pleasant side to the picture. If love keeps pace with knowledge, the result is an ever-growing, solid spiritual structure; mere knowledge puffs up, but love builds up solidly.[5] Not a hardened conscience, but a deeper spiritual insight is the result when a person lives his beliefs; his perception and grasp of spiritual things is sharpened. Of this St. Augustine writes: "For this [understanding] is the effect of pure and simple love of God, which gives the greatest power of vision in moral matters." [6]

Therefore it will help greatly if our reading of the following chapters is meditative and accompanied by prayer. This will be particularly the case in the first eight chapters, which are primarily dogmatic. Some of the truths in them can be properly appreciated only with the help of thought and prayer. That means an effort — but the effort will be found worth while, for solid devotion, such as we hope to learn in the second group of chapters, can be built only upon the firm ground of dogma.

This meditative approach is already a large step toward using our knowledge as a means to love. In so doing, we will not resemble the Jewish theologians who could point out the place where Christ was to be found and yet not find Him, but we will imitate Mary who "kept all these words, pondering them in her heart." [7]

NOTES

1. I Cor. 13:12: "We see now through a glass in a dark manner; but then face to face."

2. Henry Edward Manning, *The Eternal Priesthood* (Baltimore, no date), 275–76.

3. When we speak of acts we do not mean only *external* activity: we mean to include *interior* activity as well, such as recollection, meditation, acts of love, and of other virtues. Some have erred greatly in virtually identifying the service of God with bustling exterior activity, to the detriment of an interior life. The spirit of recollection and love withers in such externalism. Outward activity not supported by a deep interior life is sterile. Pope Pius XII speaks of this distorted emphasis on feverish activity as "the heresy of action." See his apostolic exhortation, *Menti nostrae* (September 23, 1950), par. 60, in the NCWC translation.

4. See St. Augustine, *The City of God*, XIX, 13: "The peace of a rational soul is the well-ordered harmony of knowledge and action."

5. See I Cor. 8:1: "Knowledge puffeth up, but charity edifieth."

6. *De Moribus Ecclesiae Catholicae* XVII, 31. Compare the sixth beatitude: "Blessed are the clean of heart, for they shall see God."

7. Luke 2:19.

Mary in Our Life

I ... The Fathers of the Church and the New Eve

A FASCINATING PROBLEM appears in the writings of the early Fathers of the Church on the Blessed Virgin. For there is a remarkably persistent title for Mary which begins to appear in the works of the Fathers when the Apostolic Age is barely ended, and which swells until it finds a place in the writings of practically all the Fathers of the following centuries. The Fathers love to think of Mary as "the New Eve." A little thought will show that many important truths about Mary and her position in the plans of God may be implied in this title. The problem is to find out precisely which ideas we may legitimately see as contained in it.

St. Paul in several places in his Epistles had used similar expressions to refer to Our Lord. Thus, for example, in writing to the Corinthians, he says: "The first man Adam was made into a living soul; the last Adam into a quickening spirit." [1] Christ is, then, the New Adam. Sin and death came into the world through the first Adam, but abundant restoration came through the New Adam: " ... by one man sin entered into this world and by sin death";[2] but " ... as in Adam all die, so also in Christ all shall be made alive." [3]

It may be that the early Fathers of the Church derived their idea of the New Eve from the oral teaching of the Apostles, or it may be that they took up the very open hints in the writings of St. Paul. Certainly it is not hard to see that if there was a New Adam, Christ, to outbalance the old Adam, there should also be a New Eve, Mary, to outbalance the old Eve. For St. Paul said that the Redemption was superabundant: " . . . where sin abounded, grace did more abound." [4]

The Fathers love to dwell on the contrast of Mary and Eve.

1

God had made great plans for the first Eve, but she, in her disobedience, blocked the original design of God. God, however,
found a remedy that would more than compensate for Eve: in
Mary He would have all that He had desired in the first Eve, and
much more.

The possibilities implied in this parallel and contrast are numerous. When God made the first Eve, He created her without
any stain of sin on her soul: she was immaculate. Hence we
wonder: Does the concept of Mary as the New Eve imply that
she, too, was to be conceived immaculate? God had planned that
the first Eve should be in the fullest sense "the mother of all
the living." [5] For she, with Adam, was not only to transmit
physical life to all mankind: she, with him, was to hand on also
all the other rich gifts of God, including the greatest gift of all,
God's grace. If, then, Mary is the New Eve in a superabundant
redemption, is she to become the channel through which all
graces will come to men? God had planned that Adam and Eve,
if they had been victorious over sin, would also have been victorious over death, so that He would take both their bodies and
their souls into Heaven immediately after their stay in this world.
Therefore we may also ask whether the New Eve, by virtue of her
share in the victory of the New Adam over death and sin, should
be taken body and soul into Heaven even before the general
resurrection.

It would be difficult for us, merely using our own reasoning
powers, to be sure that such truths as these really are contained
in the Fathers' concept of a New Eve. We can come to certainty
only through the interpretations of the Church, the living guard-
ian and interpreter of the revelation given to us in Scripture and
Tradition. For before He died, Our Lord promised to send the
Holy Spirit to the Church: " . . . He will teach you all things,
and bring all things to your mind, whatsoever I shall have said
to you." [6]

This is not a promise that the Church is to receive any new
public revelation[7] through the promised guidance of the Holy
Spirit. What Our Lord meant is that the Church is given an ever-

deepening appreciation of the truths contained in the original revelation. Truths that were always present, but were seen only dimly, were to be illuminated more and more clearly at opportune times throughout all succeeding ages. Therefore the Church at various times is enabled by the divine guidance to make clear and explicit statements on truths that were only implicitly contained or dimly perceived in the original revelation.

In this way the Church has, in our own day, given us the answers to the questions we have just raised. Yes, Mary, the New Eve, was conceived immaculate: Pope Pius IX in 1854 defined that truth, and in the very bull of definition told us that the Fathers had used the Eve-Mary comparison to show Mary's original innocence.[8] And ninety-six years later Pope Pius XII solemnly defined that the New Eve was taken body and soul into Heaven. In the document of definition, the Holy Father gave the New Eve teaching of the Fathers as one of his principal proofs.[9] We likewise wondered whether Mary as the New Eve was also to be the new "mother of the living," so that all graces would pass through her hands. Although they have not yet declared it in the form of a solemn definition, many recent Popes have taught in a binding and authoritative manner[10] that Mary really is the Mediatrix of all graces.

But there is another, even more striking possibility in the New Eve concept: the Fathers assign to Mary a certain role in redeeming us. Before trying to determine precisely what that role involves, it is well to define a few terms. There are two stages in the Redemption: the first consists in Christ's atonement and once-for-all *acquisition* of the entire treasury of all grace for mankind.[11] This was accomplished through the whole life and death of our Saviour, culminating on Calvary, and is called the *objective redemption*. The second stage is the *distribution* of that forgiveness and grace to men; it is called the *subjective redemption*.

It is obvious at once that Mary co-operated in the objective redemption, *at least remotely*, by being the Mother of the Redeemer. But did she also share *immediately* in the objective redemption by serving in the role of the New Eve on Calvary it-

self? If she co-operated immediately in the objective redemption
on Calvary, *then what the Eternal Father accepted was a JOINT
OFFERING, made by the New Adam, and, through Him, with
Him, and subordinate to Him, by the New Eve.* We shall try to
find out, therefore, if the Fathers really do extend their idea of
the New Eve to Calvary itself.

One of the earliest writers to compare Mary to Eve is St. Justin
the Martyr. This learned saint — for he was a philosopher before
he became a Christian — was born in Palestine not long after the
year A.D. 100. Thus he was probably born not long after the
death of the Apostle St. John; certainly he lived in an age when
memories of the preaching of the Apostles were fresh. In his
Dialogue with Trypho he says that Christ

> . . . was made man of the Virgin, so that the disobedience
> brought on by the serpent might be cancelled out in the same
> manner in which it had begun.

St. Justin continues, contrasting the disobedience of Eve with the
obedience of Mary:

> For Eve . . . conceiving the word from the serpent, brought forth
> disobedience and death. But Mary . . . when the angel announced
> to her that the Spirit of the Lord would come upon her . . .
> answered: Be it done to me according to your word.[12]

We notice that St. Justin not only thinks of Mary as the New
Eve; he considers it part of God's plan that the disobedience of
Adam and Eve should "be cancelled out in the same manner in
which it had begun." This statement is of crucial importance. In
the fall of our first parents, *two* persons had taken part. One was
Adam, the real head of the human race. If he alone had fallen, it
would have been enough to plunge mankind into original sin.
Eve, on the other hand, was not head of the race. If she alone had
sinned, we would have had a bad example but would not have
contracted original sin.[13] But the actual fact is that *original sin was
a joint work;* both Adam and Eve co-operated in it, if in different

ways. Only Adam could ruin us — but Eve did what she could. In her inferior way she shared in the fall. . . . It seems quite possible that St. Justin is implying that *the objective redemption was also a joint work,* in which the New Eve shared *as immediately* as the first Eve had shared in the fall.

The words of another Father of the second century, St. Irenaeus, carry special weight. For St. Irenaeus not only traveled widely throughout the Christian world, residing at different times in both Asia Minor and in Gaul, but he was also a friend of St. Polycarp — and St. Polycarp had been a disciple of St. John the Apostle. Thus St. Irenaeus is but one step removed from the Apostle. Moreover, he is known to have listened eagerly to St. Polycarp's recollections of St. John.[14] There are several passages[15] in the writings of St. Irenaeus in which Mary is compared to Eve. Probably the most important of these is found in his work *Against Heresies:*

> Just as she . . . being disobedient, became a cause of death for herself and the whole human race: so Mary . . . being obedient, became a cause of salvation for herself and the whole human race.[16]

These words of St. Irenaeus could imply that Mary was associated with Christ as the New Eve even on Calvary. But he continues with a comparison that is even more suggestive:

> . . . for in no other way can that which is tied be untied unless the very windings of the knot are gone through in reverse: so that the first joints are loosed through the second, and the second in turn free the first. . . . Thus, then, the knot of the disobedience of Eve was untied through the obedience of Mary.

We are asked to imagine a complex knot. To untie it, we must make the rope pass through the same movements that were used in tying the knot — but in reverse. Mary, says St. Irenaeus, undoes the work of Eve. *Now it was not just in a remote way that Eve had been involved in original sin: she shared in the very ruinous act itself. Similarly, it would seem, Mary ought to share in the very act by which the knot is untied — that is, in Calvary itself.*

St. Irenaeus and St. Justin are witnesses of what was believed in the second century in the Church in Asia Minor, Gaul, and Palestine. In addition, St. Irenaeus provides us, through St. Polycarp, with an especially close link to the Apostle St. John. The belief of the Church in Africa during the same period is attested to by Tertullian, who, in his work *On the Flesh of Christ,* also compares and contrasts Mary and Eve, and, like St. Justin and St. Irenaeus, points out the similarity between the manner of the fall and the manner of the restoration:

> ... God, *by a rival method,* restored His image and likeness. ... For into Eve when she was yet a virgin had crept the word that established death; likewise, into a Virgin was to be brought the Word of God that produced life: so that what had gone to ruin by the one sex might be restored to salvation by the same sex.[17] [*Emphasis added.*]

The compact expression "by a rival method" means that the method that God intended to use in the restoration was one that ran parallel to the way in which the fall had taken place. Now, in the fall there was *a joint work shared by two,* though in different ways; and the implication is that the same sharing was found in the restoration.

By means of these three witnesses, then, we see that in the second century, when memories of the preaching of the Apostles were still vivid, the Church in every land in which it existed taught that Mary is the New Eve. Each of these three writers, though in different ways, pointed out the parallel between the fall and the restoration. But someone may object that these early Fathers had in mind merely the remote co-operation of Mary in the objective redemption by the fact that she was Mother of the Redeemer. It is true that some of their words do refer especially to the Annunciation, and it is true that Mary shared in the objective redemption *at least* by being the Mother of Christ. But we must not forget that these early writers were accustomed to think of the Redemption as *a unified whole,* embracing the entire life of Our Lord, beginning at the Annunciation, and culminating on Calvary. For although the Redemption was not to be accomplished without Calvary, yet we must not forget that Christ merited for us throughout *all* His life, not only on the Cross. Therefore, since the Fathers had this *unified* character of the objective redemption so firmly in mind, and since the words they use can easily be understood as applying to the whole process of the restoration, why should we make a restriction or limitation where they make none? Why should we not suppose that the New Eve principle extends even to Calvary?

It is true that our own unaided reasoning cannot give us certitude that the Fathers meant to imply that Mary was the New Eve even on Calvary. But, just as the guidance of the Church has solved other questions for us, telling us that Mary was conceived immaculate, that she was assumed into Heaven, that she is the Mediatrix of all graces, so we hope that a study of the papal documents [18] will bring us the answer to this remaining question.[19]

NOTES

1. I Cor. 15:45.
2. Rom. 5:12.
3. I Cor. 15:22.
4. Rom. 5:20.
5. Gen. 3:20.
6. John 14:26.
7. On private revelations, see chap. XXI.
8. In the *Ineffabilis Deus,* Pope Pius IX said: "And therefore, to prove the original innocence and justice of the Mother of God, they [the Fathers] not only compared her very frequently with Eve, while the latter was still a virgin, still innocent, and still undefiled, and not yet deceived by the death-dealing snares of the treacherous serpent, but they also put her ahead of Eve, using a wonderful variety of thoughts and expressions. For Eve miserably obeyed the serpent, and fell from original innocence and became his slave, but the most Blessed Virgin, constantly increasing the original gift, not only never gave ear to the serpent, but with the strength that was divinely given her, completely destroyed his power and strength." See also J. Keuppens, *Mariologiae Compendium* (2d ed.; Menin, 1947), p. 95.
9. The words of Pope Pius XII are quoted and discussed in chap. VI.
10. See chap. V. The papal teaching on Mary as Mediatrix of all graces

is found in encyclicals and similar papal documents. On the doctrinal authority of such texts, see the first part of chap. III.

11. For more theologically precise definitions, see Appendix III **A**.
12. St. Justin Martyr, *Dialogue with Trypho*, 100.
13. *ST*, I–II, q.81, a.5.
14. See J. Quasten, *Patrology* (Westminster, 1950), I, 287, 297–99.
15. Other passages are quoted in Appendix I.
16. St. Irenaeus, *Against Heresies*, III, xxii, 4.
17. Tertullian, *On the Flesh of Christ*, 17.
18. This examination will be made in chap. III.
19. For additional New Eve passages, see Appendix I.

II ... *Gabriel and the Mother of Christ*

IN SPEAKING of Mary as the New Eve, the Fathers have shown us that Mary in some way co-operated in redeeming us. Only the guidance of the Church can tell us whether or not Mary's role as the New Eve extended even to Calvary, but before we examine the words of the Popes on this matter, it is worth while to look more carefully at that part of her share that is entirely clear: the divine motherhood.

Mary could not, of course, merit that the Incarnation should take place, nor could she merit that she be chosen Mother of Christ, for these are part of the very foundation on which all merit depends. But she could and did merit an acceleration of the time of the Incarnation. Even the saintly patriarchs in the Old Testament had done this; how much more she must have done! Now if Mary could not, strictly speaking, merit that she should be chosen to be the Mother of Christ, how is it that in the hymn, the *Regina Caeli*, we sing: "For He whom thou didst merit to bear . . . has risen"? St. Thomas gives this explanation:

> The Blessed Virgin is said to have merited to bear the Lord of all, not that she merited that He be incarnated, but that she, by means of the grace given her, merited that degree of purity and holiness so that she could be *fittingly* the Mother of God.[1]

That is, with the initial grace given her as a foundation, she merited such a degree of sanctity as was fitting for the Mother of God to have, so that it was becoming that God's gratuitous choice of her be put into effect.[2]

Let us try to reconstruct the scene. Mary is a young girl, probably about the age of fifteen. She is known by her neighbors in the insignificant town of Nazareth as a very good person, but remarkable in no other way. We do not know for how many years she may have lived at Nazareth; a very old and quite respectable tradition states that she spent her early life at the temple in Jerusalem. We are certain, from the institution of the feast of the Presentation on November 21, that she was presented there. And it is quite probable that the old tradition is correct.[3]

Whether her early years were spent in the temple or elsewhere, she obviously was a devout girl, meditating carefully on whatever instruction she was able to obtain, and on the Scriptures that she heard read in the synagogues or temple. Mary was betrothed to Joseph, who, in spite of the many unfortunate portraits of him, was probably a young man (the idea that he was old is based on a thoroughly unreliable tradition found in some apocryphal works). This betrothal had all the legal effects of a marriage, except that it was not customary for the betrothed persons to live together until after another ceremony, the marriage itself. Mary had obviously made a vow of virginity, and, doubtless, Joseph had learned of this and agreed.[4]

For many centuries all God's works had been aimed at one day — the day on which He sent His archangel Gabriel to the house of Mary at Nazareth. The angel greeted her: "Hail, full of grace, the Lord is with thee; blessed art thou among women." Such a greeting, coming from a messenger of the heavenly court, was an overwhelming honor. It was a jolt to the humility of Mary. No wonder that she "was troubled." The angel continued:

> Fear not, Mary, for thou hast found grace with God. Behold thou shalt conceive in thy womb, and shalt bring forth a son: and thou shalt call his name Jesus. He shall be great, and shall be called the Son of the Most High.

Imagine the impact of these words on Mary's mind. God had endowed her with a good mind [5] and she had used it well, pondering in her heart all the words of the Old Testament. She would naturally think on this occasion of the awful might of the omnipotent God who appeared to Moses in the burning bush, the

God who destroyed the armies of Egypt, the God who gave such glory to the face of Moses that the people could not look on his face when he came down from Mount Sinai. Yet the angel tells her that her Son is to be "the Son of the Most High"! She must have thought of the Messianic Psalm 2, in which the seventh verse said, "The Lord hath said to me, 'Thou art my son; this day have I begotten thee.'"

Gabriel continued:

> The Lord God shall give unto him the throne of David his father, and he shall reign in the house of Jacob forever, and of his kingdom there shall be no end.

Could Mary have forgotten the words of the prophet Isaias:

> For a child is born to us, and a son is given to us, and the government is upon his shoulder: and his name shall be called, Wonderful, Counsellor, GOD THE MIGHTY, the Father of the world to come, the Prince of Peace. His empire shall be multiplied, and there shall be no end of peace: he shall sit upon the throne of David and upon his kingdom; to establish it and strengthen it with judgment and with justice, from henceforth and forever.[6]

We who have become so accustomed to the idea of carrying God in our hearts in Holy Communion that many people, for no reason at all, omit remaining after Mass for a short thanksgiving; we have lost the sense of awe for the terrible power of the God within us. Not so Mary: her matchless fidelity to all the graces given her made her realize what a staggering proposal was being made to her.

But now she remembers her vow of virginity. Not doubting the power of God, but rather by way of inquiring what is God's will in regard to that, she asks: "How shall this be done, because I know not man?" Gabriel quickly reassured her:

> The Holy Ghost shall come upon thee, and the power of the Most High shall overshadow thee. And therefore also the Holy which shall be born of thee shall be called the Son of God.

Even before Gabriel had finished speaking, Mary's thoughts probably went back to that other line of the Prophet Isaias: "Behold a virgin shall conceive, and bear a son, and his name shall be called Emmanuel." [7] Gabriel states that Mary's Son is to be called "the Son of God." Isaias says He will be Emmanuel, which, translated, means: God with us.[8]

As the Fathers never tired of retelling, Eve had ruined us by disobedience. Now, at the beginning of the restoration, all is obedience. Mary looked to the depths of her soul. She, the blessed among women, the one full of grace, the only one conceived immaculate, the Mother of God — what is her reaction? "Behold the handmaid of the Lord!" The word *handmaid* is but a poor translation of the original Greek word *doúlē*. For to us the word handmaid means merely a hired servant. But *doúlē* meant a slave girl. Here is an obedient humility to balance the proud disobedience of Eve. Mary had just been raised to the peak of all creation, yet she replies by calling herself a slave girl: "Be it done to me according to thy word." Heaven itself waited in obedience for this obedience. For, as St. Thomas Aquinas tells us, "At the Annunciation, the Virgin was asked to give her consent in the name of the whole human race." [9] The world had been created by the *fiat* of the Word of God. Now the beginning of the re-creation in grace is ushered in by the *fiat mihi secundum verbum tuum* of the one who calls herself the slave of the Lord.

At this moment Mary became the Mother of Christ. Now Christ, the Son of Mary, is the New Adam. He is the new head of the human race. He is the head of the Mystical Body. Hence, at this time Mary became the spiritual Mother of the Mystical Body as well as the human Mother of the Head of that Body. It is true, the formal announcement came later, when on the cross the dying Son said: "Woman, behold thy son." [10] But the reality began long before, on the day of the Annunciation. Speaking to the Marian Congress at Ottawa, Canada, on June 19, 1947, Pope Pius XII said:

> But when the little maid of Nazareth uttered her *fiat* to the
> message of the angel . . . she became not only the Mother of God

in the physical order of nature, but also in the supernatural order of grace she became the Mother of all, who . . . would be made one under the Headship of her divine Son. The Mother of the Head would be the Mother of the members. The Mother of the Vine would be the Mother of the branches.[11]

One of the early heretics, Nestorius, denied that Mary could be called the Mother of God. For, he objected, Mary is only the mother of the human nature of Christ. At first sight the objection seems difficult. For it is not to be denied that Mary did not produce the Divinity itself. But the answer lies in the fact that Christ, the Son of God, though He has two natures, divine and human, is yet *only one person, a Divine Person*. Mary, being the mother of Him who is a Divine Person, may therefore rightly be said to be the Mother of God. For her Son is God. A comparison may help: the mother of an ordinary son produces only his body, not his soul. God directly creates the soul. Yet we say, without hesitation or qualifications, that she is His mother. This reasoning was brought out centuries ago by St. Cyril of Alexandria, and echoed by countless others since him. Nestorius and his heresy were condemned by the Council of Ephesus in A.D. 431.

Mary is the Mother of God, and Mary is full of grace. Which of the two is the greater prerogative: the divine motherhood or the fullness of grace? Some have thought to find the solution in the answer that Our Lord gave to an unknown woman in the Gospel. For when this woman cried out one day in a crowd: "Blessed is the womb that bore thee . . ." His reply was: "Yea rather, blessed are they who hear the word of God, and keep it." [12] It might seem at first sight that Mary's Son is saying that it is greater to be a son of God by grace, obeying His word, than to be the Mother of God. Even, then, of course, Mary would still be the greatest of those who "hear the word of God and keep it." But there is another explanation.

The woman in the crowd probably thought of Christ merely as a great prophet, rather than as divine. Therefore He might well answer her according to her own form of thought, and assure her that it is greater to have grace than to be the mother of a prophet. But even if the woman recognized His divinity, there was need to correct a too carnal way of looking at things, such as the Jews commonly had. For if Mary had been Christ's mother only in the physical sense, without being holy, her motherhood would have been of a lower order than grace.[13] The truth, however, is that Mary's motherhood was more than merely physical: it was accomplished by a free and meritorious consent to the mystery of the redemptive incarnation. She really did conceive Christ by hearing the word of God and keeping it: her Son is the Word of God.

Recent Popes have made it clear that Mary's divine motherhood, properly understood, is her greatest dignity. Pope Pius XI is quite explicit in his encyclical written for the 1500th anniversary of the Council of Ephesus (the council that defined Mary's divine motherhood):

> ... from this dogma of the divine motherhood as from the font of a hidden gushing spring flows the singular grace of Mary and her dignity, second only to God. In fact, as Aquinas writes: "The Blessed Virgin from the fact that she is the Mother of God, has a sort of infinite dignity from the infinite good that God is." [14]

Pope Pius XII, in his historic encyclical in which he announced the Marian Year of 1954, echoed the very words of Pope Pius XI, and singled out for special mention the relation of the divine motherhood to the unique grace by which Mary was ever free from all sin:

> ... it is clearly apparent ... that she obtained from God this most singular privilege, never granted to another, because of the fact that she was raised to the dignity of Mother of God.[15]

Since she was the Mother of God, Mary needed to be *full of grace*. We say that Mary was full of grace, not in the sense that she had as much grace as Christ Himself, for His fullness was absolute, so as to be incapable of any increase: His humanity had the closest kind of union to the Divinity itself. But Mary comes next in order, for she was closest of all to Him. Her fullness was relative to the mission God gave to her: her grace was such as was a worthy preparation for the divine motherhood.

Her fullness of grace was not, however, such as to exclude future increases, for her *capacity* for grace [16] could and did increase constantly throughout her life. It is difficult to conceive the rapidity with which her grace must have grown all during her life on earth. It will help us to get some slight idea of her spiritual growth if we recall that among the principles regulating the growth in grace of any person, one of the most important is this: *The increase we obtain depends not so much on the greatness of the things we do as on the fervor of love with which we do them, and on the grace we already have when we do them.* Now, since Mary's grace increased in proportion to the grace she already had, on that ground alone the increase is staggering to imagine. Add to this the fact that all her actions were performed with the maximum love and generosity, and it becomes impossible for us to imagine how great her grace became, especially when we remember that this increase continued steadily throughout her life.

We can only be certain that from the very beginning of her life Mary possessed greater grace than that which the highest of angels and men have at the culmination of their growth, when they enter Heaven. It is likewise certain [17] that her final fullness of grace, now that she reigns in Heaven, is higher than that of all angels and saints combined. Indeed, according to most theologians, it is likely that even her *initial* grace — the grace with which she began — surpassed the *final* grace of all angels and saints taken together. The incomparably exalted position in which God has placed Mary seems to call for so great a measure of grace as this, for her dignity is, as St. Thomas says,[18] in a certain sense infinite. No wonder then that Pope Pius IX, in the document in which he defined the Immaculate Conception, could assert of her fullness of grace that, ". . . none greater under God can be thought of, and no one, except God, can comprehend it." [19]

NOTES

1. *ST*, III, q.2, a.11, ad 3.

2. Mary could not merit the very decree by which God chose her (merit in the order of intention) but she could, in a certain way, merit that that decree, once made, should be put into effect (merit in the order of execution). But even in the order of execution, she could not offer to God a price in any way equal to the divine motherhood (condign or *de condigno* merit). Her merit could only be a merit of fittingness (congruous or *de congruo* merit). Some say it was congruous merit in the strict sense — a merit founded on the claims of friendship: Mary perfectly fulfilled the will of God, her Friend, and so it was fitting that God should carry out His plan to give her the divine motherhood. Others say it was congruous merit only in a broad sense — a fitting request of the generosity of God: Mary was the friend of God, but that friendship depended on the Incarnation and Redemption; that is, she could not merit the very principle of merit. Billuart, Garrigou-Lagrange, and others hold for the broad sense only; Hugon, Bittremieux, Merkelbach, Lercher, Roschini, and others hold for the strict sense. For further details, see Gabriel M. Roschini, O.S.M., *Mariologia* (2d ed., Rome, 1947), II, 44–48; and R. Garrigou-Lagrange, O.P., *The Mother of the Saviour*, trans. B. J. Kelly (St. Louis, 1953), pp. 23–24.

3. For more details on this matter and an evaluation of probabilities, see D. O'Shea, *Mary and Joseph* (Milwaukee, 1949), pp. 46 ff.

4. On the marriage of Mary and Joseph, see J. Mueller, S.J., *The Fatherhood of St. Joseph*, trans. A. Dengler (St. Louis, 1952), pp. 17–95.

5. Most theologians believe that God had also given her infused knowledge of all that she needed to know at any given stage of her mission. Further, it is clear that she was immune from ignorance of the things she had to know, and immune from error — for this privative ignorance and error would be a penalty and result of original sin, from which she was free. See Roschini, *Mariologia* (2d ed., 1948), III, 184–94; and Garrigou-Lagrange, *op. cit.*, pp. 123–30. See also Appendix II.

6. Isa. 9:6–7.

7. Isa. 7:14.

8. As to whether Mary realized the divinity of Christ at this time, see Appendix II.

9. *ST*, III, q.30, a.1.

10. John 19:26.

11. English text as given in *AAS* 39:271. On the spiritual motherhood, see *Marian Studies*, III (1952), 14–217.

12. Luke 11:27–28.

13. We are forced to think of the relatives of Christ mentioned in the Gospel, who did not believe in Him.

14. Pope Pius XI, *Lux veritatis* (December 25, 1931), *AAS* 23:513 (quoting *ST*, I, q.25, a.6, ad 4). Compare Leo XIII, *Quamquam pluries* (August 15, 1889), *ASS* 22:66: "Certainly, the dignity of the Mother of God is so lofty that there can be nothing greater." See also Garrigou-Lagrange, *op. cit.*, pp. 17 ff.

15. Pope Pius XII, *Fulgens corona gloriae* (September 8, 1953), *AAS* 45:580.

16. See *ST*, II–II, q.24, a.7, c.

17. This is clear from the words of Pope Pius XII, *Mystici Corporis* (1943), AAS 35:247: "...the Virgin Mother of God whose most holy soul, more than all other creatures of God *combined*, was filled with the divine Spirit of Jesus Christ." For a full discussion of the degree of Mary's initial and final grace, see Roschini, *Mariologia*, III, 127–33; and Garrigou-Lagrange, *op. cit.*, pp. 41–151, esp. pp. 67–77.

18. In *ST*, I, q.25, a.6, ad 4. See the quotation of note 14 above.

19. Pope Pius IX, *Ineffabilis Deus* (December 8, 1854).

III . . . *The Popes and the Co-redemptrix*

In THE FIRST CHAPTER we saw that the Fathers of the Church spoke of Mary as the New Eve, thereby giving her a title that holds many important truths about Mary. To learn precisely which truths are contained in the patristic concept we must turn to the guidance of the Church. Now, although this guidance is sometimes given in the form of solemn definitions, such as those of the Immaculate Conception and the Assumption, a great part of the Church's teaching is promulgated in other forms.

A curious misunderstanding often appears even among educated Catholics: it is thought that nothing less than a solemn definition carries any binding force for Catholics. This error had become so common that the Holy Father himself saw fit to strike at it. In his encyclical, *Humani generis,* of August 12, 1950, Pope Pius XII wrote as follows:

> Nor must one think that the things which are taught in Encyclical Letters do not of themselves demand assent, on the pretext that in them the Popes do not exercise the supreme power of their teaching authority. For these things are taught with the ordinary teaching authority, in regard to which it is also correct to say: "He who heareth you, heareth Me." [1]

Most of the teachings found in encyclicals are on matters that are already settled and accepted in Catholic doctrine. But if the Pope reaches beyond that area, and deliberately gives, in an encyclical or other official document, a judgment on a doctrinal matter that was up to that time controverted, then all Catholics must consider the controversy as settled. They must accept what the Holy Father teaches, giving true internal assent to his words.[2] The fact that these statements are not in the form of solemn

18

definitions does not destroy their binding force; after all, the preaching of the Apostles was not in the form of definitions: yet of it Our Lord said: "He who heareth you, heareth Me." [3]

It is now time to face the problem of whether or not Mary's role of New Eve extended even to immediate co-operation with the New Adam on Calvary. It is well to state the problem as accurately as possible at this point. We have already learned the distinction between the objective and the subjective redemption: the objective redemption consists in Christ's atonement and once-for-all *acquisition* of the entire treasury of grace for us. The subjective redemption is the *distribution* of that forgiveness and grace. It is beyond doubt clear that Mary co-operated *at least remotely* in the objective redemption. She did this by being the Mother of the Redeemer. For she, as representative of the human race,[4] gave flesh to the Divine Victim so that He might be able to suffer and die for us.

But now the question is: did Mary also co-operate *immediately* in the *objective* redemption? If we say that Mary was present on Calvary much in the same way as John, as a patient spectator, suffering at the sight of the pains of her Son, offering up her sufferings in union with Christ in much the same way as John did, this would not necessarily mean that she co-operated immediately in the objective redemption. For if her atonement and merit were of the same type as John's, her offering would be valuable, very valuable, but it would belong to the order of the subjective redemption only.[5] *It would not constitute part of the price accepted by the eternal Father.* Therefore, if we wish to prove that Mary did co-operate *immediately* in the *objective* redemption, we must show that her merits and sufferings were not merely those of a saintly but private person; we must show that they were those of a person appointed by God the Father to co-operate officially with the work of the Son. She would then share in *a joint work,* just as the Old Eve had shared in the joint work of original sin.

Of course, we would not thereby imply that the price paid by Christ Himself was in any way insufficient. We would merely mean that one and the same thing — redemption — would be earned on two different titles: the one a perfect and, in itself, completely adequate title; the other, a title of a lower order, quite insufficient of itself. Then the Redemption would really be parallel to the fall: in both we would have a head of the race, whose work alone was sufficient and necessary, joined by an inferior sharer, whose work alone would be definitely insufficient.

There are various ways in which a papal text might make clear that Mary shared in the Redemption on Calvary in this official way. One way, of course, would be to say that Mary was present on Calvary as the New Eve. Another way would be to say that Mary merited the same thing that Christ merited. There are also other ways, as we shall see.

Theological interest in the question of Mary's co-operation in the Redemption has not been restricted to modern times. Medieval theologians also discussed it, but it is only within the past century that papal pronouncements on the matter have become numerous. Pope Pius IX and Pope Leo XIII gave us several texts that could easily be understood to mean that Mary did share in this immediate and official way in the sacrifice on Calvary, but unfortunately their words are not so clear as to exclude readily all reasonable doubt.[6]

To Saint Pius X belongs credit for giving us the first really clear statements about Mary's role on Calvary. This saintly Pope chose as the motto of his reign: To restore all things in Christ. Before the first year of his pontificate was over, he had issued a memorable encyclical, *Ad diem illum,* in which he made clear that the prime means by which he hoped to restore all things in Christ was through Mary. But he also gave priceless light on the problem we are investigating. After quoting a statement of St. Bonaventure that Mary on Calvary would have much preferred to suffer in place of her Son, Saint Pius X goes on:

> Now from this common sharing of will and suffering between Christ and Mary, she "merited to become most worthily the Reparatrix of the lost world"[7] and therefore Dispensatrix of all the gifts which Jesus gained for us. . . .[8]

These words are so clear that no commentary should be needed: the Holy Father simply refers to Mary on Calvary as the Reparatrix of the world. But, as though fearing that some theologian might scruple over his meaning, the Holy Father, somewhat further on, gives still another, more forceful statement of the same truth:

> . . . since . . . she was associated by Christ with Himself in the work of human redemption, she merited for us congruously, as they say, what Christ merited condignly. . . .

Here we can see how meticulously careful the holy Pontiff is: not satisfied with having called Mary "Reparatrix of the lost world," he now repeats the same idea in two other ways, saying that Christ associated her with Himself in the Redemption, and that she merited, in a lesser way, what Christ merited in strict justice.[9] But there is more: the little phrase "as they say" gives notice to theologians that the Holy Father wants his words on the relation of Mary's merit to Christ's merit to be understood in the sense in which such words are commonly used by theologians. He is obviously alluding to the fact that quite a number of Marian theologians had been using just that same balance of terms on merit to describe the co-operation of Mary with Christ.[10] Therefore Saint Pius X has told us in several very precise ways that Mary was officially associated with her Son even on Calvary — in other words, that the role of New Eve extends even to the great sacrifice of Calvary.

The next two Popes, Benedict XV and Pius XI, could hardly hope to improve on the precision of Saint Pius X. They did, however, make many more statements which we might analyze.[11] We may quote but one brief passage from Pope Benedict XV:

> With her suffering and dying Son, Mary endured suffering and almost death. She gave up her Mother's rights over her Son to procure the salvation of mankind, and to appease the divine justice, she, as much as she could, immolated her Son, so that one can truly affirm that together with Christ she has redeemed the human race.[12]

The last words, " . . . together with Christ she has redeemed the human race," are forceful enough, even though not couched in the more theological language of Saint Pius X.

Pope Pius XII has been justly called "the Pope of Mary." To him we are indebted for several texts of lucid clarity on Mary's role of Calvary; but for the present we shall content ourselves with quoting two of them.[13] The first, from his great encyclical on the Mystical Body, is especially forthright:

> She it was who, free from all sin, original and personal, and always most intimately united with her Son, as the New Eve, offered Him on Golgotha, together with the holocaust of her maternal rights and love. . . . [14]

Here indeed is a simple and direct answer to our question. We asked whether we might extend the New Eve concept of Tradition so far as to include an immediate and official sharing in the sacrifice on Calvary. Now the living voice of the Church, which alone can pronounce on the correct interpretation of Scripture and Tradition, tells us that Mary *"as the New Eve,* offered Him on Golgotha. . . . "* Surely this is the solution we have been seeking.

A text of special beauty is found in a passage on the Queenship of Mary. On May 13, 1946, Pope Pius XII sent a Cardinal legate to represent him at Fatima, to place a crown on the statue there. He himself spoke to the crowds over the Vatican radio:

> Jesus is King throughout all eternity by nature and by right of conquest: through Him, with Him, and subordinate to Him, Mary is Queen by grace, by divine relationship, by right of conquest, and by singular election.[15]

There is a brilliant turn of expression in this text which might escape the attention of the reader. We note that the Holy Father says that Jesus is King "by nature and by right of conquest." This is easy to follow: He is King by nature since He is God. The expression "by right of conquest" is familiar to theologians. Mankind had been in the captivity of the devil. Christ loosed us from that captivity by the Redemption; hence we are His "by right of conquest." There is nothing new in this reference to Christ. But note what follows: After making provision for due subordination, the Holy Father gives us various titles by which Mary is Queen. Among them we find "by right of conquest." Now it is a general law of the interpretation of language that when the *same speaker* uses the *same words* in the *same context,* he ought, unless he makes clear otherwise, to mean them in the *same sense.* In the present passage, the Holy Father states clearly what differences in meaning he intends when he applies the words "by right of conquest'" to Mary as well as to Christ. For he says, "Through Him, with Him, and subordinate to Him, Mary is Queen . . . by right of conquest." Hence, since the Holy Father himself has given us the necessary qualifications to be made in his use of the expression, no one ought to add any others. The conclusion is easily drawn: when applied to Christ, the expression refers to the very culmination and heart of the objective redemption, Calvary itself; when applied to Mary, it means that through Him, with Him, and subordinate to Him, she also co-operated in the objective redemption on Calvary itself.[16]

To sum up, then, Saint Pius X stated that Mary, the Reparatrix of the lost world, was associated with Christ even on Calvary, and thereby merited in a lesser way what He merited for us in strict justice. Pope Benedict XV, in striking language, said of Mary that together with Christ she has redeemed the human race; and finally, Pope Pius XII, in the most forthright manner possible, told us that Mary acted as the New Eve on Calvary, and therefore reigns as Queen with her Son by title of conquest. Hence we can see a certain pattern unfolding: Mary is most intimately associated with her Son not only at the beginning of His course, the Annunciation, but also in the sacrifice of Calvary. In succeeding chapters we shall see the further evolution of this constant sharing.

NOTES

1. *AAS* 42:568.
2. On the doctrinal authority of encyclicals, see articles by J. C. Fenton in *AER,* August and September, 1949 (pp. 136–50 and 210–20); July, 1950 (pp. 59–67); March, 1953 (pp. 177–98, esp. p. 189); April, 1953 (pp.

287–301). Note especially, in the July, 1950 issue, p. 65: "At least in an indirect manner, however, every rejection of an authoritative doctrinal pronouncement contained in a papal encyclical is opposed to the theological virtue of faith itself." It is clear, then, that to reject a doctrinal statement made in an encyclical is a matter of sin.

The source in which encyclicals and other similar pronouncements of the Popes are to be found is the official Vatican journal, the *Acta Apostolicae Sedis (AAS)*. An early series of the same journal, with its own set of volume numbers, appeared under the name, *Acta Sanctae Sedis (ASS)*. In the *Humani generis*, the Holy Father makes clear that not only encyclicals but other papal pronouncements published in the *AAS* also carry the same authority. See *AER*, 128, 187.

3. Luke 10:16.

4. See *ST*, III, q.30, a.1: " . . . at the Annunciation, the Virgin was asked to give her consent in the name of the whole human race." This text of St. Thomas is quoted with approval by Pope Pius XII in the Mystical Body encyclical. See NCWC edition, par. 110.

5. We must note that if Mary was the New Eve on Calvary, then her merits went toward the *acquisition* of the great treasury of grace; whereas John's merit could apply only toward the *distribution* of that treasure. For more precise details see Appendix III A.

6. The texts of Pope Pius IX and Pope Leo XIII are given in Appendix III B.

7. The internal quotation is from Eadmer, *De Excellentia Virginis Mariae*, 9.

8. Saint Pius X, *Ad diem illum* (February 2, 1904), *ASS* 36:453–54. Some Mariologists, even though they admit that Mary certainly did co-operate immediately in the objective redemption, maintain that Saint Pius X was not the first to make that fact clear; they are slightly doubtful of the meaning of his words. See Appendix III.

9. The terms *congruous* and *condign* refer to two kinds of merit. Merit in general is a claim to a reward. Now if the claim is based on the fact that a strictly equivalent payment is made for the reward, the reward is due in *justice;* this is *condign* merit. But if the payment is not so great as what the reward is worth, the reward may still be granted, out of the *friendship* or *generosity* of God; this is *congruous* merit.

Mary's congruous merit in the objective redemption differs from the congruous merit of the ordinary faithful not only in that it belongs to the objective rather than to the subjective redemption, but also by virtue of its exalted nature as a result of her unique role and her wonderful sanctity. Hence some theologians, without in any way denying the truth of the teaching of Pius X, have sought for a more expressive description in other words. For a survey of the chief opinions, see Gabriel M. Roschini, O.S.M., "On the nature of the coredemptive merit of the blessed Virgin Mary," *Marianum* XV (1953), pp. 277–87.

10. For citations of the numerous theologians who used this formula to describe the merits of Mary and Christ, see Roschini, *Mariologia*, II, 272–77; and E. Druwé, S.J., "La Médiation universelle de Marie," in H. Du Manoir,

S.J., ed., *Maria* (Paris, 1949), I, 446–48. Not long before the appearance of the *Ad diem illum,* Cardinal Lepicier's *Mariology* had appeared (in 1901), bearing a laudatory letter from Pope Leo XIII, and containing precisely this formula.

11. For texts of Pope Pius XI, see Appendix III B.

12. Pope Benedict XV, *Inter Sodalicia* (March 22, 1918), *AAS* 10:182.

13. A very important, conclusive text from the *Munificentissimus Deus* will be discussed in chap. VI. Further texts are to be found in Appendix III B.

14. Pope Pius XI, *Mystici Corporis* (June 29, 1943), *AAS* 35:247.

15. Quoted in *AER* (November, 1949), *AAS* 38:266. See also a discussion of Mary's Queenship, based on a more complete quotation from the same passage, in chap. VII.

16. While a small minority of Catholic theologians (about a dozen) do not yet believe that the immediate co-operation of Mary in the objective redemption has been established, the majority — more than 200 from the twentieth century alone — do accept it. For details and answers to the objections of the minority, see Appendix III, especially C.

IV ... *Mary on Calvary*

THE PAPAL TEXTS of the preceding chapter make it clear that Mary really did co-operate immediately as the New Eve in the great sacrifice of Calvary. It remains for us to try to penetrate more deeply into the meaning of this great truth.

We must refer once again to the fall of our first parents. Scarcely had the fall taken place when God promised a Redeemer to come. God could have lowered the human race to the merely natural level, forever cutting off all hope of heaven; the truth is, however, that He wished to restore to us the opportunity for a supernatural reward. In general, three ways were open to God to provide this opportunity for us, aside from the possibility that He might have forgiven the sin without exacting any reparation (a thing He did not do).[1] He could have demanded strict payment of the debt; He could have accepted an inadequate payment; or He could have arranged that both an adequate and an inadequate payment be made together.

For any adequate payment of the debt, the incarnation of a divine person was strictly necessary; for sin has a sort of infinity about it, from the fact that the person offended is infinite. But only one who is an infinite person — i.e., divine — could pay an infinite debt; and only one who is at the same time human could pay it in such a way that it would profit the human race. Had God wished to accept an inadequate reparation, He could have designated some holy person to offer a sacrifice, or perform some other prescribed action; such a reparation would have been insufficient to pay the debt, but God, nonetheless, could have chosen to accept it.

The truth is that God wished to combine both adequate and inadequate reparation in order to exercise better His infinite mercy. That is, He freely decreed that what He would accept as the price of the Redemption was the joint work of two: the one, a divine person, who alone could really pay the debt, and whose work by itself would be fully adequate; the other, the greatest of all mere creatures, whose work would not add anything to the intrinsic value of the infinite reparation of the God-man, but whose labors, nonetheless, were ordained by the Father to be accepted with, through, and subordinate to those of the great Redeemer. The fall had come about through two: Adam, the head of the race, who alone was able to ruin all his posterity; and Eve, who alone could not bring on original sin, but who could and did co-operate in her own subordinate way in effecting the disaster of original sin.

It was fitting, therefore, that the restoration should follow the pattern of the fall. In the beautiful hymn, the *Pange lingua gloriosi,* which the Church sings on Good Friday, we find the parallel of the fall and the restoration extended even to the wood of the cross.[2] Despite its poetic form, this ancient hymn most fittingly expresses the truth of this parallel.

De parentis protoplasti	Our Maker, grieving
Fraude, Factor condolens	Over the deception of our first parent
Quando pomi noxialis	When, by the bite of the baneful fruit
In necem morsu ruit:	He fell to death:
Ipse lignum tunc notavit	Marked then the wood,
Damna ligni ut solveret.	To repair the damage done by the wood.
Hoc opus nostrae salutis	Order had called for
Ordo depoposcerat;	This work of our salvation,
Multiformis proditoris	That wisdom might undo cunning
Ars ut artem falleret,	And find a remedy
Et medelam ferret inde	In the means
Hostis unde laeserat.	By which the enemy had inflicted harm.

And so it appears that the debt had been contracted by two in co-operation; and that it would be paid by a parallel co-operation. Adam had been, as we have said, the first head of the race; Christ was to be, as St. Paul tells us [3] (see chap. I), the New Adam, the new head of the race, for if He were not the head of the race, humanity as a whole would not have a claim on His merits and reparation. It was through Mary that Christ became the head of the human race, for, as St. Thomas observes: " . . . at the Annunciation, the Virgin was asked to give her consent in the name of the whole human race." [4]

Mary, then, in giving flesh to the future Victim of Calvary, acted as the representative of mankind as a whole. Pope Pius XII, in the encyclical on the Mystical Body, makes this interpretation his own, and quotes from St. Thomas:

> . . . and she consented "in the name of the whole human race," so that "a sort of spiritual marriage exists between the Son of God and human nature." She it was who in a marvelous way gave birth to Christ the Lord, the font of all heavenly life, who had already been adorned in her virginal womb with the dignity of Head of the Church. . . . [5]

Hence it is entirely clear that Christ became the New Adam, the new head of the human race, from the fact that He received human flesh from the womb of the Virgin.

The heavenly Father could have accepted the least action of the life of Christ in reparation, for, since Our Lord is divine, even His least acts have an infinite dignity; but, to show better the love of God for man, it was decreed that the reparation should consist primarily in a sacrifice. Hence our next task is to make sure that we understand the true nature of sacrifice.

St. Augustine points out that there are two components in a sacrifice: "The visible sacrifice is, then, the sacrament, that is, the sacred sign of the invisible sacrifice." [6] Thus a sacrifice belongs to the general class of things that we call signs. The function of a sign is to show something outwardly. According to St. Augustine's statement, the external sacrifice is the outward sign of what he calls an invisible sacrifice.

The invisible sacrifice is the more essential of the two. It is the *internal* disposition of the heart which loves and adores God, expresses its sorrow and desire for reparation, its thanks, its peti-

tion for help. The victim offered in a sacrifice serves as a sign of
the internal dispositions. In the sacrifices of the Old Law, the
animal sacrificed was, by virtue of its immolation, removed from
the use of men, and that very fact signified that it was being
given to God. But the idea was not merely to give an animal to
God: otherwise He might speak as He is poetically represented
as speaking in Psalm 49:

> Hear, O my people, and I will speak: . . . I will not reprove thee
> for thy sacrifices: and thy burnt offerings are always in my sight.
> I will not take calves out of thy house: nor he goats out of thy
> flocks. For all the beasts of the woods are mine: the cattle on
> the hills, and the oxen. . . . If I should be hungry, I would not
> tell thee: for the world is mine, and the fullness thereof. Shall
> I eat the flesh of bullocks? or shall I drink the blood of goats?
> Offer to God the sacrifice of praise. . . .

A real gift should represent the giver: the animal given to
God is worthless unless it represents the gifts of the heart and the
whole being of the giver, who acknowledges the absolute rights
of God over him. The external offering in a sacrifice must be a
sign of the internal sacrifice, of the inner dispositions of love,
adoration, contrition, thanks, petition, on the part of the one
who offers.[7]

Now we turn to the scene on Calvary. There we see a true
sacrifice being accomplished. The New Adam, Christ Himself,
is both priest and victim. The outward sign is His painful death.
The inward dispositions of His Heart toward His Father — dispositions of love, adoration, reparation, thanksgiving, petition —
are wonderfully expressed by this outward sign. With Him[8] is
the New Eve, in what Saint Pius X called a "common sharing
of will and suffering" with Him. In what precisely does
this "common sharing" of hers consist? In many things. First of
all, it was through her, as we have seen, that Christ became the
New Adam, the new head of mankind. It was through her that
He had flesh in which to suffer and die: she had literally provided
the Victim, for Christ as God could not suffer and die. She herself

is obviously suffering profoundly at this sight. Such is her co-operation in the outward sign.

Her union with the inner dispositions of Christ is most perfect: she joined inwardly in offering Him. As Pope Benedict XV expressed it:

> With her suffering and dying Son, Mary endured suffering and almost death. She gave up her Mother's rights over her Son in order to procure the salvation of mankind, and to appease the divine justice, she, as much as she could, immolated her Son, so that one can truly affirm that together with Christ she has redeemed the human race.[9]

Or, as Saint Pius X stated it:

> " . . . there stood by the cross of Jesus, His Mother," not merely occupied in looking at the dreadful sight, but even rejoicing that "her only Son was being offered for the salvation of the human race: and so did she suffer with Him, that, if it had been possible, she would have much more gladly suffered herself all the torments which her Son underwent."[10]

And, let us remember, she does this not as a private person, but as the New Eve, as the one officially marked by the Father to co-operate in this way with the Son, so that the Father regards the sufferings of both as forming but one offering, for her suffering is offered only through and with His. We recall the words of Pope Pius XII:

> She it was who, free of all sin, original and personal, and always most intimately united with her Son, as the New Eve, offered Him on Golgotha, together with the holocaust of her maternal rights and love. . . . [11]

We note in the last two passages that both Pope Benedict XV and Pope Pius XII spoke of Mary's surrender of her "maternal rights" over her Son.

At this point someone may object that once a son reaches legal age, his mother has a right to be heard respectfully, but that no real consent on her part is required for his actions. Mary's position, however, was not just that of an ordinary mother, and the redeeming sacrifice was not in the line of the ordinary relations of son and mother. Just as, in accordance with the positive decree of God the Father, the Incarnation was not to take place without the consent of Mary, the representative of all mankind, so also the culmination of the Redemption, to which the Incarnation was directed, was not to take place without the consent of Mary. This consent of hers to the sacrifice of Calvary was both a continuation of the *fiat* of Nazareth and a silent but loving renewal of that original consent. In this spirit she united most intimately with the dispositions of the heart of her dying Son, so as to join with Him in a "common sharing of will and suffering." [12] She offered Him as something of herself: she would have greatly preferred to die in His stead. [13]

The prophet Jeremias spoke these words of lament over the desolation of Jerusalem:

> To what shall I compare thee: or to what shall I liken thee, O daughter of Jerusalem? to what shall I equal thee, that I may comfort thee, O virgin daughter of Sion? for great as the sea is thy destruction: who shall heal thee? [14]

In the Office of the Feast of the Seven Sorrows, the Church applies these words to Mary. As St. Alphonsus points out, [15] it is very fitting to compare her grief to the sea, for the sea is vast in extent and all bitter to the taste: there is not a drop of sweet water in it. The words "who shall heal thee?" are yet more expressive: when the martyrs suffered, they were often given relief by God, so that some of them seemed not to feel any pain. But God did not mitigate the pain of Mary. The thought of the passion of Christ consoled the martyrs; but for Mary the very passion was the cause of her suffering. Their love for God was a solace to the martyrs; but for Mary her very love for her Son, more boundless than the sea, was the measure of her bitter compassion.

Many were scandalized at the passion of Christ. St. Paul says it was foolishness to the Gentiles, and a scandal to the Jews.[16] Similarly, some, when they are first brought face to face with the fact of the co-redemptive role of Mary, are shocked at the thought that a mere creature, however pure, could share in redeeming us. But the same love of God that spared not His Only Son is also the reason for the co-redemption: of herself, Mary could do nothing to save us.[17] It is only the incomprehensible love and generosity of God that contrived such a method as this, in which:

Order had called for	Hoc opus nostrae salutis
This work of our salvation	Ordo depoposcerat;
That wisdom might undo cunning	Multiformis proditoris
And find a remedy	Ars ut artem falleret,
In the means	Et medelam ferret inde
By which the enemy had inflicted harm.	Hostis unde laeserat.[18]

NOTES

1. See *ST*, III, q.l, a.2, esp. ad 2; and III, q.46, a.2, esp. ad 3.

2. There is even a legend that the cross was made from a tree descended from the original forbidden tree — pretty, but impossible to prove.

3. See, for example, Rom. 5:12.

4. *ST*, III, q.30, a.1.

5. *AAS* 35:247.

6. *City of God* X, v. See *ST*, III, q.22, a.2,c.

7. We may profitably make an application of these principles to the Mass. The Mass represents Calvary, but in an unbloody way. On Calvary, the bloody death of Christ expressed the perfect dispositions of His Heart. In the Mass, the mystical separation of Body and Blood by the two consecrations expresses the same dispositions of His Heart. Those who assist at Mass may unite both with the external rite and with the interior dispositions of the Heart of Christ. It is obvious that the interior is the more essential of the two phases of their union. For further details, see chap. XVI.

8. Christ accomplished our salvation in four modes: by way of merit, satisfaction, sacrifice, and redemption. Mary, the Mother of God and the New Eve, by offering up her Son, abdicating her Mother's rights, and joining to this her own sufferings, co-operated in all four modes: 1. *Merit:* "She merited congruously, as they say, what Christ merited condignly" (Pope Pius X); 2. *Satisfaction:* "To appease the divine justice, she as much as she could, immolated her Son" (Pope Benedict XV); 3. *Sacrifice:* "She . . . most intimately united . . . offered Him on Golgotha" (Pope Pius XII); 4. *Redemption:* "One can truly affirm that together with Christ she has redeemed the human race" (Pope Benedict XV). See *AER*, 125:1–6, 120–29, 196–207.

9. *AAS* 10:182.

10. *ASS* 36:453.

11. *AAS* 35:247.

12. Mary had not only an extrinsic deputation for her role on Calvary. God also provided for a special intrinsic worth to her actions by giving her the dignity of the Mother of God who is full of grace. Of course, all the value of her acts depended ultimately on the positive decree of God and on the merits of her Son.

13. Such is the thought of St. Bonaventure, quoted by Blessed Pope Pius X in *ASS* 36:453. See the text in Appendix III, B, 3.

14. Lamentations (of Jeremias) 2:13.

15. St. Alphonsus Liguori, "Sermon on the Dolors of Mary," *The Complete Works of St. Alphonsus* (4th ed., Brooklyn, 1931), vols. VII–VIII, 482–92.

16. See I Cor. 1:23.

17. It is helpful to compare the role of Mary on Calvary to that of a layman who devoutly assists at Mass, and who, in addition, through a Mass offering, provides the bread and wine for the sacrifice. In providing the material for Mass, the layman in a faintly similar way imitates the fact that Mary provided the Victim. The layman also tries to join in the dispositions of the Victim being immolated on the altar. Mary joined in the dispositions of Christ, but in a much more perfect way. The differences between Mary and the layman thus far are great. But there is a more striking difference: the position of the layman is not *unique and official,* as Mary's was. For she was the New Eve. In addition, the layman is taking part in the re-presentation of Calvary, in the means of the distribution of the fruits of Calvary. But Mary took part in the original Calvary, in the once-for-all earning of those fruits. She on Calvary was sharing in the objective redemption; the layman is sharing in the subjective redemption. Of her, and her alone, could it be truly said: "She merited congruously, as they say, what Christ merited condignly." Of her alone could it be said that "Through Him, with Him, and subordinate to Him, Mary is Queen . . . by right of conquest."

18. From the *Pange lingua.*

V ... *All Grace Through Her Hands*

SINCE Mary shared with her divine Son in atoning for us and in meriting [1] the inexhaustible treasury of grace for us, she now shares with Him in the distribution of all graces. As Pope Pius XII observed in a sermon delivered before his election as Pope, "The unity of the divine plan demands" that "Mary should co-operate equally in the two phases of the same work." [2]

This doctrine that Mary is the Mediatrix of all graces is very old. It is implicitly contained in the New Eve concept, for the first Eve, according to God's original plan, was to have been, with Adam, the means of the transmission of sanctifying grace to all their descendants. But fairly clear, explicit statements of this doctrine appear much earlier than they did on the matter of Mary's role in the sacrifice of Calvary. Thus, for example, in a prayer which is almost certainly by St. Ephraem, the fourth-century Syrian Doctor of the Church, we note that Mary is called "dispensatrix of all goods." [3] Or again, Theodotus of Ancyra, one of the most prominent of the Fathers at the Council of Ephesus (A.D. 431), called Mary "dispensatrix of good things." [4] Basil of Seleucia († c. A.D. 458) addressed Mary as the "Mediatrix of God and men." [5] It would be easy to add other quotations from the patristic period.

The first writer to dwell clearly and at length on this doctrine, however, was the great Cistercian Doctor of the Church, St. Bernard († A.D. 1153), who speaks of the universal mediation in many places. He does so at great length in his famous sermon "On the Aqueduct," [6] but it will be sufficient for our purpose to quote one short but clear passage from another work of St. Bernard. In a sermon on the Vigil of Christmas, the Saint said: "God wished us to have nothing that would not pass through the hands of Mary." [7] Another great theologian of the universal mediation of Mary is St. Bernardine of Siena († A.D. 1444). Pope Leo XIII made his own the doctrine of St. Bernardine: speaking of the fact that in the Rosary we first say the *Our Father,* and then the *Hail Mary,* Pope Leo XIII wrote:

> ... after invoking Him with excellent prayers, our voice of supplication turns from the throne of His Majesty to Mary, precisely in accord with this rule of conciliation and deprecation which has been expressed thus by St. Bernardine of Siena: "Every grace which is communicated to this world has a threefold course. For, in accord with excellent order, it is dispensed from God to Christ, from Christ to the Virgin, from the Virgin to us." [8]

Saint Pius X likewise prized the teaching of St. Bernard and St. Bernardine, and in his great encyclical, the *Ad diem illum,* he said:

> ... Mary, as St. Bernard fittingly remarks, is the "channel," or even the neck through which the body is joined to the head, and likewise through which the head exerts its power and strength on the body. "For she is the neck of our Head, by which all spiritual gifts are communicated to His Mystical Body" [St. Bernardine].[9]

A very forceful passage is found in another encyclical of Pope Leo XIII:

> And therefore no less correctly can one affirm that absolutely nothing of that great treasury of grace which the Lord brought us (for "grace and truth came by Jesus Christ") — nothing of it is given to us except through Mary, for such is the will of God: so that just as no one can go to the Most High Father except through the Son, in much the same way (*ita fere*) no one can come to Christ except through His Mother.[10]

It would be a simple matter to multiply passages stating the same truth from the saints of the past and the Popes of our own era. Although some few theologians [11] dispute the immediate co-operation of Mary in the objective redemption, yet there is no dispute over the fact that Mary is Mediatrix of all graces. In fact, the unanimity of theologians on this matter has been officially noted in the decree of the Congregation of Rites by which Pope Pius XII approved two miracles for the canonization of St. Louis de Montfort. After speaking of the doctrine that "God wished us to have all through Mary," the text of the decree continues: "All theologians now agree in holding this most tender and salutary doctrine." [12]

As we have noted, there is no dispute over the *fact* that Mary is Mediatrix of all graces. But it is one thing to agree that the doctrine is true that *in some way* Mary serves as Mediatrix of all graces but quite another to explain *in precisely what way.* The expressions commonly used to state this doctrine are largely metaphorical. It is said that all graces come through the *hands* of Mary, or that Mary is the *channel,* or is in the position of the *neck* in the Mystical Body. The problem is to find what literal truth is contained in these figures of speech.

All theologians admit a certain fundamental truth in this matter: Mary is the Mediatrix of all graces *at least* through her intercession, through the fact that she asks for all graces for us by her prayers.[13] Some theologians, however, would go farther, and add a statement that Mary actually serves as a physical instrument, through which grace literally passes. We might make the difference clear by a comparison. Suppose that the son of a poor man goes to the queen of his land, and asks her to help him obtain from the king a considerable sum of money needed to provide medical help for his father. The queen intercedes with the king, and obtains the grant of the needed sum. In sending the money to the poor man, the king might hand it to the queen, and she in turn could pass it on to the poor man. Or the king might merely send a servant to the poor man, so that the money would not actually pass through the hands of the queen.

If the queen merely obtains the favor, but does not actually handle it on its way to the poor man, she is acting only by way of intercession. But if she also handles the money after the king has granted it, she serves as a physical instrument in its transmission. Similarly, if Mary not only obtains graces by her intercession, but also as it were "handles" them on their way from her Divine Son to us, she is a physical instrument of grace. If grace literally and physically passes through Mary, then the texts alluding to her as the "channel" or the "neck" of the Mystical Body have a much fuller and richer sense.[14]

It does not seem possible at the present time to be sure whether or not Mary, in addition to her intercession, also serves as a physical instrument. We can, however, bring forth two considerations which, though inconclusive, do favor the idea of physical instrumentality.

First of all, a similar problem exists when we think of the sacraments, since the Council of Trent said that the sacraments contain the grace that they signify. In attempting to explain this statement of the Council, theologians employ theories that are precisely parallel to those we have just examined in regard to Mary's influence in distributing grace. In the case of the sacraments, we have the weighty authority of St. Thomas favoring the idea that the sacraments serve as physical instruments.[15] Of course, the fact that St. Thomas favors that theory for the sacraments does not prove he would favor such a theory when applied to Mary's influence; since the two problems are parallel, however, it does at least show that it is not impossible that Mary could have such a role. The Thomists are even willing to say that a priest giving absolution is a physical instrument of grace, and surely Mary is no less closely united to God than is the priest who absolves!

The second consideration favoring the idea of Mary as a physical instrument is the fact that this view seems to accord better with the papal texts and with the words of the saints of the past on this subject. Especially does this view fit well with the passage cited above in which Pope Leo XIII quotes St. Bernardine of Siena as saying:

> Every grace . . . has a threefold course. For, in accord with excellent order, it is dispensed from God to Christ, from Christ to the Virgin, and from the Virgin to us.

Of course it is possible, though somewhat difficult, to understand this text as meaning mere intercession; but the text has a more natural and full meaning if we suppose that grace, after originating in the Divine Nature, and passing through the Sacred Humanity of Christ, next passes physically through Mary's instrumentality. In spite of these considerations, however, we must openly admit that in the present state of the evidence it seems to be impossible to prove which of these theories is correct. One thing we do know: Whatever be the manner, Mary certainly is the Mediatrix of all graces.

A question is sometimes asked about what place the sacraments occupy, in view of the fact that Mary is Mediatrix of all graces. Since the sacraments really contain and produce grace, as the Council of Trent says, where is there room for Mary? The answer is obvious. Whatever grace is dispensed through the sacraments (1) has been earned by both Christ *and* Mary, as we have seen, and (2) its application has been obtained through Mary's power of intercession. These facts alone are sufficient to answer the question, but, in addition, we may note that Mary also leads us to frequent the sacraments, and obtains for us the disposition to profit from them. Whether or not we may go still further depends on which view is true about Mary's influence in the dispensation of all graces. If we think her role is mere intercession, we cannot go further. But if she is a physical instrument of grace, we can trace the course of grace thus: Grace begins in the Divine Nature, passes through the Sacred Humanity of Christ (a physical instrument), passes through Mary (also a physical instrument), and finally passes through the sacrament (also a physical instrument). So we have here another argument for the view that Mary serves as a physical instrument of grace.

Another question sometimes asked about Mary's distribution of all graces is this: How can Mary, being a creature, know the needs of all men? The answer again is quite simple. St. Thomas gives the principle: "No blessed intellect fails to know . . . all the things that pertain to itself." [16] That is, anyone who enjoys the beatific vision sees God Himself. God is the abyss of all knowledge, and all things are contained in that vision. Each one who beholds that vision by the light of glory sees all the things that concern him. Hence we may say that although Mary is a creature, yet, in the vision of the divine essence, she sees all that pertains to her. But she has been constituted Mother of all men — hence, obviously, the needs of all do pertain to her, and therefore she sees the needs of all of us. The fact that there are so many for whom she must care is not a problem — though many, the number is not infinite, and so does not exceed the capacity of a finite mind enlightened by so enormous a degree of the light of glory in the vision of the divine essence.

This is a consoling doctrine to think upon, for it makes clear to us that it is no mere figure of speech to say that Mary is our Mother. The function of a mother is to give life to a child, and then to take care of it. Mary has literally given life to us: supernatural life, which she, though only through and subordinate to her Son, earned for us, and which she dispenses constantly to us, since she is enabled, by the vision of the essence of God, to know all our needs. Hence we see another sense in which Mary is the New Eve: she is in an especially true sense the "mother of all the living." [17]

Let us cite one more passage from Pope Pius XII, one that shows us forcefully that we must make no exceptions to Mary's influence. At the descent of the Holy Spirit on Pentecost, we do not merely find Mary with the Apostles, but in addition,

> She it was who, by her most mighty prayers, obtained that the Spirit of the Divine Redeemer, already given on the Cross, should be bestowed on the new-born Church on the day of Pentecost, in the company of miraculous gifts.[18]

NOTES

1. Note that the term *merit* has a different sense when we speak of the merits of Christ and Mary on Calvary from what it has when any one of us merits. The merit of Calvary filled up a great reservoir of grace once and for all. Nothing is ever added to that treasury. When anyone merits now, he does not earn that new grace be added to the treasury, but that something be withdrawn from the treasury and distributed.

2. For the complete text, see Appendix III, B, 6.

3. St. Ephraem died in A.D. 373. The text is quoted from Druwé, "La Médiation universelle de Marie," Du Manoir, *Maria*, I, 543.

4. *Ibid.*, p. 544.

5. *Ibid.*

6. PL 183:437–48.

7. PL 183:100.

8. September 8, 1894, *ASS* 27:179.

9. February 2, 1904, *ASS* 36:454.

10. September 22, 1891, *ASS* 24:195–96.

11. See note 16 on chap. III and Appendix III, esp. C.

12. January 11, 1942, *AAS* 34:44. At times one meets with a statement expressing doubt on this doctrine, in an out-of-date work, or by some writer who is either careless, or who, not being a professional theologian, is not acquainted with recent theological developments. As the decree just quoted implies, all professional theologians agree that the papal texts are so categorical and clear that the matter is inescapable.

13. In addition, we may note that even if Mary had no role in the actual distribution of graces, her share in earning all graces would justify the title of Mediatrix of all graces.

14. According to the first theory, Mary is merely the moral cause of the distribution of grace; in the second theory, she is a physical-instrumental cause. There is a third theory in which she is an intentional-dispositive cause, that is, she produces in us, before we receive grace, a special sort of disposition, or rather, a designation or title that in a certain way calls for grace. Not many theologians favor the third theory.

15. *ST*, III, q.62, a.4.

16. *Ibid.*, q.10, a.2.

17. Gen. 3:20.

18. *Mystici Corporis* (June 29, 1943), *AAS* 35:248.

VI ... *Death and Assumption of Mary*

For while the deaths of others may be caused by infirmities or length of days, when these souls die, although it may be from some infirmity, or from old age, their spirits are wrested away by nothing less than some loving impulse and encounter far loftier and of greater power and strength than any in the past, for it has succeeded in breaking the web and bearing away a jewel, which is the spirit. And thus the death of such souls is very sweet and gentle, more so than was their spiritual life all their life long, for they die amid the delectable encounters and sublimest impulses of love, being like to the swan, which sings most gently when it is at the point of death.

S UCH is the description given by the "mystics' mystic," St. John of the Cross, of the death of those souls that reach the highest states of love of God possible on this earth.[1] Now if any person ever literally died of love of God, that one was Mary. Whose love of God was anything but a pale shadow compared to the living flame of her love? For the love of God might be compared to a powerful magnet, attempting to draw the soul toward God. The assaults of this force become ever stronger and stronger in the purest souls, until finally a state is reached in which, as it were, the soul, being no longer able to resist that drawing force, leaves the body.

St. John of the Cross speaks of loving impulses and encounters. These expressions suggest violent movements and assaults. And so it is in other souls — that is, in all others who reach such a height, except Mary. For in her case, death must have come without a shock. Such is the opinion of St. Francis de Sales:

> ... we must not suppose an impetuosity of agitation in this celestial love of the maternal heart of the Virgin; for love, of

41

itself, is sweet, gracious, peaceful, and tranquil. If it sometimes deliver assaults, if it give shocks to the spirit, this is because it finds resistance there. . . . It was so, then, that holy love employed its force in the virginal heart of the sacred Mother, without effort of violent impetuosity, because it found no resistance or hindrance whatever.[2]

For we must remember that Mary's love of God was from the very start at a higher level than that of the greatest saints at the end of their lives. St. Francis de Sales brings Mary's death into relation with Calvary. Speaking of her at the foot of the cross, he says:

The sorrow of the Son at that time was a piercing sword, which passed through the heart of the Mother, because that Mother's heart was glued, joined, and united to her Son, with so perfect a union that nothing could wound the one without inflicting a lively torture upon the other. Now this maternal bosom, being thus wounded with love, not only did not seek a cure for its wound, but loved her wound more than all cure, dearly keeping the shafts of sorrow she had received, on account of the love which had shot them into her heart, and continually desiring to die of them, since her Son died of them, who as say all the Holy Scriptures, and all Doctors, died amidst the flames of his charity, a perfect holocaust for all the sins of the world.

. . . Love had given at the foot of the cross to this divine Spouse the supreme sorrows of death, and therefore it was reasonable that at length death should give her the sovereign delights of love.[3]

Before the definition of the Assumption, the opinion of the majority of theologians was that Mary actually did die. A few, however, defended the view that she never died at all.[4] The chief argument of the smaller group was based on the fact that death is a penalty of original sin: but, they said, Mary never was infected with original sin; therefore she did not suffer death, the result of original sin.

The argument is interesting. The sufferings of Jesus and Mary, however, were the result of all sin, even though both were completely free of sin. Jesus accepted death for us. Mary is, as we have seen, the sharer in the lot of her Son at every step. Hence she must have died. Few of the Fathers and modern theologians have thought the doubt about her death serious enough to disturb them. Nonetheless, the constitution defining the Assumption, the *Munificentissimus Deus,* carefully refrained from defining, or even stating flatly, that Mary did die. Yet the same document does quote numerous Fathers who take it for granted that Mary died; and since the whole tone of the text shows the general belief that Mary did die, it seems difficult to continue to hold the view that she was exempted from death. On the other hand, a heated controversy has flared up since the definition. Some theologians believe that they have an argument for Mary's immortality in the very fact that the Holy Father carefully refrained from defining that she died.

Since there is no unanimity as to whether Mary died at all, we must not expect to find any general agreement on the details of her death. There are two places competing for the designation as the place of her death: Jerusalem and Ephesus.[5] The claim of Ephesus would rest chiefly on the fact that Mary had been entrusted to the care of John, and that John later resided there. But this argument is far from conclusive: we do not know the date of her death, and so we do not know where she may have been at the time. If Mary went with John to Ephesus, she probably would have been between sixty and eighty years old at the time. The traditions associated with Jerusalem seem to have far better support, and consequently most students of the question today defend the claims of Jerusalem.

But let us leave these insoluble though interesting matters and turn to the Assumption itself. Since the most authoritative work we have on the subject of the Assumption is the above-mentioned constitution of definition, let us review some of the chief points of this document.[6]

It is obvious that one of the thoughts most strongly in the

foreground of the Holy Father's mind was the principle of
consortium: the constant sharing of Mary, at every point, from
beginning to end, in the life and work and lot of her Son, for he
makes use of this principle both at the beginning and at the
end of the document. In the opening section he shows the relation
of the Assumption to the Immaculate Conception:

> For these two privileges are most closely related to each other.
> Christ has overcome sin and death by His own death; and one
> who is reborn in a heavenly way through baptism has, through
> Christ Himself, conquered sin and death. However, in accord
> with His general rule, God does not wish to grant the full effect
> of victory over death to the just until the end of time shall
> have come. . . .
>
> Yet God wished that the Blessed Virgin Mary be exempt
> from this general law. For she, by a completely singular privi-
> lege, conquered sin in her Immaculate Conception, and thus
> was not liable to that law of remaining in the corruption of the
> grave, nor did she have to wait for the end of time for the re-
> demption of her body.[7]

The Holy Father then goes on to show some of the reasons
for the definition. He tells us that he had asked the opinions of
all the bishops of the world on this matter. Their response was
almost unanimous in the affirmative. This universal teaching of
the authorities of the Church by itself, he tells us, supplies us with
a proof. For this teaching is a reflection of the faith of the
Church, the depositary of Tradition, which, since the beginning,
has preserved the divine revelations, under the guidance of the
Holy Spirit. He reviews for us some of the outstanding statements of Tradition down through all the centuries. The teaching
that Mary was assumed into Heaven is found at a very early date
in the ancient books of the liturgy; it is found in the teachings of
the Fathers. After the patristic age, the same doctrine is studied
in detail by the scholastic theologians. For example, the Holy
Father quotes the words of St. Bernardine of Siena who,

> . . . gathered up and carefully treated everything that medieval
> theologians had said and discussed on this matter. He was not

satisfied to repeat the chief considerations which doctors of previous times had already proposed, but also added others of his own. For the likeness of the Mother of God and the Divine Son in regard to nobility of soul and body — a likeness which forbids the very thought that the heavenly Queen should be separated from the heavenly King — absolutely demands that Mary "must not be anywhere but where Christ is." And furthermore, it is reasonable and fitting that not only the soul and body of a man, but also the soul and body of a woman should have already attained glory in heaven. Finally, since the Church has never sought for bodily relics of the Blessed Virgin, nor exposed them for the veneration of the faithful, we have an argument which can be considered as "practically a proof by sensory experience." [8]

The Holy Father also thought the words of St. Francis de Sales worthy of special attention in this matter:

Similarly, St. Francis de Sales, after stating that it would be wrong to doubt that Jesus Christ has kept in the most perfect way the divine commandment that children honor their parents, puts this question: "What son, if he could, would not bring his mother back to life, and take her, after death, into paradise?" [9]

The samples which we have just quoted form but a small part of the review of the earlier teachings given in the *Munificentissimus Deus*. Following this survey the Pope offers some comments of his own, in the paragraphs immediately before the definition itself:

All these arguments and considerations of the Holy Fathers and the theologians rest on the Sacred Writings as their ultimate foundation. These place the revered Mother of God as it were before our eyes, as most closely joined to her Divine Son, and always sharing in His lot. Hence it seems practically impossible to think of her who conceived Christ, brought Him forth, gave Him milk, held Him in her hands and pressed Him to her heart as being separated from Him after this earthly life in body, even though not in soul. [10]

Here again we encounter the principle of *consortium* with which the document had opened. The Holy Father continues, endorsing the argument which he had quoted earlier from St. Francis de Sales:

> Since He is the most perfect observer of the divine law, Our Redeemer, being the Son of Mary, could not do other than honor His most beloved Mother next to His Eternal Father. But since He had the power to adorn her with the great honor of keeping her untouched by the corruption of the grave, we must believe that He really did so.[11]

We have already seen two passages in which the Holy Father makes use of the principle of *consortium*. We also noted his statement that the arguments of the Fathers and theologians were ultimately based on Scripture. He next amplifies this last point, and shows us that it is the New Eve concept which he has especially in mind — and this concept is really but another way of stating the principle of *consortium*. We have already studied it at some length insofar as it applied to the earlier phases of the life of Mary. We noted that it implied the Immaculate Conception, that it applied to the Annunciation, and, especially, we tried to see its application to Calvary. We now see the Holy Father making a further application of it:

> We must remember especially that, since the second century, the Virgin Mary has been presented by the Holy Fathers as the New Eve, who, although subject to the New Adam, was most closely associated with Him in that struggle against the infernal enemy which, as foretold in the protoevangelium, was to result in that most complete victory over sin and death, which are always correlated in the writings of the Apostle of the Gentiles. Wherefore, just as the glorious resurrection of Christ was an essential part and final sign of this victory, so also that struggle which was common to the Blessed Virgin and her Son had to be closed by the "glorification" of her virginal body; for, as the same Apostle says, "When this mortal body hath put on immortality, then shall come to pass the saying that is written: Death is swallowed up in victory." [12]

The thought is crystal clear: Mary is "most closely associated" with Christ in the struggle against the devil. That struggle won victory over sin and death. The victory over sin was won on Calvary. Mary shared in it, as we saw in an earlier chapter. The victory over death was, for Christ, the Resurrection, for Mary, the Assumption. The "struggle . . . was common to the Blessed Virgin and her Son." The Resurrection was "an essential part . . . of this victory." Hence, he infers, since Mary had taken a common part in the struggle that won the victory, she must also have shared in the fruit of the victory, the conquest of death — the Resurrection — which was "an essential part . . . of this victory." She did this by means of the Assumption. In the mind of the Holy Father, the lives of Jesus and Mary might be represented by two parallel lines. They are, in his thought, not merely parallel in all things, from the start on earth to the finish in the glory of Heaven, but there is also a common sharing: the struggle is "common" to both. *It is precisely because the struggle was common to both that the Assumption, which was Mary's way of sharing in the Resurrection, had to take place.* Here we see the grand sweep of the New Eve concept: nothing is an exception to it; it embraces every step from beginning to end of the Redemption.

In passing we may note what a difficulty it would be for a theologian who wished to deny Mary's immediate co-operation on Calvary to explain away the words of this document of definition. We would have two lines parallel at beginning and end, but not in the middle: only a gap in the middle of Mary's line. We would have to suppose the Holy Father argued that Mary, having had a common share with Christ *in all but the struggle,* would thereby be expected to share in the victory. We would have the Assumption parallel to the Resurrection, although the Resurrection is an "essential part" of the victory of Calvary, in which victory Mary would have no immediate part!

The definition of the Assumption is especially fitting and beneficial in this our age. For we live in an age given to gross materialism and the excessive cult of the body. By showing us the true destiny and worth of the body, the Holy Father provides us with a powerful weapon against our modern diseases. For if Christ is the first fruits of those that sleep,[13] so also is Mary: their resurrection and assumption show us vividly the true destiny and purpose of our own bodies.

NOTES

1. St. John of the Cross, *Living Flame of Love* I, xxx, *The Complete Works of St. John of the Cross*, trans. E. Allison Peers (Westminster, 1946), III, 135.

2. St. Francis de Sales, *Treatise on the Love of God*, trans. H. B. Mackey (Westminster, 1949), VII, xiv (p. 322).

3. *Ibid.*, VII, xiii–xiv (pp. 321 and 324).

4. See M. Jugie, A.A., "Assomption de la Sainte Vierge," in Du Manoir, *Maria*, I, 621–58.

5. See Robert North, S.J., "Mary's Last Home," *AER* 123 (October, 1950): 242–61.

6. See the complete text of the definition, *AER* 124 (January, 1951): 1–17. See also *ibid.*, Bishop John Wright, "The Dogma of the Assumption" (February, 1951), 81–96; and Juniper B. Carol, O.F.M., "The Apostolic Constitution *Munificentissimus Deus* and Our Blessed Lady's Coredemption," *AER* 125 (October, 1951): 255–73.

7. *AAS* 42:754.

8. *Ibid.*, 42:765–66.

9. *Ibid.*, 42:766.

10. *Ibid.*, 42:767–68.

11. *Ibid.*, 42:768.

12. *Ibid.*, 42:768.

13. See I Cor. 15:20.

VII . . . *The Queenship of Mary*

THE BEGINNINGS of the concept of Mary as Queen appear very early: the opening chapter of St. Luke's Gospel contains clear implications of her Queenship. In the account of the Annunciation, we read that Mary's Son is to be King forever, and Elizabeth at the Visitation salutes her as "the Mother of my Lord." Now if her Son is both Lord and King, surely Mary must be of queenly rank.

The Fathers of the Church were not long in developing these implications. For example, a text that is probably by Origen († 254) gives Mary the title *Domina*.[1] *Domina* is merely the feminine form of the Latin word for Lord, *Dominus*. We commonly translate it merely as "Lady," but in its fullest sense the word stands for "Sovereign Lady." The same title *Domina* also appears in many other early writers, such as St. Ephraem, St. Jerome, and St. Peter Chrysologus.[2] The word "queen" itself makes its appearance about the sixth century, and becomes common thereafter.[3]

But there is no need to seek for proof of Mary's queenship. The conclusion is obvious, and spontaneously flows from the dogmatic truths about Mary that we have already learned. It is an idea thoroughly familiar to us in our prayers, such as the *Hail, Holy Queen*, which we recite after every low Mass.

We may, however, seek to penetrate more deeply into the nature of Mary's Queenship. First of all, we must note that the titles of king and queen may be bestowed in either a metaphorical or a literal sense. In a metaphorical sense, we confer them upon those beings that excel in some way. Thus, for example, we call the lion the king of beasts, the rose the queen of flowers. It is obvious that Mary deserves the title of Queen in this broad sense of the word, for she is the highest of all mere creatures.

But not only in this loose, metaphorical sense is Mary a Queen: in the strictest literal sense also she is a Queen — and for many good reasons, which we shall discuss. Before doing so, however, we may note certain inadequate reasons that have been proposed. These inadequate reasons posit Mary's Queenship: 1. By right of natural inheritance; 2. By right of original justice; 3. By her relationship to the Father and the Holy Spirit.

Some theologians have reasoned thus: Mary is the daughter of David, King of Israel, and Jesus is of the same line. Hence, Jesus and Mary have a hereditary right to the throne of Israel. These theologians forget that not every child of a king becomes a king or a queen. Furthermore, it seems likely that Mary descended from David, not through Solomon, who inherited the throne, but through Nathan, who did not inherit it.[4] Thus it seems that a claim to merely temporal royalty for Jesus and Mary must be abandoned; but even if such a claim could be proved, it would be a poor title indeed to use for the King and Queen of Heaven.

The second inadequate reason for Mary's Queenship is her freedom from original sin. Some have argued that Adam and Eve possessed a domination over all things, according to the words of God in the book of Genesis:

> . . . let him have dominion over the fishes of the sea, and the fowls of the air, and the beasts, and the whole earth, and every creeping creature that moveth upon the earth.[5]

Now, it is argued, Mary was in the same position of innocence in which Adam and Eve were first created. We readily admit this,[6] and recall the New Eve parallel. But the royalty of Adam and Eve was largely metaphorical. Adam was the first head of the race in the sense that all were to descend from him and to inherit God's gifts through him. But he was not king in the sense of having legislative, executive, and judicial power over all humans. We note that the text of Genesis speaks of domination over animals, but not over human beings. There is no mention of a domination over all mankind.

The third inadequate reason is Mary's relationship to the Father and the Holy Spirit. She is rightly called the eldest daughter of the Father, and the spouse of the Holy Spirit. Hence, it is argued, she shares in their royalty. A perfectly valid argument for the Queenship of Mary can be drawn from her relation to the Son, as we shall see, but her relation to her Son is much different from her relation to the other two Persons of the Holy Trinity. To the Son she is related by real consanguinity, in the first degree and in the direct line; whereas her relations to the Father and the Holy Spirit are only relations of affinity. Therefore, it would seem that although this relation to the other two Persons is indeed glorious, and gives her a peerless eminence, the title of royalty it confers would be more metaphorical than literal.

Now that we have disposed of these inadequate reasons, it is time to search for the real, the adequate reasons for Mary's title of queen. We are indeed fortunate in that Pope Pius XII has, in recent years, given us a very clear statement on the matter. We have already seen part of it in an earlier chapter, for a related purpose. But it is necessary here to examine it in more detail:

> He, the Son of God, reflects on His heavenly Mother the glory, the majesty and the dominion of His kingship, for, having been associated to the King of Martyrs in the ineffable work of human Redemption as Mother and co-operatrix, she remains forever associated to Him, with an almost unlimited power, in the distribution of the graces which flow from the Redemption. Jesus is King throughout all eternity by nature and by right of conquest: through Him, with Him, and subordinate to Him, Mary is Queen by grace, by divine relationship, by right of conquest, and by singular election. And her kingdom is as vast as that of her Son and God, since nothing is excluded from her dominion.[7]

Let us analyze this beautiful passage. The Holy Father begins by giving the titles by which Christ is King. He is King "by

nature and by right of conquest." The Incarnate Word, Christ,
is one Person (the Second Person of the Holy Trinity) in two
natures: divine and human. These two natures are united in such
a way that the two natures remain distinct and not confused;
yet there is only one Person. We call this state "hypostatic union."
It is necessary to use a special term to describe it, since there is no
other example of this kind of union. The union of body and soul
to form a mere human being is in a way similar, but, in an ordinary human being, the person is composed of the two elements
in such a way that before the union took place, the person did not
exist. In the hypostatic union, the Person, a divine Person, always
existed, even before the union, from all eternity.

Now Christ, by virtue of the hypostatic union, is King "by nature," for in the fullest and strictest sense of the word, God Himself is the absolute King of all creatures. But in Christ there is only
one Person, a divine Person. By very nature that divine Person is
King of all. So much for the first title "by nature." As to the
second, "by right of conquest," we have already commented on it
in chapter III. We noted that it referred to the fact that Christ, by
His death, bought the human race back from the captivity of
the devil. Hence, having reconquered all, Christ is King "by right
of conquest."

In explaining Mary's Queenship, the Holy Father sets down
at the outset that she is Queen only "through Him, with Him,
and subordinate to Him." This qualification is obvious and needs
no explanation. Mary's Queenship is fundamentally a participation in the royalty of her Son. But the Holy Father goes into detail for us by specifying the precise titles on which her royalty
rests: "By grace, by divine relationship, by right of conquest, and
by singular election." Let us consider each title separately.

In saying that Mary is Queen by grace, we have a reason that
is valid in both the metaphorical and the literal sense. For Mary
is full of grace; yet, as we have explained in chapter II, her capacity and her actual degree of grace continued to grow at a staggering rate throughout her whole life. She is not merely of a
wonderfully higher degree of grace than all other creatures, her

dignity belongs to the hypostatic order, for it was in her womb that the hypostatic union, in virtue of which her Son is King by nature, was accomplished.

Mary is Queen "by divine relationship." Again, the title is valid in both the broad and the strict sense. In the broad sense it includes Mary's relations to the Father, as His eldest daughter, and to the Holy Spirit, as His spouse — relations of affinity, yet immeasurably great. But this divine relationship also, and especially, includes the fact that she is mother of the King. She is, as we have said, literally related to Him in the first degree, in the direct line of consanguinity. Further, since He had no human father, her relation is even more exclusive than that of other mothers. The objection is sometimes raised that, in earthly kingdoms, the queen-mother does not have royal power. This is true, but Mary is more than a mere queen-mother. For she is, as we have noted, the *sole* human parent. And, what is of special importance: earthly queen-mothers merely give birth to a child who *later* will become king. Mary gave birth to Him who *by very nature, from the very beginning,* was and is King of all. Hence she is in a position much different from that of an earthly queen-mother.

The next title "by right of conquest" has already been explained in chapter III. We noted that it is parallel to the same title mentioned for the Kingship of Christ — with the proper subordination. It uses the very same words. In reference to Christ, the title is quite familiar: it refers to His redemptive death, the very focal point and essential part of the Redemption. Therefore, in the case of Mary, it must express a co-operation in precisely the same thing: in the redemptive sacrifice on Calvary itself. In other words, it refers to Mary's immediate co-operation in what we have called the objective redemption (the great atonement and once-for-all earning of all graces). The Holy Father himself gave us the necessary qualification: "Through Him, with Him, and subordinate to Him." We should not presume to add any others.

It is possible to become a temporal king or queen by choice of the people. Jesus and Mary were rejected by their people, but the Father in Heaven accepted them. The second psalm speaks of the appointment of the Messias as King over Sion — meaning, of course, not merely the earthly Sion, but all men:

> . . . I am appointed king by him over Sion, his holy mountain. . . . The Lord hath said to me: "Thou art my son, this day have I begotten thee. Ask of me, and I will give thee the Gentiles for thy inheritance, and the utmost parts of the earth for thy possession." [8]

Mary likewise is Queen by divine appointment, by special choice ("singular election") of the Father.

How extensive is Mary's domain? The Holy Father tells us: "And her kingdom is as vast as that of her Son and God, since nothing is excluded from her dominion." Mary rules over the earth: all graces are distributed through her hands. No request that she makes of her Son, the King, is ever refused. She rules over Purgatory: she prompts the faithful on earth to pray for them. She herself applies to them the fruits of the Redemption earned by both Jesus and herself in co-operation. Her Queenship extends even to Hell. The demons are powerless against her. It is especially humiliating for the devil to be beaten by her, for, although he must rightly expect to suffer defeat at the hands of God Himself, it is galling that a mere creature should also foil him so thoroughly. Finally, her Queenship extends to Heaven itself. All who enjoy Heaven do so by virtue of the graces earned by Jesus and Mary in co-operation, as we have seen. Even the just of the Old Law were saved only in anticipation of the merits of Calvary, in which she co-operated. She also contributes to the *accidental* blessedness of those in Heaven. For though the *essential* joy there is the direct vision of God, there is accidental happiness also from the presence of the angels and saints, whose Queen is Mary.

Hence we may say that Mary is Queen of all things,[9] without limit to her domain, in the strict sense of the word. Let us thank God for giving us a Queen who is *par excellence* the "Mother of Mercy."

NOTES

1. See *Marian Studies,* IV (1953), 87.
2. See *ibid.,* IV, 87–91.
3. See *ibid.,* IV, 91–94.
4. See G. M. Roschini, O.S.M., "Royauté de Marie," Du Manoir, *Maria,* I, 614.
5. Gen. 1:26.
6. Except that Mary, though free of sin, was so only by anticipation of the merits of Christ, while Eve was in need of redemption only *after* the fall.
7. Radio message to Fatima (May 13, 1946), *AAS* 38:266. Quoted from *AER,* November, 1949, p. 358.
8. Ps. 2:6–8.
9. In general, see all of Vol. IV of *Marian Studies* on Mary's Queenship.

VIII ... *The Necessity and Extent of Devotion to Mary*

Good Catholics sometimes wonder how much attention they ought to give to Mary in their prayers and other religious practices. They do not put the question so mathematically as to ask what percentage of a holy hour, for example, should be devoted to prayers to Mary, for if the question were stated in that way it might imply that prayers to Mary are said at the expense of devotion to her Son — which would be ridiculous. *If our devotion to Mary were to take away anything from devotion to Him, it would have to be rejected.* But such is not the case. To discover the correct answer to the question, we need to recall what place God Himself has assigned to Mary in His plans, for surely, we can do no better than to imitate His ways. Accordingly, it might be profitable to sum up briefly the conclusions we have reached in our study of the dogmatic truths about Mary.

From all eternity God had laid his plans for Mary. The Church in her liturgy often applies to Mary a beautiful and fitting passage from the Old Testament:

> The Lord possessed me in the beginning of his ways, before he made anything from the beginning. I was set up from eternity, and of old before the earth was made.[1]

Of course the Church does not mean to tell us that Mary always existed. Since God, however, had in mind from all eternity each creature that He planned to make, then, for the greater reason, He must have planned for this most excellent of all mere creatures, and decided all the graces and favors He would lavish on her.

He planned in advance to make her the associate of the Redeemer, for at the time of the fall of our first parents He at once promised the Redeemer, and spoke of a "woman" who, being at enmity with the serpent, would share in the struggle and in the victory against the enemy of mankind.[2] He already had in mind to provide a New Eve as well as a New Adam. He planned that the New Eve should be conceived immaculate, by the anticipated application to her of the merits of her Son.

On the day of the Annunciation God sent a great archangel to honor her in His own name. He decreed that the Incarnation should take place only after asking her consent, only at her *fiat*. He decreed that although His time had not yet come, the Son should nonetheless work His first miracle at her request at Cana of Galilee. He decreed that on Calvary Mary should stand, not as a mere spectator, but as the one who had furnished the flesh in which the Victim would be offered, as one joining in the sentiments of the heart of the Victim, so that with Him and through Him one joint offering should be made to the Father. He decreed that on Pentecost the Holy Spirit should be given to the new-born Church through her mighty prayers. He decreed that, after the end of her earthly life, she should be taken up to Heaven in body as well as in soul, there to be crowned Queen of all, and to distribute absolutely all graces to men. Finally, according to a prophecy of St. Louis de Montfort,[3] God has planned that just as Christ came to us the first time through Mary, so also His second coming will be preceded by an age of Mary.[4] Many scripture scholars think this fact is also foretold in the mysterious vision of St. John in the Apocalypse in which he saw a woman clothed with the sun.[5] For it seems probable that the woman represents both Mary and the Church, indicating thereby that the Church is to take on an especially Marian character during the age before the second coming of her Son.

To sum up, we can see that the place God has given to Mary

is all-embracing: her influence appears throughout every phase of the Redemption, from its first prophecy in Eden to the distribution of the last graces at the end of time and the coming of the Son of Man to judgment.

Mary, of course, was not necessary to God. Still, although the merits of the Redeemer alone were infinite and superabundant, so that He alone would more than suffice without the help of Mary or of any other saint, God freely willed to associate Mary most intimately with Jesus both in the acquisition of all graces and in their distribution. It is perfectly true that, in the nature of things, God could have done well without Mary. Nevertheless, He has made it abundantly clear that He actually wishes to employ Mary as His inseparable associate and helper in the work of our redemption. So when we ask how much attention we ought to give to Mary, what place we should assign to her, the answer is: If we wish to imitate the ways of God as perfectly as we can, we will try to give her an all-pervading place in our lives.

If our attention to her detracted at all from the honor of her Son, we should have to ignore her completely. But the truth is that whatever honor we pay to Mary redounds to the glory of her Son, and whatever good works we give to Mary, we offer through her, for she passes them all on to Him. As St. Louis de Montfort expresses this truth:

> She presents these good works to Jesus Christ; for she keeps nothing of what is given her for herself, as if she were our last end. She faithfully passes it all on to Jesus. If we give to her, we give necessarily to Jesus. If we praise or glorify her, she immediately praises and glorifies Jesus. As of old when St. Elizabeth praised her, so now when we praise her and bless her she sings: "My soul doth magnify the Lord." [6]

He who uses Mary to go to Jesus, imitates Jesus Himself, who used and still uses Mary to come to us. Furthermore, the act of humility implied in not willing to approach Him alone, but only in the company of Mary, pleases Him greatly. For humility is one of the virtues which, as we shall see,[7] most effectively draws down the favor of God on us.

Someone may object that if we never pray except through Mary, we are excluded from intimacy with Our Lord, His heavenly Father, and the Holy Spirit. To answer this difficulty we must note that there are two ways in which we might understand the expression "to pray through Mary": 1. We pray through Mary when we, as it were, come to her and make our prayer, and ask that she convey it to God for us: in this way we do not speak directly to God; or, 2. We speak directly to God Himself, but relying on the intercession of Mary for the granting of our prayer, since all graces come through her. Even when we pray in this second way, although it is very good, it is not required that we expressly ask her intercession each time: the invocation of Mary is at least implicit in every request for a favor, since everyone who prays rightly intends to ask in accordance with the order of salvation which God has established.[8] In this order, as we have seen, God intends to grant nothing except through Mary. It is clear that we may and should use both methods, according as the occasion and the inspirations of grace suggest. Thus we see that to pray through Mary not only does not detract from our intimacy with God, but promotes it, for we can approach God our Father, and Christ our Brother, and the Holy Spirit with all the more confidence in the company of the Mother of God, the Spouse of the Holy Spirit.

But it is not only through abstract principles that we see that devotion to Mary promotes the honor of her Son; history teaches the same lesson. For the greatest devotion to Mary is found in the greatest saints, while Protestantism, which began by rejecting Mary, has now, in some of its branches, rejected the divinity of her Son. Since God distributes no graces without Mary, and since the majority of Protestants ignore Mary, are they thereby deprived of all grace? Certainly not. Mary is a good Mother — she obtains various graces for all sorts of men for which they have not prayed at all. And so she will pray even for those who ignore her, provided they are in good faith. In this connection we may also recall that, as stated above, anyone who prays well, at least implicitly calls on Mary, whether or not he realizes that fact. But, of course, the more fully one falls in line with God's plan of the distribution of all graces through Mary, the more he pleases God, and the more grace he will receive.

But, one may object, if Mary's intercession is so universal, what becomes of the other saints? Are they not then useless? Are we not taught to believe in the Communion of Saints? The answer is quite easy. We have noted above that, strictly speaking, in view of the boundless treasures of the merits of Christ, God *could have* left Mary out altogether. Merely because His goodness wished it, however, He has so arranged things that He uses Mary's co-operation in all stages of the Redemption. The case is somewhat similar with the saints. Strictly speaking, God could do without them, just as He could do without Mary. Yet it is idle to speak of what God could do but does not do; the important thing is to find what He actually does. What He does is this: He has freely willed that we should make use of the intercession of the saints as well as of Mary, with this difference: Mary's intercession is always at work, her realm is universal, while the domain of any other saint is limited, and, in a way, occasional. Therefore we not merely may, but should, pay honor to various saints, our patron saints, the patron of our school, of our parish, and various others according to our own position, wishes, and needs. When we ask a favor through one of the other saints, that saint, whether or not we ask him to do so, will not ask it without the aid of the intercession of Mary, for, as we have seen, it is God's will that no graces should be given except through her.

Furthermore, the type of honor we pay to Mary is not merely of a higher degree than the honor we pay to other saints: it is of a higher kind. For the honor given to the saints in general is called *dulia,* while that paid to Mary is called *hyperdulia.*[9] The reason for the distinction is this: Mary, by being Mother of God, belongs to the hypostatic order; the other saints do not.[10]

Especially do we rely on Mary's protection and help to obtain for us that grace which the Council of Trent calls the great gift: the gift of final perseverance, which alone is sufficient and necessary to make our death a happy death. Now the age-old tradition of the Church tells us that anyone who is devoted to Mary will obtain this most necessary gift. Not that one could practice some devotion to Mary and then, relying on it for safety, live a sinful or careless life. No, such a "devotion" would really be not devotion but presumption. St. Alphonsus and many another saint and Doctor of the Church tell us that it is morally impossible for anyone who is really devout to Mary to be lost. We shall have more to say on this subject in our treatment of the Brown Scapular of Mount Carmel.[11] For the present, let us listen to the solid and authoritative assurance given us by the words of Pope Benedict XV that our trust in Mary to obtain this great gift for us is well founded:

> With her suffering and dying Son, Mary endured suffering and almost death. She gave up her mother's rights over her Son in order to procure the salvation of mankind, and to appease the divine justice, she, as much as she could, immolated her Son, so that one can truly affirm that together with Christ she has redeemed the human race. Now since for this reason every kind of grace which we receive from the treasury of the Redemption is ministered as it were through the hands of the Sorrowful Virgin, no one can fail to see that *it is from her also that we must look for a holy death,* for it is precisely by this gift that the work of the Redemption is effectively and eternally completed in each individual man.[12]

Even more striking are the words of Pope Pius XI:

> . . . nor would he incur eternal death whom the Most Blessed Virgin assists, especially at his last hour. This opinion of the Doctors of the Church, in harmony with the sentiments of the Christian people, and supported by the experience of all times, depends especially on this reason: the fact that the Sorrowful Virgin shared in the work of the redemption with Jesus Christ.[13]

The Holy Father not merely makes his own the opinion that we may justifiably put our trust in Mary's help to obtain final perseverance, but he enlarges on the theme, pointing out that actual experience throughout all ages has confirmed its truth. It is the view of both the laity and of the Doctors and saints of the Church. And its support is most solid: Mary shared in the work of Redemption. Since it was with her co-operation that every grace, including the grace of final perseverance, was earned for all, it is logical that we should with the greatest confidence seek that grace at her hands.

Hence we can now see that devotion to Mary is not to be considered as optional or as a luxury item in the spiritual life. At least a certain basic filial devotion to Mary is a necessity, even for salvation (unless, of course, one is excused by ignorance). This follows from the fact that God has made Mary the constant subordinate helper of His Divine Son throughout all the work of the Redemption, so that He dispenses no graces except through her. No one can say that he loves the Son who ignores the Mother. Certainly it would be a great disorder for anyone to go directly contrary to the plans of God and neglect Mary. Pope Leo XIII expressed this idea with special force when he said:

> Such is the greatness of Mary, such the favor she has with God, that he who when in need of help would not run to her, would wish to fly without the aid of wings.[14]

Of course, as we have already said, it is not necessary that we ask explicitly for the intercession of Mary each time we pray.

Most Catholics, even those whose devotion to Mary is not especially strong, have learned an excellent prayer, which is a good means of showing the soul's desire to correspond with the plans of God for Mary. It is the morning offering of the Apostleship of Prayer, which begins:

> O Jesus, through the Immaculate Heart of Mary, I offer You my prayers, works, joys, and sufferings of this day, for all the intentions of Your Sacred Heart. . . .

It is to be recommended that every Catholic make some such offering as this at least at times. Just as God has willed to give all to us through Mary, so, by such an offering, we give whatever we have to offer back to Him through Mary.

Marian devotion begins most naturally in the home. Parents can confer a priceless favor on their children if from earliest years they teach them to take a childlike attitude to God our Father and Mary our Mother. A child's very notion of the meaning of the words father and mother depends largely on what sort of persons its parents are. If the parents are all that they should be, children easily learn to look upon God as the best of fathers, and to love Mary their Mother. An outstanding example of the powerful good influence of parental example of this kind can be seen in the life of St. Thérèse of Lisieux. On the other hand, the poor example of parents, or the lack of good example, is a spiritual hindrance to the children. In this connection we should point out that if parents for a great part of the time give their children into the hands of baby-sitters, the children can easily learn to think of father and mother as persons who do not wish to be bothered. Such children are handicapped in forming a correct idea of the Fatherhood of God and the Motherhood of Mary.

Are all souls obliged to adopt a form of spirituality in which they enter into special intimacy with Mary, so that they live in ever increasing consciousness of her presence, call on her lovingly in everything, and do everything to please her? Definitely no. There are legitimate differences in spiritual attractions on this point.[15] Those whose devotion to Mary is of a less intimate kind can not only grow in holiness, but can even become saints. Even in these souls, however, devotion to Mary will necessarily grow as they advance in grace, even though it does not take the intimate form.[16]

Within the area of specially Marian forms of spirituality there are many degrees and variations. The most complete form of Marian spirituality calls for a total consecration, such as that of St. Louis de Montfort,[17] but even within this realm some souls reach more advanced degrees than others, as St. Louis himself remarks.[18] To attain the highest and closest form of intimacy with Mary, the special action of the Holy Spirit, received through the

Gifts, is needed; for it is this Divine Spirit, the Spouse of Mary, who produces in the most thoroughly Marian souls a truly Christ-like love for the Mother of Christ.[19]

Although it is possible for souls to reach sanctity by paths that do not involve close intimacy with Mary, yet the more thoroughly Marian the way, the greater the advantages for a soul. Speaking of the total consecration, St. Louis de Montfort wrote:

> There have been some saints, but they have been in small numbers, who have walked upon this sweet path to go to Jesus, because the Holy Ghost, faithful Spouse of Mary, by a singular grace disclosed it to them. Such were St. Ephrem, St. John Damascene, St. Bernard, St. Bernardine, St. Bonaventure, St. Francis of Sales, and others. But the rest of the saints who are the greater number, although they have all had devotion to our Blessed Lady, nevertheless have either not at all, or at least very little, entered upon this way. *That is why they have had to pass through ruder and more dangerous trials.*[20] [*Emphasis added.*]

Souls that walk in this Marian path go by a way that is shorter, easier, safer, surer, and yet more perfect and more meritorious than those who do not.[21] In this our day, the age of Mary,[22] this privilege of a thoroughly Marian life is being given to a great many souls. May God grant it abundantly to us.

NOTES

1. Prov. 8:22–23. The text literally referred primarily to Divine Wisdom, but is fittingly applied to Mary.

2. Gen. 3:15: "I will put enmities between thee and the woman, and thy seed and her seed." On the Marian interpretation of this passage, see Appendix IV A.

3. See St. Louis de Montfort, *True Devotion to the Blessed Virgin Mary*, trans. F. W. Faber (Bay Shore, N.Y., 1941), §§49–59, 158.

4. Pope Pius XII, in a private conversation with the Director of the General Secretariate of all Sodalities in Rome, stated that we are now in the age of Mary (reported in *Our Lady's Digest*, August–September, 1951, p. 119). Of course no one knows whether the age of Mary is to last a few years or a few centuries.

5. The vision is narrated in Apocalypse 12. On the view that the vision represents Mary and the Church, see Appendix IV B.

6. St. Louis de Montfort, *op. cit.*, §148.

7. See chap. XI.

8. See Roschini, *Mariologia*, IV, 29.

9. *Dulia* is a Greek word meaning "service." The prefix *hyper* means "above."

10. For the term "hypostatic union" see chap. VII.

11. See chap. XXII.

12. *AAS* 10:182.

13. *AAS* 15:104.

14. *ASS* 30:133.

15. See Ven. Michael of St. Augustine, "The Mariform and Marian Life, in Mary, for Mary," in *Life with Mary*, ed. Thomas McGinnis, O.Carm. (New York, 1953), pp. 21–22; and St. Louis de Montfort, *op. cit.*, §152.

16. The reason is that all virtues in their perfect form advance together. Furthermore, the Gift of Piety, by which we love all that God loves, will, in the upper levels of the spiritual life, bring forth a manifest growth in the love of Mary whom God loves so dearly. On the Gifts in general see chap. XIX.

17. We shall treat this total consecration in chap. XVIII.

18. St. Louis de Montfort, *op. cit.*, §119.

19. See chap. XIX.

20. St. Louis de Montfort, *op. cit.*, §152.

21. See R. Garrigou-Lagrange, O.P., *The Three Ages of the Interior Life*, trans. Sr. Timothea Doyle, O.P. (St. Louis, 1948), II, 268–71.

22. See note 4 above.

IX ... *Mary Teaches Us to Love and to Grow*

IN EVERY ASPECT and part of our spiritual life God's graces come to us through Mary. Clearly, the more we on our part cooperate with this all-pervading influence of Mary, the more we shall please God, and the greater the good to our souls. Those who have received the privilege of an intimately Marian form of spirituality will live in a closer, more familiar way with Mary. But each in his own way will benefit greatly from making full use of her help. To see how this can be accomplished, let us examine, with Mary's help and example, some of the more basic facts about the spiritual life in general.

Many a well-intentioned person, seriously desiring to improve himself spiritually, to grow in grace, sets out to do so with strangely confused ideas of how to go about it. If he turns to certain books on spirituality, the very richness of their detail may confuse him. There are many pitfalls to his spiritual progress. One may specialize in fasting or other forms of mortification. He has read glowing descriptions of the heroic mortifications of the saints, and quickly concludes that spiritual growth and penance are the same thing. At the same time he may overlook the fact that he has become irritable to family and friends, and indulges in uncharitable words and acts. Still another thinks that interior progress consists in multiplying prayers. If formerly he said one Rosary a day, he now says three. And, since he knows that he should advance constantly, never stopping for fear of falling back, he is prepared to double the number of his prayers each year or two, or at least to increase them indefinitely, until he has reached a staggering total. The very same person may think little or nothing of exchanging the latest gossip whenever the opportunity presents itself.

66

Others become attached to giving away their money to the poor or to the missions. This, they think, is charity, and charity is the greatest of the virtues. Yet, hidden in their hearts, and not too far beneath the surface, may lie bitter resentment for what they consider wrongs done them by their relatives or neighbors or friends. They will draw forth these lurking memories whenever the original offenders commit any new "crime," and recite the complete litany of abuses perpetrated against them. Or, indeed, they may boast of their almsgiving.

These are but some of the varied and subtle distortions that may creep into the idea of self-perfection. The disturbing thing is not merely that these false notions may hinder progress, but, what is worse, that they may easily lull one into a false sense of security so that he does not realize that he is falling into really grave faults.[1]

Far be it from us to give the impression that there is anything wrong with mortification, with many prayers, with giving generously to the poor. These acts are not only not wrong; actually they are among the outstanding means to perfection, and many people use these means without falling into any of the vices that we have mentioned. *The danger lies in confusing the means with the end.* We must always keep in mind in what perfection and spiritual growth really consist, and if we do, we shall be in a better position to evaluate and utilize the means to that end.

On one occasion Our Lord was asked to explain what is the great commandment, the one that sums up all else. We all know the answer:

> Jesus said to him, "Thou shalt love the Lord thy God with thy whole heart, and with thy whole soul, and with thy whole mind. This is the greatest and the first commandment. And the second is like to this: Thou shalt love thy neighbor as thyself. On these two commandments dependeth the whole Law and the Prophets." [2]

Mary understood and practiced this commandment more perfectly than all other human beings. Other hearts appear cold compared to the flame of her love. Everything depends on love: love of God, and of neighbor for the sake of God. One who really loves God will not fail to love neighbor for God's sake. Hence, in practice, there is only one commandment, to which all else may be reduced: *Love.* Everything else — penance, almsgiving, prayers, sacraments, even devotion to Mary — all are means to that great end of love of God; and among them, some are more effective than others. *Devotion to Mary, properly understood, is the means that permeates all other means, and causes us to obtain more benefit from them.* Therefore, devotion to Mary does not compete with the other means to spiritual growth; it makes all others more fruitful.

The very essence of perfection is perfect love of God, to which is joined love of neighbor. Obviously, then, to grow in the spiritual life is to grow in the love of God — and in practice this is the same as to grow in sanctifying grace. But the very word *love* is often misunderstood. In our day it has been mangled almost beyond recognition in popular songs. We easily absorb the impression that love is largely an emotion — or, at least, that it must have an emotional accompaniment. Such is not the case: pure love consists in an attitude of will. The presence or absence of emotion is an accidental feature. This truth is easy to see when we reflect that if love really required emotion, it would be virtually impossible for us to love certain of our neighbors; it would even be impossible to love God most of the time, for most of us do not often feel emotion toward God. Yet God has commanded us to love Him always, above all things, and to love even our enemies. Were emotion required, He would be commanding an impossibility.

Love consists fundamentally in an attitude of our will. St. Thomas says that to love is to will good to someone.[3] It is obvious that this sort of love is much more solid, more noble, more lasting and permanent than a flickering emotion. Now there are chiefly two aspects or kinds of love of God: we may love God because He is *good for us,* that is, because He is our eternal reward: this is called *love of desire;* and we may love God because He is *good in Himself:* this is called *love of benevolence.* There is no conflict between the two: the same God who is infinitely good in Himself, who *is* love, is also infinitely good for and to us.[4]

It is easy enough to understand the nature of the *love of desire;* in it the soul longs for God, its eternal Good. As for the *love of benevolence,* we may note three stages of its full development. First of all, this love of benevolence begins when the soul sees how good God is, and when it takes pleasure (not necessarily emotional pleasure) in the fact that God not merely possesses, but *is,* Infinite Good. From this beginning there naturally arises the wish to do good to God. If it were possible, the soul would wish to increase the goodness that God has and is in Himself; but since it knows well that this is impossible, it at least wishes to increase the manifestation of His goodness, so that all creatures may know, love, and serve Him. But a love that would go no further than merely wishing well would be ineffective indeed. Hence the third stage is one of *doing.* The soul not only loves and serves God Himself, but labors to make others do the same. Thus love is by its very nature apostolic. The stronger the love, the greater the lengths to which the soul will go to please God and to induce others to please Him. Little love will be satisfied with giving little; great love will give much; perfect love will give all. Strong love feeds on difficulties, even on suffering. As St. Augustine says, "In love there is either no difficulty, or the difficulty itself is loved." [5]

In stating that love goes forth into action, we are not implying that love must always be busied in exterior works: no, the heart of love is found in the will.[6] Love springs forth into action according as various circumstances call for it. To identify love with external activity would be a great error, sometimes referred to nontechnically as the "heresy of good works." Love does tend to action, but that activity must be fed by interior love, or it will bear no fruit.[7] We must remember that those who live in contemplative communities, although apparently not active, are really promoting the glory of God in a wonderful way by their prayer and penance.

Our love of God is really a friendship. Friendship involves two things: mutual love of benevolence known to both, and a mutual exchange of good things, tending toward union. It is obvious that between God and the man who has charity this friendship does exist. For there is a mutual love of benevolence, which God has shown to us, and which we show to Him. There is also an interchange of favors, tending toward the perfect union of the beatific vision. As for the interchange of good things, God's favors to us are enormous. On our side, although, strictly speaking, He cannot gain anything from us, yet we can strive to promote the manifestation of His goodness in ourselves and in others, so that His great desire to give His goodness and love to us may not go unrealized. This zeal pertains to *doing* for God, the third stage in love of benevolence.

There is no conflict between these two kinds of love of God — the love of benevolence that considers Him as good in Himself, and the love of desire that considers Him as good to us, as our eternal blessedness. Rather, they go together. It is the same God who is good in Himself and good to us, and our eternal beatitude is a means to the glory of God as well as good to us. It is merely necessary that we preserve the proper proportion between the two, and that in every desire for our own eternal good we avoid making ourselves the ultimate end; i.e., we refer even our happiness to God, desiring to be with Him to glorify Him forever. Therefore we ought to desire God as our eternal good chiefly and primarily for His sake, for the manifestation and spread of His goodness and glory. But we do not thereby exclude the desire of God for our own happiness as a secondary end. Even in perfect souls both loves are found. But the love of desire undergoes a shift of emphasis: even in seeking its own happiness, a soul advanced in love thinks of the possession of God in Heaven not so much as a reward, but as a union with the object of its love. Thus the reward aspect tends to recede into the background as one develops.[8] In this way a soul forgets itself, as it were, in thinking of its Beloved. Yet, at least in an implicit way, the legitimate desire for our own good is always present, though one does not

always advert to it. In fact, in Heaven, although the blessed love
God principally and immeasurably more because He is good in
Himself, they also love Him as their own happiness (referring
this also ultimately to Him who is their friend). Thus St. Anselm
says that a soul in Heaven,

> . . . will love God incomparably more than self and all others
> with self; [and] so will rejoice immeasurably more over the
> blessedness that God has than over its own blessedness and that
> of all others with it.[9]

As St. Thomas observes, if God were not *our* good, we could
admire Him, but not love Him.[10] To hold that pure love should
positively sacrifice the desire for salvation would be the heresy of
the Quietists.[11] Hence we see that not all self-love is wrong.
When spiritual writers speak of it as evil, they mean a *disordered*
love of self, one that is out of proportion or that at least in practice subordinates God to self rather than self to God.[12]

We should love God more than ourselves. Deep within the
human soul there is a tendency to love God more than self.[13]
Original and personal sin have weakened and obscured this tendency. But it is still there, even in the natural order. This does
not seem strange when we recall that a parent may readily sacrifice his or her life to save that of the child. Grace gradually heals
the wounds of sin, and elevates the natural tendency to the
supernatural plane, making it possible for us to love God more
than ourselves in the supernatural order. In fact, as we have said,
in generous souls the love of desire changes its orientation, so
that even in seeking their own happiness the fact that Heaven
is a reward is overshadowed by the fact that it is a union with
the Beloved. On this point St. Thérèse says:

> There is a verse in the Divine Office which I recite each day
> with reluctance: "I have inclined my heart to do Thy justifica-
> tions for ever, because of the reward." I hasten to add in my
> heart: "My Jesus, Thou knowest I do not serve Thee for sake
> of reward, but solely out of love and a desire to win Thee
> souls." [14]

◁ She loves to think of God as love, who desires most earnestly to give Himself, though He gains nothing out of so doing.[15] She tries to imitate that Divine generosity.[16] (In the language of a saint on fire with love we must not look for the nice precision of language of a theologian who is concerned with avoiding Quietistic errors.)

So we see that perfect love does not exclude the well-ordered self-love just described: it merely refines self-love and subordinates it, at an enormous distance, to the love of benevolence.[17]

In another sense, we may distinguish three kinds of perfect love of God. The first kind would love God as much as He deserves. No creature is capable of that. The second would love God with all its powers, constantly, at every moment, without any intermission or slackening. This is possible only in Heaven. The third kind is that which is possible on this earth. It is a love that puts our wills perfectly in harmony with His,[18] and excludes all that hinders the soul from loving God with all its strength. It is a love whose activity excludes not only mortal and deliberate venial sin, but also every voluntary imperfection.[19] In such a state, the soul will still commit some venial sins of frailty or surprise, as well as slight imperfections (also in frailty or surprise). Such occasional slips cannot be avoided in this life. For although a man has, strictly speaking, the strength (with the help of grace) to avoid any one sin taken by itself, he cannot have the perseverance to avoid all together, except by a most special favor of grace.[20] These occasional failings do not alter the fact that a soul may *habitually* have perfect love.

The distinction of deliberate venial sins from sins of frailty and surprise is of capital importance. For fully deliberate venial sins are serious obstacles to perfection, and, if we commit them out of an affection for them, we set up a complete block to our spiritual growth: no actual increase in the love of God is possible until we resolve to give up these deliberate sins.[21] There are some souls whose attitude, if clearly expressed, would be something like this: I do not intend to commit any mortal sins, nor do I plan to commit every venial sin that presents itself to me. But, on the other hand, I do not plan to avoid every venial sin: sometimes it would be inconvenient to avoid lying,[22] and it is good fellowship to join at times in a bit of uncharitable conversation. Such a soul does not really intend to avoid certain venial sins all the time. Its attitude shows a considerable lack of generosity, a callousness toward God's love. A soul cannot advance in love in the presence of such a deficiency.[23] But venial sins of frailty or surprise are not such an obstacle. For if we are sincerely trying to avoid all sin, and after each sin of frailty or surprise we humble ourselves, make a fervent, fully deliberate act of contrition and renew our good resolve, God will draw good out of evil and make these small faults into steppingstones for us.

We said that perfect love excludes deliberate imperfections. What is an imperfection? It is a morally good act, which can be used remotely as a means to love, but which lacks a certain perfection suitable to spiritual progress. Countless examples of imperfection could be listed, such as: *remiss acts* — that is, acts that fall below our habitual degree of love, as when an advanced soul makes an act of love or receives the sacraments with no more than the fervor proper to beginners;[24] *merely natural activities* — things not forbidden, yet not perfectly subjected to grace, such as certain needless amusements, small attachments to books, places, persons, kinds of food; many restless and useless *desires;*[25] and *omissions* of good things which are not commanded, but which we could easily perform.

As we have said, an imperfection is not morally evil: it is only something *less* good, but still *basically* good. Consequently, if an imperfection is performed for a good motive, it will not be sinful, it may even be slightly meritorious.[26] The merit that may possibly be obtained will, however, give us at most only a *title* to a *future* increase in love: the *actual increase in love* is not given until sometime later, when the soul is properly disposed.[27] For imperfection does not give us the disposition for immediate growth; rather, it inclines us, in a sense, toward venial sin. The motive for which we perform these less perfect acts needs careful watching. For if the motive is not good, then venial sin will accidentally be present. Such an unreasonable motive for doing a lesser good would be, for example, mere sloth, or contempt for spiritual values, or a whim of pleasure.

Any imperfection for which we keep an affection is a great hindrance to our spiritual progress. We cannot actually reach perfection until this affection is renounced. Of this St. Francis de Sales says:

> It is true . . . that we can never attain to perfection while we have an affection for any imperfection however small it may be, even nothing more than the harbouring of an idle thought. . . . and one fault, however small it may be, for which we keep an affection, is more contrary to perfection than a hundred others committed inadvertently and without affection.[28]

The commandment, "Be you therefore perfect, as also your heavenly Father is perfect," [29] is given to *all*. But despite its unequivocal wording, it is open to misinterpretation. One error would suppose that all were obliged to attain *at once* the maximum possible perfection. The other would restrict the command to those who enter the religious life, or would treat it as a mere counsel, not a command. But it is the teaching of St. Thomas Aquinas, confirmed by many theologians, and, in our own times, by Pope Pius XI, that this text is a command, and does apply to all.[30]

This command of Our Lord sets before us the perfection of God Himself as matter for imitation. It is obvious that we can never decide that we have gone far enough. We must advance constantly throughout our entire lives. For the very limitless character of this goal indicates that He does not demand that we attain it at once. It can only mean that we ought to grow constantly up to the very end. The force with which this obligation applies to any person varies according to his state in life, the graces God gives him, and his present state of progress. It is obvious that it applies more forcefully to priests and religious than to the laity. *But it does apply to all.* There should not be two classes of Catholics: those who wish to grow, and those who wish merely to "get by." All are called to perfection: hence perfection is possible in all states of life, as we can see from the calendar of saints: for there we find not only priests and monks and nuns, but married saints and other layfolk as well.

It is less easy to understand the latitude in its application according to one's present degree of progress. We might illustrate the problem by a comparison. A two-year-old child butchers its native language: hardly a word comes out without being badly mangled and distorted in the process. Strictly speaking, this is far from perfect. Yet those who hear it are not only not displeased; they may even enjoy it. Why? Because the child is acting as befits his age. On an *absolute* scale, he is far from perfect. But on the *relative* scale, relative to what can be expected of a child of that age, his performance is satisfactory. But suppose that ten years later, at the age of twelve, the same child is still speaking in the same way. He is no longer attractive; he is a tragedy, a freak; his parents will probably put him into an institution for professional treatment. The case is similar in the spiritual life. God has a certain standard and rate of progress to which each ought to conform, according to his ability, his graces, and his state in life.

Progress is ordinarily gradual.[31] To attempt to take a large leap all at one time would probably result, not in progress, but in a fall, perhaps to a level even lower than that from which the leap began. But all must constantly advance: he who does not go forward inevitably goes backward: he becomes a distorted freak in the spiritual life.

Let us not forget to avoid the dangers mentioned at the start of this chapter. Other things being equal, a fervent man will say more Rosaries, practice more penance, spend more time before the Blessed Sacrament, than a less fervent man. There is no limit to growth in interior perfection; but there is a limit on mere multiplication of *external* practices. Prudence sets this limit. *The essential part of progress consists in growth in the love of God which we habitually possess and which we put into all that we do.* There is a limit to the multiplication of practices; there is no limit to love.

The rate of progress depends on the degree of grace we already possess, on what new graces God offers to us, and on the generosity and fervor of love with which we respond to God's new offers. Just as a stone dropped from an airplane increases steadily in speed as it approaches its goal, so also should a soul advance more rapidly the closer it comes to God. God is generous with the generous: ". . . to everyone that hath shall be given." [32] Imagine the staggering rate at which Mary advanced in grace, being so close to God from the very start, being faultlessly faithful in corresponding to every new opportunity presented to her. She who lived so close to her Son, who grew so rapidly herself, is a safe and effective helper for us who wish to grow to be like her Son.

In loving God we need to learn to take the attitude of a small child to the best of fathers. In varying degrees, a dread of God's might and justice, or at least a deficiency in the proper childlike confidence, hinders our advance toward our good Father. Mary, who is pre-eminently the Mother of mercy, can teach us to know and trust Him, for she makes us learn His loving fatherliness by experience. She shows us that His Heart is like hers — or, rather, it is immeasurably more loving. The Apostle John, in whose home Mary lived so long, learned well, for he wrote, "God is love." [33] Mary teaches us that although we will certainly want to do everything we can to please God if we really love Him, yet, we do not, as it were, have to "buy" His love. Imagine any child who would say to itself: "I must do this and that about the house and yard, and so I will get my father and mother to love and take care of me." A really loving child will do all it can to show its love, and the parents will appreciate and reward such efforts, but the real reason why its father and mother love it is not because the child is good, but because they are good.

Finally, Mary will not let us forget that we are not the only children in the family: we must love all the children of God because He loves them. If we think we love God and do not love our brothers and sisters, we deceive ourselves. As St. John says, "If any man say, 'I love God,' and hateth his brother, he is a liar."[34] He who does not love Mary, the greatest of all the adopted children of God, who is at the same time God's Mother, does not love God Himself.[35] Since she is the closest of all to God, we shall approach Him in the measure in which we are led by her to His love, to Him who is love.

NOTES

1. For a brilliant development of the thoughts just presented, see St. Francis de Sales, *Introduction to the Devout Life*, I, 1; or L. Scupoli, *The Spiritual Combat*, §1.

2. Matt. 22:37-40.

3. *ST*, I–II, q.26, a.4. c. For an excellent study of love, see St. Francis de Sales, *Treatise on the Love of God*.

4. I John 4:16: "God is love." [*Confraternity version.*]

5. St. Augustine, *De Bono Viduitatis*, XXI, xxvi.

6. Unfortunately, the language we use in speaking of the love of God must include many words that have a connotation of emotion. It must be constantly kept in mind that love of God may be perfect, and still no emotion may be present. The precise role of emotion in this matter will be considered in the next chapter. For the present it is sufficient to note that we may have great emotion and no love, and, conversely, great love and no emotion. Of course, both may be present together.

7. See Pope Pius XII, *Menti nostrae* (September 23, 1950), §60 in the NCWC translation.

8. There are, as we have seen, two kinds of love:

    1. The love of benevolence, which is not self-seeking;

    2. The love of desire, which is self-seeking, for by it we desire God for our own happiness. But within this self-seeking love we may have two ways of looking at the attainment of our goal, the possession of God:

        a) We may think of that goal as a reward;

        b) We may think of it as union with the Beloved. This latter aspect is still self-seeking, for in it the lover wants the Beloved for his own satisfaction, but it is more closely allied to the love of benevolence than is the thought of Heaven as a reward. See also Garrigou-Lagrange, *The Three Ages of the Interior Life*, II, 425.

9. St. Anselm, *Proslogion*, 25. See also H. Lennerz, S.J., *De Novissimis* (Rome, 1940), §53 (p. 35); *ST*, II–II, q.26, a.13, and Suppl. q.44, a.3.

10. *ST*, I, q.60, a.5, ad 2.

11. See A. Tanquerey, S.S., *The Spiritual Life*, trans. H. Branderis (Westminster, 1930), §§1482-88 (pp. 696-99).

12. St. Thomas tells us (*ST*, II–II, q.26, a.4, c) that we ought to love our own salvation more than that of neighbor: we are closer to ourselves than to others.

13. *ST*, I, q.60, a.5, c.

14. "Counsels and Reminiscenses," in *St. Thérèse of Lisieux, An Autobiog-*

raphy (New York, 1927), p. 317. See also M. Philipon, O.P., *The Message of Thérèse of Lisieux,* trans. Ross (Westminster, 1950), pp. 68–69.

15. See I John 4:16: "God is love."

16. See her *Autobiography,* chap. 8 (p. 148, Kenedy ed.), and A. Combes, *The Spirituality of St. Thérèse,* trans. P. Hallett (New York, 1950), p. 50.

17. The fact that we know what the highest motives are does not mean that we should scorn to use any lower motives when needed. It is far better to avoid sin out of fear of hell than to sin. Furthermore, imperfect souls must be led *gradually* upward, through the use of many good but imperfect motives.

18. In what this conformity or harmony consists will be made clearer in chap. XV.

19. As one advances, he will find his eyes opening more and more to small faults and attachments in himself of which he was not formerly conscious. Perfect love will, of course, want to hunt out and uproot these. On perfect love, see also *ST,* II–II, q.184, a.2.

20. See R. Garrigou-Lagrange, O.P., *Christian Perfection and Contemplation,* trans. Sister Timothea Doyle, O.P. (St. Louis, 1946), p. 168.

21. Garrigou-Lagrange, *Three Ages of the Interior Life,* I, 399; and Tanquerey, *The Spiritual Life,* §§729–33.

22. We do not have in mind lawful evasions and mental restrictions.

23. As we shall explain in chap. XVII, an actual increase in the love of God can be received only when we are disposed to receive it. But this sort of permanent affection to sin prevents a soul from being properly disposed to receive an actual increase in love, even though such a soul might merit to have some such increase at some future time.

24. That is, fervor of will, not necessarily fervor of emotion.

25. On desires and attachments see chap. XV.

26. Some theologians (e.g., J. C. Osbourn, O.P., *The Morality of Imperfections,* Westminster, 1950) have maintained that a deliberate imperfection is always a venial sin. But the view of Garrigou-Lagrange seems sounder. See *The Love of God and the Cross of Jesus,* trans. Sister Jeanne Marie (St. Louis, 1948), I, 318–44; and *Christian Perfection and Contemplation,* pp. 428–34. The principles that determine the morality of an action are three: the object (the thing done); the purpose of the one who does it; and the circumstances. If we take care that these three are good, we need not focus attention on the fact that imperfection is a *lesser* good; we should remember that the lesser good is still *good.*

27. On this matter, see chap. XVII.

28. St. Francis de Sales, *The Spiritual Conferences,* trans. under supervision of Gasquet and Mackey (Westminster, 1945), VIII, 130, 131. See also St. John of the Cross, *Ascent of Mt. Carmel,* I, xi, 4.

29. Matt. 5:48.

30. See Garrigou-Lagrange, *The Three Ages of the Interior Life,* I, 202–05.

31. The rate of progress should be in accord with God's plan for our current position. Some err by attempting to go too fast (impatience). St. John of the Cross (*Dark Night,* I, v, 3) warns them against trying to become saints in a day. But more commonly we are too patient about our own

progress, as St. John also warns us (*ibid.*). See also the remarks of St. Teresa of Avila on this matter: *Autobiography* XXXI, in *The Complete Works of St. Teresa of Jesus*, trans. E. Allison Peers (New York, 1949), I, 211–12. But we must note that God does not ordinarily permit us to know our exact state of progress. See St. Francis de Sales, *The Spiritual Conferences*, VIII, 135–36.

There are two cases in which progress is not a matter of gradual change. First, in breaking off a habit of sin, it is not necessary that the break be gradual, with falls becoming less and less frequent only over a long period. A break can be made at once, even in a habit of long standing. The experience of many, especially that of the Alcoholics Anonymous group, has demonstrated this fact thoroughly. The supposition that a sudden break is impossible rests on a false psychology that views the will as though it were a sort of bodily muscle. The prime factor in such a change is a strong and realized *motive:* such a motive is, with the help of grace, always available. God will always give the strength to avoid formal grave sin. It is essential that those who are enmeshed in a habit realize this fact, for the conviction that reform must be a long, slow process would certainly tend strongly to bring on many further falls. Cf. T. J. Gannon, *Psychology, the Unity of Human Behavior* (Boston, 1954), pp. 404–07, 423–24.

The second case is on the more positive side. Even in ordinary souls, God commonly sends within a lifetime certain special graces such that if a soul cooperates, it makes a rapid advance in a short time (e.g., the grace to resolve to avoid all deliberate venial sin, and the grace to resolve to work towards perfect detachment). Now it is always safe and good to propose to avoid all deliberate venial sin and to be generous in necessary trials and humiliations, but in other matters great caution is needed. A soul must not dare to make a great change without the approval of a spiritual director, for the danger of deception is great.

32. Luke 19:26.

33. I John 4:16.

34. I John 4:20.

35. Of course a man may love God who, out of ignorance, fails to have any conscious explicit love for Mary.

X ... *Aridity, Consolations, and the Presence of Mary*

WE HAVE SEEN that the very heart of the spiritual life is love of God and love of neighbor for God's sake, and that this love is rooted in an attitude of will which tends to be carried over into action. The more intense the inner love, the greater the difficulties it will surmount externally. And we have pointed out that the presence or absence of emotion with love is an accidental feature — that is, it does not belong to the essence of love. Nevertheless we ought to know what to think and do about the presence or absence of emotion in our religious practices.

Precisely what is the relation of emotion to our soul-life? Spiritual writers make common use of two terms to describe the states of feeling in which we may find ourselves: consolation, and aridity. We are said to have consolation whenever we find any enjoyment in prayer or in the thought of God, or in any religious exercises. If we except the higher levels of the spiritual life, which very few ever reach, this pleasure lies primarily in the emotions or in the senses. Hence it is sometimes called *sensible* consolation — although along with sensible consolation an actual grace may give a light to the intellect and an attraction to the will. When we lack this enjoyment in religion, we are said to be in aridity or dryness. In dryness a soul may also suffer from distraction, and may not think of God at all, but dryness and distraction in themselves are two different things.

When we read certain spiritual writers, we may get the impression that the normal state for a beginner in the spiritual life, if he is sincerely striving to please God, is a state of consolation. It is true that God is very generous in distributing these consolations to souls who are trying to give themselves to Him without reserve. Yet even such souls sometimes find themselves in dryness, and that without any fault of their own. The classic example of constant aridity in a soul of real generosity is St. Thérèse of the Child Jesus.[1] For example, in her *Autobiography* we read:

> Do not think that I am overwhelmed with consolations. Far from it! My joy consists in being deprived of all joy here on earth. Jesus does not guide me openly: I neither see nor hear Him.[2]

But we must not make the mistake of supposing that lack of emotion must involve forgetfulness of God: St. Thérèse thought of Him almost constantly even in her dryness. We may also note that a divinely infused purifying trial, the Dark Night, played a large role in the life of St. Thérèse. We shall sketch the nature of this special type of aridity in a later chapter.

Three influences are at work in the production of consolations and aridity — ourselves, the devil, and God.

One important reason for variances in the frequency of consolation is to be found in ourselves. Some persons by natural temperament are much more prone to emotionalism than are others. In general, Americans seem but little inclined to intense emotion in religion. This lack may be due in part to the manifold distractions which our materialistic civilization provides, in part to a failure of generosity toward God, in part to our natural temperament. Then, too, one cannot help wondering if perhaps it may not be part of God's plans for our age or our nation that we should enjoy less sensible consolation. Is it not conceivable that St. Thérèse, one of the greatest saints of our age, was raised up as an example and a model of the way in which it pleases God to work in some souls at the present time? Yet even Americans do experience a degree of emotional pleasure in religion, particularly if they are living in seminaries or in the novitiates of religious orders. It is of capital importance for such persons to learn the correct principles involved, for if they do not know how to handle consolations properly, they may cultivate an illusory, unsolid, and largely apparent spiritual growth, which they may later lose when consolations become rarer after ordination or final profession. Then in their dryness they may sigh in vain for a "first fervor" that cannot be recaptured, and, not finding it, they may settle down into a lukewarmness or mediocrity that frustrates any real progress. But if these persons make proper use of consolations, much profit can be gained from them. For consolations are apt to come to generous souls striving to practice habitual recollection and detachment from all things.[3]

It is possible for consolations to come from ourselves by way of imagination or self-deception. For example, some persons of strong imagination, after reading the life of a saint, may imagine themselves like this saint — particularly if they happen to have a calm mood in prayer. Then they may take pleasure in "contemplating" themselves as they pray, thinking themselves holy. They may even reach the point of identifying themselves with their saint. Of course it happens in a subtle way in the case of consolations of imaginary origin: the person involved does not realize that he is deceiving himself, for it is easier to deceive oneself than to deceive others.

Sins, deliberate imperfections, and, in general, self-indulgence and lack of generosity may cause aridity. Various organic indispositions may also cause it, even without fault on our part. Thus, for example, faulty digestion, lack of sufficient sleep, and many kinds of ill-health may help to bring on dryness. The same must be said of various psychological indispositions, even in individuals who suffer from no abnormality. For example, worry or preoccupation with certain business matters may prevent the appearance of consolations. Such preoccupations and worries, however, are often not entirely without fault: they often reflect attachments or lack of confidence in God.

We can readily believe that the devil may contribute to our aridity by causing us temptation or distraction. That consolations in devotion may also come from the devil is somewhat harder to grasp: to think that he would actually make prayer sweet to us, that he would encourage us to form good resolutions! Yet it is true that he does so, and not rarely. St. Paul warns us of this danger when he says, ". . . Satan himself transformeth himself into an angel of light." [4] Satan can afford to give us pleasurable emotion in prayer,[5] for he knows well that emotion is not the essence of love, but is only a resonance that may be beneficial or harmful, according to the use that is made of it. Therefore, if he sees a chance to further some devilish scheme by encouraging pleasure in devotion, he will give us that pleasure. He is even willing to see some solid good results flow from it. When we apply the Gospel principle, "By their fruits you shall know them," we must consider the *over-all, long-term* results. For just as God is willing to *permit* evils when He can bring out more good than evil in the long run, so, conversely, the devil is willing to permit some apparent good (consolation) and even some solid good as well, as long as he hopes to produce more evil than good in the long run.

What are the ways in which the devil hopes to produce evil? It would be presumptuous for us to try to list all his wiles, for he has the brilliant mind of an angel — a fallen angel, yes, but still possessed of an intelligence far more powerful than ours. But we can give some typical examples of the way in which he works. The most common deception he uses in consolations is to make us think that we are already saints, or practically so; or, if the temptation does not go quite that far, it at least makes us believe that we are making fine progress toward sanctity. For there is a strong tendency in the minds of many to identify emotions with sanctity; and now that they themselves have the rather new (to them) experience of emotion in devotion, they compare themselves favorably to the saints of whom they have read. The truth is that even in the case of the saints, *sanctity consists in the love of God, which resides in the will: any emotion is an accidental accretion.* Further, this thing we call sensible consolation is not at all rare among *beginners* in the spiritual life. Even if it be sent by God, it proves nothing as to the state of progress of the soul receiving it. It comes closer to being a proof that one is still on the lower levels of the spiritual life, for at the very highest levels things are much different. Hence we must take care to avoid the temptation to pride in consolations. Consolations that cause pride bear the stamp of the devil.

Another common snare laid by the devil through consolations lies in a presumptuous urge to undertake projects beyond our strength. The normal law of the spiritual life is that each one should make *gradual* progress: the rate of speed is greater for some than for others, and in everyone it should increase as one approaches more closely to the goal. But progress should be gradual — not in broad jumps. Especially does the devil counsel us to take on great mortifications. He knows well that these over-ambitious projects are beyond our strength, at least at that time, though we may and should hope to advance in mortification gradually, in due time. Hence, if we try to jump too high in one leap, we will probably fail to make it, and, as a result, fall down to a point lower than that from which we started. The remedy against such dangers as these is simple: no one, with or without the urging of consolations from the devil or even from God, should undertake any major or long-range change in his spiritual program without the approval of his spiritual director. It is very desirable that souls should have the assistance of a spiritual direc-tor. The guidance of a prudent director protects us against many an error and imprudence. We should pray earnestly that Mary, who knows all the artifices of the ancient serpent, may guide both the director and us.[6]

There is another very subtle danger that the devil may seek to exploit in consolations — and he may even attempt in this way to pervert consolations inspired by God: he may lead us to love the consolations of God more than the God who sent them. In other words, consolations are a means; we ought to profit by them, but not become attached to them. They should help us to God, not replace Him. We should serve Him for His own sake, not merely for the pleasure we get out of it. Otherwise we are merely indulging in a refined form of self-seeking, telling our-selves that we are serving God, when really we are just pleasing ourselves. This is not to say that it is wrong to enjoy consolations: no, but we must keep them in true perspective, and take care that we really use them to help us serve God better, lest we accept the service of God to help us the better to obtain consolation.

Finally, consolations may come from God. We understand, of course, that He regularly operates through secondary agents. Every grace is given through Mary, as we have seen, and Mary herself may employ any of the angels to serve her purposes, for she is Queen of Angels. Why does God grant us consolations? Chiefly as a temporary help to encourage us in His service, and to wean us more easily from earthly pleasures. St. John of the Cross aptly compares sensible consolations to toys.[7] He says that if we wish to induce a child to let loose an object that he holds in one hand, we do so by putting something else into his other hand. So also sensible consolations help us to detach ourselves from earthly things. If we are sufficiently generous with God in detaching ourselves from all things, including consolations (this does not mean that we may not enjoy them), we will reach a point at which God will complete the work of detachment by putting us into the passive night of the senses, in which infused contemplation supplants the sensible consolations (see chap. XIII). Meanwhile, however, if we know how to use consolations well, they may be of great help to us.

What, then, should be our attitude when we receive consolations? First of all, let us realize that they prove nothing of our spiritual state. We may even receive them when we are in the state of mortal sin. We must make it our immediate concern to *avoid any pride*. We need not be overanxious to determine from which source they come. Our chief concern is to make good use of them with humility.[8] If we do this, then, even though the consolation may have been sent by the devil, God will turn it into a grace for us. Let consolations help us to pray with more attention, let them help us to wean ourselves from earthly pleasures,[9] let them encourage us to make good resolutions to better our life in the future (always remembering that any notable change must be approved by our director). Let us also realize that consolations will not last forever: most likely they will be of short duration in us. Let us prepare for our usual dryness, and recognize that although prayer offered in a state of consolation may seem better to us, it may easily be of less value than one made in dryness, for the chief measure of the value of an action is the amount of love we put into it. Now love is an affair of the will, not of the emotions. *It is fervor of the will that counts.* Hence, when we struggle against dryness or distaste for prayer or for serving God in some other way, we may actually have to put more will, more love, into it than when it is all pleasant for us.[10]

St. Francis de Sales has some excellent advice in this matter of consolations:

> Moreover, we must from time to time make acts of renunciation of such feelings of sweetness, tenderness, and consolation, withdrawing our hearts from them and protesting that, although we accept them humbly and love them, because God sends them to us, and because they stir us up to love him, yet we seek not them, but God and his holy love: not the consolation but the Consoler. . . . [11]

St. Francis apparently fears that we may become attached to consolations if we never deny ourselves in this direction, or if we give ourselves over to them too completely or too eagerly. In the same chapter, he also cautions that if we should have an extraordinary abundance of consolations, or if there is anything at all extraordinary in them, we should consult our director.

We should certainly thank God when He sends us consolations, but we should also thank Him if He sends us dryness. For, as St. Paul says, for those who love God, "all things work together unto good." [12] We should try to determine whether the dryness is really sent by Him or whether we have brought it on by our own fault — by sin, imperfections, lack of generosity, lack of recollection. But whether it is a result of a personal failing, or has been sent by God and is inculpable, He will turn the dryness into a grace for us if we humbly ask pardon for the fault (if it is a fault), and then work *at least as hard* at loving and serving God as we would if we had consolation.

There are certain advantages to be had from dryness. For one thing it is easier to exclude self-seeking from our prayers when there is no pleasure in them. It is also easier to avoid many a subtle plot of the devil — although the devil can plot even in dryness to make us feel proud. For he may make us think, "We are strong souls who can walk in dryness: consolations are for the weak."

Dryness is simply a lack of consolation in our prayer-life. It is not the same as distraction. We may experience dryness with or without distraction, though the two tend to go together. As to distraction, we need constantly to remind ourselves — for we naturally keep forgetting it — that *involuntary* distractions do not destroy the essential value of prayer. We refer here to vocal prayer; special comment on distractions in mental prayer appears in chapters XII and XIII. In fact, if we struggle against distractions, even though they keep returning, we may actually be more pleasing to God than when we abound in consolations. But observe that distractions may be voluntary in an indirect way — that is, we may invite them by our lack of recollection, by our sins, imperfections, and attachments. When we are especially preoccupied with any matter, we ought to spend a minute or two recollecting ourselves before attempting to pray.[13]

All souls are spiritually close to Mary their Mother whether or not they realize it. Many souls succeed in developing a more or less constant loving consciousness of her presence. This is very conducive to a spirit of union with Jesus and Mary. In our treatment of mental prayer, we shall give some very specific suggestions on how to cultivate this realization, but now we must ask: In what sense can Mary be present to souls?

Any mere spirit, an angel, or God Himself, is present wherever he acts. Wherever God's power makes itself felt, He is present. Now the presence of Mary is not precisely like this. Mary's soul, since the Assumption, is united to her body in Heaven. Hence in that sense it is present there and there only. Yet there is a *virtual* or *dynamic* type of contact between Mary and us, insofar as she distributes all graces to us. The exact nature of this contact is difficult to determine: the idea one forms will depend on what view he holds as to the manner in which Mary works in the distribution of all graces (see again chap. V). It is obvious that if Mary is a physical instrument of grace, the contact is especially close. Furthermore, although in one sense the soul of Mary and our souls as well are present only where our bodies are, yet, in another sense, the soul, insofar as it is a spirit, transcends the body, and is not, as such, in a place. Hence Garrigou-Lagrange writes:

> From this point of view, *all souls,* in the measure in which they grow in the spiritual life and become detached from the senses, *by bringing themselves spiritually nearer to God,* bring themselves spiritually nearer to one another as well. Thus is explained the *spiritual presence* of Christ's Holy Soul and that of Mary in us. . . . [14] [*Emphasis in the original.*]

But there is also what is called an *affective presence* of Mary. The deeper our love for her, the more intimate does this become. For love has a unitive force. There are two ways in which this affective presence takes place: 1. We go out of ourselves, as it were, to be in Mary: this is true inasmuch as we rejoice greatly in seeing her interests furthered, and in promoting them in ourselves and in others; 2. Mary is in us by the pleasure she gives us through the thought of her. It is obvious that the first form of the affective presence is the safer, the more disinterested, the more valuable. The second is also good, but since sensible consolation tends to be strong in it, we will have more need to observe the cautions we have just outlined. Especially must we beware, as to the second form, that we do not, by our own imagination, and out of self-love, counterfeit this sort of affection, or fall into a kind of spiritual greediness in it: that would consist in loving the consolations we derive from the thought of Mary rather than loving Mary herself.

Of course, we must not suppose that a loving realization of

the presence of Mary is merely a kind of consolation: actually this awareness may be either arid or consoled. It is best considered as a form of recollection or informal mental prayer, but we have thought it opportune to discuss certain aspects of it at this point because of its relation to consolations.[15]

In conclusion, consolations and aridity are both useful means to the love of God, if we use them well. But there are also, as we have seen, many dangers to be avoided; to avoid these, and to make the best use of whatever God wills to send us, we must rely both on the direct help of Mary and on the help of a good director, who must also be guided by her.

NOTES

1. See A. Combes, *The Spirituality of St. Thérèse*, pp. 103–18, 161–62.
2. *St. Thérèse of Lisieux, An Autobiography*, chap. 13 (p. 196, Kenedy ed.).
3. By habitual recollection a man strives for an almost constant consciousness of God's presence, and, at the same time, works toward the goal of shutting out other things, insofar as duties permit him to do so, and insofar as these other things do not help him toward God. For further development, see chaps. XII and XIII.
4. II Cor. 11:14.
5. The devil, though fallen, is a fallen angel, and he still retains great powers that are merely natural to him. He can easily work on our imagination or senses.
6. Authors do not agree on the degree of necessity of a director. Direction is not necessary for salvation, but is a normal means for reaching perfection and is of great efficacy. The rules of religious orders commonly make provision for direction in various forms, but lay persons and others who cannot have frequent and extensive help should at least consult a confessor or other competent guide when they have problems, for the formation of general rules of life, and for guidance in their reading. Authors do not agree whether submission to a director is an act of obedience in the strict sense or only of prudence and humility. While we cannot give a director the same blind obedience as we give a religious superior, yet we are ordinarily safe in following his guidance, safer than when following our own judgment. If we should ever think him in error, we should not disobey without the approval of some other director. See St. Francis de Sales, *Introduction to the Devout Life*, trans. A. Ross (Westminster, 1948), I, iv; J. de Guibert, S.J., *The Theology of the Spiritual Life*, trans. by P. Barrett (New York, 1953), pp. 155–86; A. Tanquerey, S.S., *The Spiritual Life*, §§530–57; and P. Parente, *Spiritual Direction* (St. Meinrad, Ind., 1950).
7. St. John of the Cross, *Ascent of Mount Carmel*, III, xxxix, 1 (I, 321).

8. See St. Teresa of Avila, *Way of Perfection*, XXXVIII.

9. On the correct attitude to pleasure and its use see chap. XV.

10. Note that it is not mere difficulty *as such* but the increased love needed to surmount the difficulty which increases the value. See Tanquerey, *op. cit.*, §245; also De Guibert, *op. cit.*, p. 94.

11. St. Francis de Sales, *Introduction to the Devout Life*, IV, xiii.

12. Rom. 8:28.

13. For a good treatment of consolations and dryness, see L. Scupoli, *The Spiritual Combat*, §59. See also, in the *Spiritual Exercises* of St. Ignatius, the "Rules for the discernment of spirits" and the "Rules for perceiving the different movements which are caused in the soul" (Rules 3–14). St. Francis de Sales, *op. cit.*, IV, xiii–xiv, is likewise valuable. On mystical aridity, see chap. XIII of this book.

14. Garrigou-Lagrange, *The Mother of the Saviour*, p. 213. See the entire section, pp. 212–15, on the presence of Mary.

15. See also the remarks on habitual recollection in chap. XII, and T. McGinnis, O.Carm., *Life with Mary*, pp. 35–37. On the presence of Mary in the higher stages of the spiritual life, above the purgative way, see the concluding parts of chaps. XIII and XIX, and: Ven. Michael of St. Augustine, "The Mariform and Marian Life In Mary, For Mary," McGinnis, *op. cit.*, pp. 11–30; V. Hoppenbrouwers, O.Carm., "The Blessed Mother Teaches Us to Pray," *Analecta Ordinis Carmelitarum* XVI (1951), pp. 259–65; L. Reypens, "Marie et la Mystique," Du Manoir, *Maria*, I, 756–63; and St. Teresa of Avila, *Interior Castle*, VI, vii.

XI . . . *The Humility of His Handmaid*

Our Lord and His holy Mother could rightly claim to possess all virtues. Yet when He described Himself and proposed Himself as a model for our imitation, He mentioned the virtue of humility as especially characteristic of Himself. "Learn of me," He said, "because I am meek, and humble of heart." [1] Mary, too, as we have already seen in our consideration of the Annunciation, showed this virtue in an outstanding way. [2] Indeed, at the very moment when she became the Mother of the Incarnate Word, she said, "Behold the *slave girl* of the Lord" (that is the precise translation of the Greek, as we have noted before).

In this chapter we shall talk about the virtue of humility. Exaggerated statements are often made in discussions of this virtue, but here, so that the reader may not feel the need of discounting the force of anything that will be said, let us agree to propose only statements that are strictly and literally true at their face value.

Let us understand at the outset that humility is by no means the greatest of the virtues; far greater are the three theological virtues: faith, hope, and especially love, which in itself sums up all. We must always keep before our eyes that the very essence of the spiritual life consists in charity — that is, love. But humility is necessary in order to make room for that love. It makes room by ridding us of extensive disorders of self. Now although we cannot, as it were, apply a measuring instrument to any virtue, and gauge it in degrees or any other mathematical unit, yet to help make the matter clear, let us use the following loose comparison: suppose I seem to have ten degrees of love. To make that safe, I ought to have ten degrees of humility. If I seem to have only five degrees of humility, then I must fear that at least five[3] of the ten degrees of love that I *seem* to have are counterfeit. For love and humility rise and fall together.

What, then, is the special claim of humility on our attention? Its position is peculiar: though it is far from being the greatest of the virtues, it is a *conditio sine qua non,* a prerequisite for all other virtues. That is, if one does not have humility, he cannot really possess any other virtues at all. Of course he may seem to have many or all of them. But they will be counterfeits if they are not grounded on humility. St. Augustine very aptly compares humility to the foundation of a building: "First think about the foundation, humility. . . . the greater the structure will be, the deeper a man digs the foundation." [4] The same St. Augustine gives another striking illustration. He proposes the question: Why was it that the Roman Empire grew so great? Basing his comments on the data of Roman history, he notices that the early Romans seemed to possess many virtues. They were satisfied with little for themselves: all was given to the service of the state. They showed prudence in their handling of conquered peoples, justice and mercy even to enemies, temperance in the management of public and private affairs, the greatest fortitude in war: an inspiring picture indeed. But, says St. Augustine, Divine Providence could not grant them a supernatural reward, Heaven, for these virtues. Why not? Because their works were not performed to gain such a reward. They were done because the people were

. . . eager for praise . . . this they loved most ardently, for this they wished to live, for this they did not hesitate to die; they crushed other desires out of their great desire for this one thing.[5]

They sought only for praise: they received what they looked for. In the words of the Gospel, "they have received their reward." [6]

The same truth is taught in the Gospels in a forceful way. Our Lord is shown to us as marvelous in His mercy, in His love for sinners. Publicans who unjustly defrauded their own countrymen are treated kindly. A woman taken in adultery is most generously pardoned. In short, every kind of sinner meets with kindness and mercy at His hands — every kind, that is, but one. The only sinners for whom Our Lord seemed to have no mercy were the Pharisees. Yet they were to all appearances the most religious of men. They zealously kept the least prescriptions of the Old Law. They gave money to the poor. They fasted much. Yet to them Mercy Incarnate said:

> Woe to you scribes and Pharisees, hypocrites! because you are like to whited sepulchres, which outwardly appear to men beautiful, but within are full of dead men's bones, and of all filthiness. So you also outwardly indeed appear to men just; but inwardly you are full of hypocrisy and iniquity.[7]

The same thought is strongly expressed in the first Epistle of St. Peter: "God resisteth the proud, but to the humble he giveth grace." [8] We note the sharp wording: it does not read, "God gives *less* grace to the proud," or "God gives *no* grace to the proud." God does not merely deprive the proud of grace. He *resists* them. If God Himself is against us, surely we are in a bad way. The only remedy is to turn from pride. For God retains mercy even for the proud in the sense that He is willing to cure them of their pride if they will accept His help.

Why is this virtue so dear to Christ and His Mother? It is *because it makes room for God.* If the essence of spirituality lies in love, love of God, then it follows that we must make room in ourselves for God. Now that room is made only at the expense of the disorderly self in us. The virtue that digs the foundations and makes room is humility. Conversely, the opposite vice — pride — is implicit in every sin. Pride attempts to claim for a creature what is really due to God. Hence *pride, as it were, aims at dethroning God and setting up a creature — self — in His place.* No wonder pride is so odious to God!

Humility is the virtue that teaches us to know our true place in the scheme of all things, and makes us willingly accept that place. Hence *humility is based on truth.* Thus it becomes apparent how it was possible for Christ and His Mother to be humble. Insofar as He is God, Christ is the Lord of all. Yet He freely wished to assume human nature. And He did not merely assume human nature, but became a member of a fallen race (though He Himself did not have a fallen nature). Having once made this choice, He would not recoil from the consequences thereof: He willingly accepted the hardships and difficulties that are the lot of a fallen race.[9] But He did not accuse Himself of sin: to do so would have been contrary to truth, and humility is founded on truth, the true estimate of one's proper position.

Now it is all too easy to misunderstand the notion that humility requires us to recognize our true position and accept it. Many of us will promptly throw out our chests and say: Yes, I am good, and I really ought to admit it. Such a statement is based on an *untrue and incomplete view* of our position. To counteract such a danger, we ought to review briefly just what is the truth about ourselves.[10]

We must recognize at the outset that we are creatures. In us there is good and evil. (Of course evil is not a positive thing: rather it is a lack of the good that ought to be there.) We must determine what in us is due to ourselves, and what is a gift of God. Let us begin with the natural order. First of all, we were made out of nothing by God. Therefore, of our initial equipment there is *nothing* that we have not received as a completely unmerited gift: how could we merit anything when we were as yet nothing? Hence, as regards the starting point, we have nothing of ourselves, everything from God. But now that we have begun to exist and live, what shall we say? The very same metaphysical principles that require the work of an Infinite Being, God, to bring us out of nothing require the unending work of that same God to keep us in existence, and to enable us to perform any action, however small. (Recall that we are at present speaking of the natural order.) But can we at least choose to do good or evil? Yes, we can, for God has given us free will — but we need His support even in the use of our free will, insofar as there is any good in it. As for the evil, we must attribute that to ourselves.

In order to grasp more clearly what is God's role and what is our role in a choice or action, let us take a crude example. Consider the act of picking up a roll of money from a table. One man, the owner, may perform the act, in which case it is a good act in every respect. But suppose a thief performs the same act: we then have a sinful act. For something is *lacking* when the thief performs it. It is the same *physical* action as when the owner did it, but the thief *lacks* a right to the money. But is the act of the thief evil in every respect? It is surely evil in the moral order; but it is not evil in the physical order.[11] Though the act is evil morally, it has a sort of physical goodness and that physical goodness *as* a good requires the support of God. But the moral evil which is a *lack* of a required quality belongs to man. In a good action, however, both the physical and the moral goodness require the support of God. Therefore, we may say that we are able to *lack* something without God, but are not able *to be or to do anything* without Him.[12]

Thus we see that what we can do of ourselves is extremely little. Yet, although our co-operation with God in producing any good action is so pitiably slight, God requires it of us under pain of sin, and rewards it richly when it is given.

We have found that we can be nothing and do nothing without God. But we can lack something — i.e., we can have evil will — without Him. We can now understand the sense in which some of the saints have said of themselves: "I am nothing, I can do nothing, I am less than nothing." Now one cannot really be less than nothing. What they mean is this: they could do no good without God, but they could be lacking in something without Him. In that sense, seeing their capacity for evil but not for good, they realized that they were less than nothing — for to commit sin is worse than to do nothing.

We have had a glimpse of the shattering sight of our position in the natural order. Much meditation is needed to bring it home to ourselves. We need to do more than just look at the truth; we need, with the help of grace, to *realize* it and *act* upon it. It is a long task to make the same examination in the supernatural order

(*The Path of Humility* may be a help in the task). But we can easily conclude that if we are so poor and helpless of ourselves even in the natural order, the same things must be even more true in the supernatural order. Hence Our Lord Himself told us: "Without me you can do nothing." [13]

Thus far we have considered only our *capacity* for sin. When we realize that *we really have sinned,* and that we have sunk still lower because of having sinned over and over again, what shall we say of our position? Surely it is not one to feel proud of. No wonder the saints could consider themselves worse than nothing. For by the realization that of ourselves we have a capacity for evil, but not for good, we can come to lack esteem for ourselves. When we add to the picture the fact that we have sinned, we can honestly have contempt for ourselves. We can justly call ourselves "unprofitable servants." [14] In fact, we easily become worse than unprofitable, for by our intractability and lack of docility we often hinder God's designs.

But yet we must not forget that there are two elements in us: that which we have from God, and that which we have of ourselves. Looking at the latter, we can properly arrive at contempt of self. But looking at our dignity as sons of God, as sharers in the divine nature through grace, and considering what we can do with the divine help, we can still conceive a proper kind of self-esteem. The right sort of humility agrees well with magnanimity, the virtue that makes a man dare to undertake great things for God and neighbor, relying not on self, but on the divine power. In this sense St. Paul says, "I can do all things in him who strengtheneth me." [15]

We have considered thus far what humility ought to be in relation to God; we see that it is founded on an attitude of truth, on reverence toward God, as well as on knowledge of our own nothingness. We must now consider what humility should be in relation to other human beings. Here the truth is more difficult to see. How can we honestly, without self-deception, follow the advice of St. Paul: "... in humility let each esteem others better than himself ... "? [16] Many confusing things have been written on this point, as if St. Paul wished us all to deceive ourselves.

For it is obvious that out of all men, only one can be the worst sinner in the strict sense of that term. All others are somewhat less bad. St. Paul is not demanding that each of us think himself the very worst sinner in the world.

St. Thomas Aquinas gives us the true solution.[17] He tells us to distinguish two things in us, as we have already done above: what we have from God, and what we have of ourselves. We can then make three comparisons: 1. If we compare what we have of ourselves to the gifts of God in others, we can and should, out of reverence for the gifts of God, defer to others, esteeming them in this way better than ourselves; 2. But if we compare the gifts that we have from God to those that others have from God, humility does not demand that we think our gifts less, since they may actually be either greater or lesser: humility demands only that we give the credit to God, not to ourselves, if they are greater in us; 3. Similarly, if we compare what we have of ourselves to the same element in others, we are not *obliged* to consider ourselves inferior to all — otherwise each would have to consider himself the greatest sinner, which is, of course, mathematically impossible, for only one can claim that dubious title. But, St. Thomas adds, we ought nonetheless to be *inclined* to *conjecture* that others have some good in them which we do not have, or lack evil that we know we have.

If we wish to be scrupulously exact on this last point we shall have to admit that we simply cannot make an accurate comparison between ourselves and others. We can, it is true, see their external acts. Thus I may see a robber who has also murdered six men; inasmuch as I have not done those external acts, I seem to have a better record. External acts are important. But even more important is the state of a man's soul. Was he fully responsible? What would he do if he had had the graces that we have had? To make an accurate comparison between ourselves and others we ought to have precise knowledge of two things: Our own state of soul, relative to the graces we have received; and the state of soul of others, relative to the graces they have received. Now our own self-knowledge is but imperfect at best;

and our knowledge of the interior state of others is even dimmer
— it is all but total darkness. Hence we really cannot make an
accurate comparison of our own spiritual worth with that of
others. Yet, without dishonesty, which must be avoided with the
greatest care, *if we have a true knowledge and appreciation of
our own weakness and failings,* we can in all truth say: "If that
robber had received the graces I have had, I wonder if he would
not be much better spiritually than I am. It is hard to see how
he could have done much worse than I, with such graces as I have
been given." St. Francis of Assisi actually did say this sort of thing,
and was honest in saying it.[18]

If we wish to understand the great lengths to which some of
the saints go in humility, we must consider the motives that impel
them. First of all, they love humility because Jesus and Mary love
it. If we really love anyone, we want to be like them. They meditate much on the humiliations of Bethlehem, of Calvary, and
on the continued humiliation of Our Lord in the Holy Eucharist,
in which He takes the appearance of a lifeless thing, at the mercy
of anyone who handles the Sacred Species. Next, they have a
powerful and quite wholesome fear of illusions and self-deception. They see in humility, which is based on truth, an excellent
protection against being ruined by any deceptions. And when
we see the saints rejoicing to receive even obviously undeserved
humiliations and insults, they are using yet another method in
addition to the desire to be like Jesus and Mary and other motives
already suggested. They can always reflect: It is true that this in-
sult, in the present circumstances, is something I do not deserve.
Still, when I consider what my past sins have deserved, the punishment I ought to have had for offending God but have not received, here is a fine chance to take this as a payment for the
past, to make reparation to the Heart of Christ for the pain[19] that
I have caused Him.[20] In addition, they realize that humiliations
inflicted by others provide them with a chance for much greater
spiritual progress in a short time than many a self-imposed humiliation. And, finally, they wish thereby to earn graces for
others.

Is it correct to say, "As soon as we think ourselves humble, we cease to be so in reality"? Some writers maintain that one who is humble cannot know that fact. It is difficult to agree with that view; it seems to suppose that humility is founded, not on truth, but on self-deception (although it is true, as we shall see, that humble persons tend to be suspicious of their own humility). We may approach the matter in this way. There are many degrees of humility. A complete absence of humility would mean that we would have formal contempt for the authority of God as such. We wonder if any one but the devil himself could reach such a depth. Perfect humility is that of Our Lord Himself. The truth about any one of us probably lies somewhere in between. A man may honestly *think to himself,* or say to his spiritual director, "I think I have some humility, not perfect humility, but some low degree, less than I ought to have." It is easy to see that our degree of humility is low: if it were high, we would be making wonderfully rapid spiritual progress. But, unless acting under a special divine inspiration, a man would probably be guilty of pride, and would surely seem ridiculous, if he were to proclaim to others: "I am humble." He would be in danger of being "proud of his humility." Yet the fact that we *know within ourselves* that we have *some* humility does not of itself destroy humility; Our Lord was humble, and admitted it; so was Mary, and she knew it.[21]

Humility is primarily a great gift of God, for which we must pray much, and St. Thomas says, "They who share in the gifts of God know that they have them." [22] But we must concede that the theologians who disagree do have a certain truth in mind, for humility is a delicate, elusive virtue. There is danger that we may indulge in a self-deceiving pride in even a lowly appraisal of ourselves and our little humility. St. Teresa of Avila gives us the wholesome advice that we ought to be suspicious of the genuineness of solid virtues that we seem to possess:

> ... when the Lord really gives one of these solid virtues, it seems to bring all the rest in its train: that is a very well-known fact.

But I advise you once more, even if you think you possess it, to suspect that you may be mistaken; for the person who is truly humble is always doubtful about his own virtues; very often they seem more genuine and of greater worth when he sees them in his neighbours.[23]

St. Teresa is not urging us on to self-deception: it is merely being realistic for us to suspect the degree of our humility. We can know, of course, that we do not have the formal contempt of God's authority of which we spoke; but whether we have much more than a bare minimum of humility is another question. For pride is able to counterfeit all virtues. And it can even contrive an appearance of humility. In our best actions, often a part of our motive is apt to be a secret desire for self-esteem or for the esteem of others though we do not realize it. We must learn to suspect the presence of such hidden pride and to seek it out. In suspecting that some of our humility may be only apparent, not solid, we are taking a precaution against self-deception, not indulging in self-deception. Therefore we must pray to God that even the little humility we possess may be *real*, not illusory.

Humility should incline us to wish to avoid even deserved praise. For praise is a danger to humility even if the praise is well earned — not that truth is dangerous of itself, but because of our normal human weakness. We may and should recognize the gifts that God has given us, but we must be careful not to take to ourselves the credit for them. If we keep in mind the explanations given above on what part is due to us, this becomes possible, though not easy.

While humility is difficult to acquire, a deep realization of our own nothingness and of the infinite greatness of God will help us develop it. But a speculative knowledge of these truths is not enough; they must be impressed deeply by much meditation. In our meditation we should also dwell long and lovingly on the humility of Our Lord and His blessed Mother. It is likewise good to think often on our past sins, but observing this caution — that we do not recall certain types of sins so vividly as to cause new temptations. Our outward actions should be such as the virtue of humility suggests, but, in general, unless we have a special inspiration of grace, it is better to be content merely to avoid, so far as we can, any singularity that attracts attention to ourselves. If humiliations from others come our way, however, it is most helpful to accept them.[24]

Prompt obedience to all lawful authority is an excellent means of growing in humility. For there is a close relation between obedience and humility: both serve to make us empty of self, and it is the function of humility to make room for love by ridding us of disordered self. Now when we obey, we also contradict self, for we are following the directives of someone else — not our own wishes. Hence we can see the great value of obedience, even when a superior gives us an order to do something that is less good and prudent than it might be. The superior may err in his judgment, for he is only human, but we, in obeying, do not err, for we thereby substitute the will of God for our own disordered self (assuming, of course, that the command is not to do something sinful). This is the reason the saints disliked accepting posts of authority: it is much safer to obey. The truly humble man will not only obey, but he will make an honest effort, so far as he reasonably can, to see things the superior's way. This is obedience of the judgment.[25] For he will recall that his own judgment is very apt to be warped in things that concern him; and, in addition, he recognizes that the superior has better access to the facts, and possesses graces of state.

As to speaking in a lowly way of ourselves, a certain caution is needed. St. Francis de Sales warns us not to do this unless we sincerely mean it,[26] as it could easily happen that we might really be seeking praise through what would seem to be humble words. We should make it a practice to speak as little as possible of ourselves, as this danger is unlikely to occur in silence about ourselves. A tendency to criticize or dispute much is often rooted in pride. Hence we do well to avoid such activities unless they are really necessary. Finally, we must constantly beg God for humility, for humility is, like all other good things, basically a gift of God.

And now a brief look at the relation of humility to the grace of final perseverance — for it is obvious that unless we persevere to the end, it will do us no good to have received all other graces. We might express our situation in this way: On what do we pin our hope that we will actually avoid grave sin and persevere so as to be in the state of grace at the end? If we attempt to rest that hope on our own ability and constancy, we are building on sand, for we are notoriously inconstant in good — and this is true of the best. We must, then, depend on God for this great grace — that is, we must depend on Him to send us such graces as will effectively insure that we will co-operate with grace without, of course, taking away our free will. How shall we obtain this great grace from Him? We cannot merit it: Scripture and Tradition offer us no text in which God has promised us the means of meriting it. But we can obtain it by *constant humble prayer*. For although we do not have the means of meriting it, we can still ask for it. As in the case of all other graces, it is through the hands of Mary that we must obtain it. To her we say many times daily: "Pray for us, now and at the hour of our death." A close attachment to her gives us solid reason for confidence that we will be given that all-important grace.

Thus humility leads us to take the attitude of little children toward God our Father and Mary our Mother. Let us recall that, as Our Lord said, if we do not become as little children, we shall not get into Heaven at all. Now a child expects to receive things from its mother, not because he, the child, is good. No, the mother, though she rewards the child for the good he does, yet gives most things to the child not because *he* is good, but because *she* is good. Similarly, though we are capable of earning, thanks to the gifts of God, certain graces, yet even the means of earning them has been freely given to us. In this sense we may say that our chief contribution is to refrain from being bad children. God gives us good things through our Mother not so much because we are good, but because He is good. And the reason Mary can serve as the channel of all graces is that she is completely empty of self: *Ecce ancilla Domini!*

NOTES

1. Matt. 11:29.

2. The interpretation of Luke 1:48 (". . . he hath regarded the humility of his handmaid") is disputed even among Catholic commentators. Some hold that the word *humility* refers to the virtue, others claim that it refers to lowly station. The second group bases their claim chiefly on two arguments: 1. The Greek word more readily refers to lowly station than to the virtue; 2. The opinion that a person who is humble cannot know or admit that fact. The argument based on the Greek is interesting but inconclusive. The second argument we shall deal with later in this chapter; in brief, we may say that humility is founded on truth. Therefore, to know that one has *some* humility does not destroy the virtue. This would be particularly true in Mary, whose fullness of grace would put her in a safer position: see *Marian Studies,* III, 228–35. But whether or not Mary meant to refer to the virtue of humility in v. 48, a later verse in the *Magnificat* shows without a doubt that Mary was aware that she was humble. For in saying (Luke 1:51) "He hath scattered the proud in the conceit of their heart," she clearly implied she was humble — for God had not scattered her, but exalted her.

3. Perhaps more than five degrees may be merely apparent — for some of the five degrees of humility may be only illusory.

4. St. Augustine, *Sermo* LXIX, i, 2.

5. St. Augustine, *The City of God* V, xii.

6. Matt. 6:2.

7. Matt. 23:27–28.

8. I Pet. 5:5.

9. For a beautiful development of this theme, see Edward Leen, C.S.Sp., *In the Likeness of Christ* (New York, 1938), pp. 173–95.

10. For a thorough treatment of this matter, and of humility in general, see the outstanding meditation book by an anonymous author: *The Path of Humility* (Westminster, 1946).

11. We say that the act has a sort of physical goodness insofar as it is an action at all. A better term would be goodness in the order of being (the ontological order). For a thing may be good or evil in two orders: in the order of being, and in the order of morality. A thing is good in the order of being insofar as it exists or has being. The opposite of this sort of goodness would be nothingness. A thing is good in the moral order if it conforms to the moral law, and (in a concrete case) if the man who does it acts with a good intention and in the right circumstances. *All good, both onto-logical and moral, needs the support of God; without the support of God we are capable only of lacking something.*

12. In other words, in the activity of our free will, there are two things to distinguish: 1. Any good (in the order of being, and in the order of morality); 2. Any evil (lack of something that should be there). Insofar as the will makes any decision at all, it does *something.* Insofar as it does something, it needs the same support of God that any action of ours needs. *This is true insofar as the will does something or chooses good.* But there is a reservation: Insofar as a will is evil, it is inclined toward a *lack* of

being (for evil is not a positive thing, it is *a lack of something that should be there*). Therefore, inasmuch as evil is not a positive thing, but a lack of something, we can lack something without God. Hence, though a decision of our will is undoubtedly free, we can do without the constant support of God only in an evil choice, and even in that evil choice we can do without Him *only insofar as we are lacking something:* not insofar as we are doing *something.*

13. John 15:5.

14. Luke 17:10.

15. Phil. 4:13. On magnanimity, see F. J. Connell, C.SS.R., "Magnanimity: A Priestly Virtue," *From an Abundant Spring:* The Walter Farrell Memorial Volume of *The Thomist,* ed. the Staff of *The Thomist* (New York, 1952), pp. 28–39.

16. Phil. 2:3.

17. *ST,* II–II, q.161, a.3.

18. See H. Felder, O.F.M.Cap., *The Ideals of St. Francis of Assisi,* trans. B. Bittle (Chicago, 1925), p. 180: " 'It seems to me that I am a greater sinner than anyone else in the world.' And when the brother replied that this was not in accordance with the truth, Francis said: 'If Christ had shown such great mercy to a criminal, however wicked he may be, he would be tenfold more perfect than I.' "

19. Of course the Heart of Christ is incapable of suffering now. But in His Passion, He foresaw all sins, yours and mine included, and suffered because of them, and to make up for them. See §15 of the encyclical *Miserentissimus Redemptor* of Pope Pius XI, in *The Sacred Heart Encyclicals,* ed. C. J. Moell, S.J. (New York, 1953), pp. 41–42.

20. See St. Teresa of Avila, *Way of Perfection,* XV.

21. See Matt. 11:29: "Learn of me, because I am meek, and humble of heart." On Mary's knowledge of her own humility, see note 2 above.

22. *ST,* II–II, q.161, a.3. See also note 31, chap. IX, on the question of a person's knowledge of his own stage of progress.

23. St. Teresa of Avila, *Way of Perfection,* XXXVIII (II, 167).

24. See *ibid.,* XXXVI (II, 158–59): "Understand then, sisters, that as these persons have already learned to rate everything at its proper valuation, they pay little attention to things which pass away. A great wrong, or a great trial, may cause them some momentary distress, but they will hardly have felt it when reason will intervene, and will . . . drive away their distress by giving them the joy of seeing how God has entrusted them with the opportunity of gaining, in a single day, more lasting favors and graces in His Majesty's sight than they could gain in ten years by means of trials which they sought on their own account."

25. For further development of obedience of the judgment, see St. Ignatius Loyola, *Letter on Obedience,* esp. §§ 9–12; and M. M. Pólit, S.J., *Perfect Obedience* (Westminster, 1947), esp. pp. 100–47.

26. St. Francis de Sales, *Introduction to the Devout Life,* III, v. Chaps. iv–vii are excellent on this point.

For an excellent study of the theology of humility, see *The Virtue of Humility,* by Sebastian Carlson, O.P. (Dubuque, 1952).

XII ... *Pondering in Our Hearts with Mary*

Twice within the second chapter of his Gospel, St. Luke tells us of Mary's habit of meditating on the great mysteries in which she was taking part. After the shepherds had left, we read: "But Mary kept all these words, pondering them in her heart." Again, after the return to Nazareth, when Jesus had been lost, and found in the temple, "His mother kept all these words in her heart." [1] These two scanty references give us but a glimpse of the soul of Mary. They show her to us as one whose communion with God in mental prayer or meditation was constant. Actually her prayer was of a loftier kind than meditation: she was engaged in contemplation, the form of prayer to which meditation ought to lead in a fervent and generous soul. For if other saints have enjoyed contemplation, certainly she who was full of grace far surpassed all others in her contemplation.[2]

In one sense we can correctly say that mental prayer is necessary for salvation: vocal prayer, if said with devotion and attention to what we are doing, includes mental prayer. Still, even if we use the term mental prayer in the more usual sense of a purely interior exercise made without vocalization, its importance is extremely great. Pope Pius XII goes so far as to say that for priests,

> It must . . . be stated without reservation that no other means has the unique efficacy of meditation, and that, as a consequence, its daily practice can in no wise be substituted for.[3]

Nor can laymen, if they are really in earnest about making spiritual progress, afford to neglect this great means. At the end of this chapter we shall discuss some of the problems of meditation for laymen, and suggest possible solutions.

Two dangers in particular are to be avoided when we are learning how to meditate. On one hand, we must not be contemptuous of all method. On the other, we must beware of enmeshing our prayer in needless complications of involved procedure. As so often is the case, the truth lies between the extremes of lack of method and overcomplexity. In the case of most people, lack of method would probably lead to no meditation at all, or else to reverie or self-deception. It is true that some of the saints, especially St. Thérèse of Lisieux, seem not to have followed a specific method, but that simplicity in prayer belongs to a higher level than that of beginners. We can hope to reach that level safely only by passing first through the lower stages, during which some method is needed.

There are many good methods of meditation and many good books [4] that provide detailed and lengthy directions for each method, so that it will be sufficient here to sketch the chief elements of meditation and the principal features of the various methods. All schools of spirituality tell us to exercise a certain freedom in our application of whatever method we may choose.

Meditation, or mental prayer, differs from vocal prayer in that it is essentially a purely interior exercise, carried on by the intellect (mind) and the will, with perhaps some help from the imagination and the emotions. [5] It aims at a union of the soul with God. Therefore its two essential parts are, first, *the work of the mind,* which reasons and ponders; and second, *the work of the will,* which, deriving motivation from the work of the mind, unites us to God in a *loving conversation with Him.* [6] It is of the greatest importance that we understand this, for no matter what method we employ, this is its purpose. Method is useful or useless to us on any given occasion according as it helps or hinders us in the accomplishment of these ends.

These two essential parts are often referred to briefly as the considerations and the colloquy (conversation). Beginners spend most of their time on the considerations. But as they grow in grace and in experience in mental prayer, they should need to spend less and less of their time in considerations or reasoning.

For the work of the mind should become simplified, so that a mere glance at the subject suffices. As this simplification progresses, a person is able to spend increasingly large proportions of the time in colloquy. Hence a good method of meditation must be flexible, so as readily to allow this simplification and increase of colloquy to take place gradually.

All methods teach us to make some immediate preparation or introduction to our meditation. It is rather generally agreed that the introduction should include at least three elements: prayer for help, realization of the presence of God, and humble adoration. Therefore, after opening with a brief prayer asking Mary to obtain for us the light of the Holy Spirit, we should place ourselves in the presence of God — for if we wish to hold a conversation with God, we must have Him present. Now, of course, God is always present everywhere, and especially is He present in the Blessed Sacrament, but we are not always aware of that fact. Hence we need to recall to mind His presence, and this we may do in many ways.[7] We may think of the fact that He is present outside of us, everywhere. Or we may recall that He is present in our souls by grace. Or, making use of our imagination, we may picture Our Lord as looking down upon us from Heaven. Or we may imagine Him in some particular scene in His life.

We need not spend too much time merely recalling the presence of God, but neither should we forget His presence when we move on to the other parts of the meditation. And, since the graces of meditation come to us through Mary, and since she is so intimately associated with her divine Son throughout all the work of redemption, we will do well to try to make our whole meditation in mindfulness of her presence as well as of His. We will resemble a child who busies himself in the same room as his mother: he does not always explicitly think of her, but he is always conscious of her presence, and he often comments to her on what he is doing or asks her help. In meditation, however, even though we are not at every moment calling on Mary, yet her help is constantly supporting us, for *all* graces come through her.

Some find it helpful to have an imaginary representation of Our Lord in some scene in their mind throughout much of the meditation, but if we use imagination in this way, some authors think it better not to entertain too vivid or detailed a representation, since that might tend to be distracting.[8]

Our realization of the presence of God should naturally invite us to make acts of adoration and of humility; thus we fall down in spirit before Him, recognizing Him as our absolute Lord (that is the meaning of adoration), and recalling our great unworthiness to speak to Him, our own nothingness and sinfulness (see chapter XI). Then, realizing our inadequacy, we ought to ask Mary to unite her priceless adoration to our poor dispositions, so that she may compensate for our deficiencies.

In offering our adoration, we may think of Our Lord in some particular episode in His life. Thus, for a meditation on humility, we might choose the scene of the Annunciation, in which He humbled Himself to become a child in Mary's womb; or, for a meditation on almost any topic, we might think of the scene on Calvary. The Passion is the most fruitful and important of all subjects of meditation.

If we are inclined to prolong the act of adoration, it is very good to do so, even though the soul does no more than to behold, in silent awe, its own nothingness and poverty as against the majesty or the beauty of God. Such an act may even develop into a brief but loving gaze at God and this, too, is very good, so long as it can be maintained; the soul should not be anxious to move on, for it has, during that time, attained to that very union of mind and will with God for which it is seeking. This adoration may also develop into a conversation with God. Although logically such a colloquy should follow after the considerations, which provide us with motivation and inspiration for it, yet it is profitable, according to the movements of grace at any particular time, to interpose bits of colloquy not only in the adoration, but throughout any and all parts of the meditation. At all times we ought to ask Mary to be with us, to help us. Remember that Mary is the channel of all graces, and that includes the graces of meditation. Even the grace of contemplation — if it is ever given to us — is granted through Mary.[9]

We have now completed the introduction to the meditation, and turn to the first of the two principal parts of the meditation — the considerations. Most people will find that they need some help from a book, although those who have practiced meditation for some time may need a book during only a small part of any meditation. Those well advanced may find enough help in merely glancing at one sentence, but beginners will probably have to do a great deal of reading. Nonetheless — and this is important — even a beginner should try to find what we might call "take-off points" in the book: that is, he should find a point at which he can put the book down, and then proceed by himself for a while. At such a point, one person will reason and develop the thought further. Another, finding a thought that impresses him in some way, will merely stop to allow it to penetrate more deeply into his mind and will. Still another, if he has been reading a Gospel passage for a while, will let his imagination represent the whole episode to him, so that he seems to see the persons and their actions, and to listen to what they say. Perhaps he may even imagine himself as speaking to Jesus or Mary, or to others in the scene. Of course two or more of these various ways of proceeding at take-off points can be combined.

Those who are more advanced will be less dependent upon a book; their meditation will be simpler; they will tend to reason less and to ponder more; they will incline to spend more time on the colloquy, the second of the principal parts of meditation. All — beginners and advanced — should feel free to indulge in free conversational prayer (colloquy) with Our Lord, with His Mother, or with the saints, at various points throughout the considerations. In any case one should also try, so far as he can, to stir up his will by means of the considerations to such an extent that he can spend some time in mere loving colloquy.

Before proceeding to the section devoted especially to colloquy, some authors would have us insert a bit of self-examination. Thus, we might compare our actual conduct in the past to the ideal we have just been considering in the Gospels or in the life of Mary or of some saint, or in a meditation on the nature and need of some virtue in itself. Obviously the correct principle to follow in this matter is to do whatever, in a given case, disposes us most effectively to a loving colloquy. That may well vary with the individual or with the day. At any rate, the examination, if made, should be short; and it should be followed by acts of sorrow, for true contrition is really love expressing its regret for sin.

The second of the principal parts of the meditation, the colloquy, is sometimes termed the "affective" aspect, but we must remember that, although the term suggests emotion, emotion is nonessential, as we saw in chapter X. In this conversation we speak to God, expressing the attitudes and acts of various virtues, especially love. We express our desire to love Him more, to prove our love. We vary it in many ways, taking our theme from the mystery we have been considering. We may speak not only to God Himself, but also to the saints, and especially to Mary.[10] We may speak freely, not only making acts of love but of other virtues as well. As we have already noted, beginners will find it necessary to spend most of their time on the considerations and will spend but little on pure colloquy. But their aim should be to shift the proportion gradually, so as to give more and more time to the colloquy.

In this colloquy we may form the words vocally if we wish, or we may speak interiorly with the movement of the heart or the will. Nor is it necessary that we speak all the time: we ought to listen to God's answer. Of course we do not expect Him to speak audibly: His answer comes in the form of graces of light to understand His ways and His truths better, or graces of love, urging us to serve Him better.

It is a good practice to stop for just a few moments toward the end of the colloquy to engage in a simple loving gaze at God. For this purpose we will ordinarily have to represent Our Lord to ourselves by our imagination. The picture we use is best taken from a Gospel scene related to the subject of our meditation. For just a moment or two we try merely to gaze on Him, letting our will express itself, with or without words (ordinarily with words, especially when we first adopt this practice). The will makes acts of any virtue that is appropriate to the scene — love, humility, sorrow, desire for amendment, confidence, admiration. As soon as we see that we can no longer hold our attention in this gaze, we return to the remaining parts of our meditation. The reason for practicing this moment of gazing will be clear later on: it is the opening wedge toward a simplified form of meditation.[11]

By way of concluding the meditation, there are various other acts which we may make, though not all are essential. We may make acts of thanksgiving, acts of self-offering, and also we may ask for various graces. Whether or not we make these various acts, we ought to form some very specific resolution as a conclusion, and beg Mary to obtain for us the grace to be faithful to it. In adopting this specific resolution, we ought to be careful to avoid dissipation of energy by letting it deal with too wide a variety of subjects on various days; this danger is easily avoided if we let our resolution be concerned each day with improvement in matters with which we are currently having difficulty. Naturally we should try to bring the resolution into relation with the subject of the meditation, so as to gain strength from the motivation provided by the considerations. Thus meditation will become a valuable help to our progress. In addition, it is worth our while to reflect often on the subject of the meditation during the day.

This, then, is meditation — in brief review. We shall not, however, be very successful in meditation unless we live our whole lives in such a way as to be disposed to meditate; we need to practice detachment from worldly things, mortification, humility, and habitual recollection, and we should never let the thought of God and His blessed Mother be far from us. For we all carry on an interior life, which some writers describe as a sort of intimate conversation with ourselves. Not that we are literally talking to ourselves, but we do consider present problems and turn them over in our mind, and we recall past events, and look ahead to coming things. This very natural tendency can be spiritualized, so that it is turned into a loving awareness of God and of Mary, to whom we often comment on whatever we are doing, even on commonplace, routine things, or on things going on about us. We cannot explicitly think of God or of Mary at every moment, but we can to a considerable extent, and the habit will grow in time. Such an interior conversation need not hinder our work. A certain train dispatcher in a large metropolitan center developed this sort of abiding consciousness of God, and yet did not make an error in his work for many years. Those whose work requires less mental effort will find such an interior life still more easy, and even pleasant, in the midst of occupations that are dull in themselves. Especially those engaged in humble tasks can think of the lowly housework that filled so much of the life of our blessed Mother. We should not forget to ask her frequently to offer up our ordinary actions to the Eternal Father, uniting them with the priceless merits that she and her divine Son won in their humble daily occupations. The *ideal* would be never to let our recollection be *completely* interrupted by anything. In this sense St. Thérèse advises us:

> We read that the Israelites, while building the walls of Jerusalem, worked with one hand and held a sword in the other. This is an image of what we should do: avoid being wholly absorbed in our work.[12]

Spiritual reading, outside of the time of meditation, is also very helpful, as it prevents our going dry, so that we are unable to form thoughts or considerations on the things of God. In addition to this remote preparation, it is important, if our meditation is made in the morning, to look over the next meditation the night before, so that, on arising, we may at once begin to turn our thoughts to the subject on which we intend to meditate.

Sometimes one finds that he cannot meditate. In the case of one who has long been faithful to meditation, and who practices great purity of heart, habitual recollection, and thoroughgoing detachment, this may be an indication that God wishes him to take up a simplified form of meditation, such as we shall describe later. But in others, the inability may come from many other causes, such as lack of preparation, recent sins, imperfections or self-indulgence, physical indisposition. At times of great difficulty in meditation we shall probably suffer not only from dryness (for it is often possible to meditate well in dryness) but especially from distractions. Now if the distractions are voluntary, the thing to do is to ask pardon for them, and beg Mary to help us to banish them. But if they are involuntary, we must make a distinction. Ordinarily distractions come and go: they are not long-lived, and we in some way manage to get back to the subject in a reasonable time. But at other times the distractions, even though involuntary, will persist, monopolizing most or all of our meditation period.

Now the first pattern, in which the distractions are brief, and in which we are somehow recalled to the subject after each distraction, is normal, and we need only exert ordinary care, especially asking Mary for help against them. But when they run on and on, and we cannot return to the subject, we should ordinarily take an *alternative* for that particular day. At times, however, we do not really need an alternative: just a slight change in procedure may help us. For example, instead of so much reasoning, we may use the imagination more, or we may stop to ponder more, to allow truths to soak in, as it were. We should be slow to change to an alternative, lest our laziness generate endless distractions every day, and so keep us from normal meditation for an indefinite period of days. In any case, St. Teresa of Avila and St. Ignatius of Loyola suggest a very good alternative: it is to recite any vocal prayer, such as the *Our Father* [13] or the *Anima Christi,* just a phrase at a time, drawing all the thought we can out of each phrase, perhaps even rising to a little colloquy in the intervals. Another alternative is to say the Rosary, with all attention on the mysteries (see chapter XXII). Or we might make the Way of the Cross. Some even find it useful to produce pencil and paper and write their meditation: curiously enough, they are able to meditate more easily with a pencil in their hand. [14]

Thus far we have attempted to describe only the first level in the development of meditation. This first level is often called *discursive meditation.* Two other levels of meditation are within the reach of all, with the more usual graces: *affective meditation* and the *prayer of simplicity.* All three kinds — discursive, affective, and simple — belong to the level of beginners, the purgative way.[15] It is part of the normal, expected development that meditation should, in due time, reach the second and third levels, provided, of course, that the soul is working with all the generosity it can muster to advance in the love of God.

There is no sharp line of division between *affective* and *discursive* meditation. In discursive meditation the considerations, the work of the mind and imagination, predominate, and consume the larger portion of our meditation period. This proportion should gradually shift, so that the colloquy tends to increase at the expense of the considerations. When finally the colloquy, or affective part, becomes dominant, we have affective meditation. In some persons this shift takes place very early in their development. Temperament may favor this shift. The final phase of affective meditation is reached when the considerations become thoroughly simplified — that is, when a mere glance at the subject, or perhaps one sentence out of our book, is enough to activate colloquy with Our Lord or His blessed Mother which will last for the entire period. Of course, the initial consideration may have to be recalled many times during the period, and there may be some little development of it. And there are still distractions. Basically, however, the intellectual side is simplified, while the acts of the will are luxuriant.

The *prayer of simplicity* is not at all likely to be found, except on rare occasions, in persons who are not working generously toward progress in the love of God. A person who *regularly* possesses the prayer of simplicity must have great purity of conscience. He must have a firm will never to consent deliberately to the slightest offense against God. He must have made considerable progress in detachment from earthly pleasures and possessions, even though the objects of the attachments may be innocent in themselves.[16] He should also be advanced in habitual recollection, trying never to allow the thought of God to be far from him, trying also to restrict thoughts on subjects that do not help him to go to God, so far as the duties of the moment permit. He should be striving for purity of motives in all his actions, watching not only the motives with which he begins an action, but also being careful lest he slip into a merely natural way of doing things in the midst of an action well begun. Of course it is not required that one be perfect in all these points, but it is necessary to be striving hard, and to have made some progress.[17]

We have already noted that in affective meditation the activity of the intellect is simplified, especially in the fully-developed form of that prayer. The prayer of simplicity is reached when the activity of the will also becomes simplified. There is a single dominant thought and a matching attitude and act of will that run all through the prayer of simplicity on any given occasion. The mind gazes at this thought, and finds that it can easily hold its attention on it. The will, at the same time, with or without the use of words, is occupied in simply repeating, with little or no development, a single act (such as love, desire, humility, sorrow, admiration). We must not think, however, that this thought is absolutely continuous for as much as a half-hour. It will be interrupted more or less often in various ways. Sometimes it merely fades, and must be consciously brought back before the mind, renewing the gaze. Sometimes it is interrupted by brief distractions — which, however, ought to vanish almost spontaneously. Sometimes the interruption comes from a slight development or variation in the thought. Similarly, the acts of will are not perfectly continuous: though for the great part they are merely repetitive, there may be some little variety in them.

For example, one might picture Our Lord crowned with thorns, as He sits before the mocking soldiers who spit in His face. He gazes at Our Lord in this state (he does not imagine that he sees the actions of the soldiers — only the resultant picture). His mind is absorbed at the thought. His will makes an act of sorrow or love, in few if any words: "Because of my sins," or "My God, I am sorry," or, "My God, I love you."

The gaze tends to fade at times, and must be recalled, and the acts of will are repeated many times. Or a distraction may interrupt briefly, or a bit of development of thought or affection may intervene. When the gaze fades, care must be taken not to sink into mere blankness, doing nothing. Whatever the interruption, there is a constant return to the dominant thought and the dominant attitude and act of will, in which the person *actively and deliberately* maintains himself.

Or, to take another example, the mind might be impressed with the general thought of the immense majesty of God, while the will repeats: "O Lord, our Lord, how admirable is thy name in the whole earth!" [18]

The prayer of simplicity may deal with practically any subject available for meditation: the virtues, our own nothingness, the four last things, the vanity of earthly things, the Blessed Virgin, the mysteries of the life of Christ, the divine nature, the Blessed Trinity. It has a tendency to develop, however, from such specific aspects of faith or the Sacred Humanity of Christ to a more abstract and general consideration of the Divinity. [19]

Should the prayer of simplicity be prepared in advance? Ordinarily the answer is yes, though the preparation may consist only in a bit of meditative reading. And not infrequently the Holy Spirit will suggest a different subject when the time comes. If He does so, it should by all means be accepted: for it is a cardinal rule in all forms of meditation that we must *look for and follow the current attraction of grace.* We must follow this attraction not only as to the subject of the prayer, but also during the prayer: we may make many or few acts or considerations, just as grace leads us.

The same principle helps us to determine whether one is called to this prayer of simplicity as his *regular* form of prayer. When grace moves one to this prayer, he should certainly follow its lead, but it would be wrong to attempt to *force* one's way into this prayer without the call of grace. Final judgment on a call to the prayer of simplicity as our regular prayer should come from our director. In general, there are two signs of a call to this prayer: an attraction for it, together with some facility and success in it; and profit resulting from it. (We are assuming that habitual recollection, detachment, and other general conditions mentioned above are present in the person's life.) As to the first sign, it does not seem to be required that the soul find it impossible to meditate *discursively,* though this condition will often be present. As to the second sign, this is in accord with the Gospel principle, "By their fruits you shall know them." The fruits may not, however, be apparent at once, but if a soul has been faithful to this prayer, within a reasonable time a general spiritual improvement will appear. Especially notable should be an increase of humility and contempt for earthly things, as well as more generosity in mortification. St. Teresa of Avila says that as a result of this prayer worldly things appear to the soul as mere toys.[20]

It is well to make resolutions at the end of the prayer of simplicity, but they will be quite general — for example, "I will be more recollected or generous to God today."

This prayer does not, as a rule, appear suddenly in the life of an individual: it is normal for it to evolve gradually from the other forms mentioned. As a rule, a number of more or less isolated occurrences of it will be experienced before it finally becomes the prevailing mode of prayer.[21]

By nature the prayer of simplicity is especially exposed to distractions. If it is accompanied by consolations, distractions will be no real problem. But if it is made in aridity, we must distinguish two cases: aridity with recall, and aridity without recall. In the first case, distractions come, and may last a little while; yet there is a certain attraction of grace which persistently brings the soul out of them, and draws it back to the dominant thought. If this is the case, it is obvious that no special measures are needed. But in the second case, when recall fails, distractions continue indefinitely, without any persistent return to the dominant thought. The soul then tends to slip into mere reverie, which must be carefully distinguished from simplicity, for reverie is vague, with no dominant thought or persistent return. When the recall fails, the person should revert to affective prayer or even discursive meditation. If this proves impossible, he must merely continue to work patiently against the distractions, begging for light and help, but being resigned to suffer the affliction so long as God wills it. Sometimes it may help to keep repeating some brief vocal prayer, for example, "My God and my All," pausing each time to try to dwell on it.

The prayer of simplicity brings a soul to the end of the purgative way, the first of the three stages in a soul's spiritual development. If a soul is generous in corresponding to all the graces that Mary will obtain for it, she can bring it across the border into the realm of infused contemplation. We shall describe that transition in the next chapter.

A note on some objections to formal meditation, and the problems of laymen

Some rather formidable objections are often made to formal meditation — that is, meditation carried on at a set period and by means of some definite method. Let us list these objections in order:

1. Formal meditation may be all right for priests and religious, but how could a working man or woman or a housewife manage to undertake so complex an exercise?

Answer: As to the complexity of meditation, all methods look far more complex on paper than they do when translated to practice. Essentially, formal meditation requires only the union of the mind and will with God for a fairly protracted time, so that the mind is occupied with thinking about God or divine things, and the will reacts accordingly, expressing its attitudes in the form of a free conversational sort of prayer. The length of time required for this exercise is quite flexible. There are few laymen who cannot find a way to spend at least fifteen minutes at it in a day if they make the effort. Unmarried persons, and even married couples before the arrival of the first child, should find no difficulty in setting aside a brief period either before work in the morning, or in the evening. For married persons with children, the only difficult years are those from the birth of the first child until the time when older children have reached an age at which they can take care of the younger children and keep them quiet at certain times. Even during this difficult period, the wife may be able to meditate while the children are having their naps. The husband may, in difficult cases, have to resort to making his meditation on the way to work, in the bus, train, or subway, or afoot. After these strenuous years have passed, the whole family can be taught to have a brief meditation period in the evening. If some of the children are too young to join in, they can be trained at least to be obedient and to play quietly during this time.

2. But formal meditation is, relatively speaking, an innovation in the Church.[22] Some of the older religious founders, such as St. Benedict, provided no place in the daily program for a meditation period.

Answer: The early monastics had almost continuous informal prayer of a simplified kind. This was carried on during both the community recitation of the Office, and also during the day, in which they practiced an habitual awareness of the presence of God, often stopping for short prayers. Furthermore, it is not quite correct to say that St. Benedict did not provide for any meditation periods: according to his rule, several hours of the day were devoted to holy reading. Concerning these periods, an early Benedictine abbot, Smaragdus, says in his commentary on the rule: "Prayer does not differ from reading, nor is reading different from prayer." [23] Strictly speaking, meditation and meditative reading are not quite the same, but it seems that these monks were using their books much in the manner in which we use meditation books. In any case, whatever the practice of early monasteries may have been, it does not prove that formal meditation should never have been introduced: there are many different forms of spiritual attractions, and there are many developments in the history of the Church. The Holy Spirit is to be with her until the end of time. This fixed time for meditation is far more necessary today than it would be for an early monk, in view of the very different conditions of our times. Much external activity today makes the *constant* prayer and the habitual recollection of the monks difficult to imitate, especially for persons living in the world. Hence we have great need of these periods of concentration, to help provide a wellspring that will feed recollection throughout the rest of the day.

3. St. Thérèse, who is so important a model for our times, had no method of meditation, and seemed to have little success with meditation.

Answer: We admit that St. Thérèse did not use a complex method, but recall again that methods look much more complex on paper than in practice. She certainly did, from an early age, apply her mind and heart to God for long periods, and that is the very essence of mental prayer. Later, in persistent dryness, she leaned heavily on reading the Gospels, she thought about them, and indulged in colloquy with God about her thoughts. Abbé Combes points out that chapters IX and X of her *Autobiography* are "a direct transcription of her meditations, suggested or fully developed, upon verses of St. Matthew and St. John." [24] And her whole day was filled with the thought of God, much as with the early monks. Hers was a naturally contemplative soul, and her prayer inevitably became simplified. Yet it seems that she reached the highest levels of contemplation, in a hidden form for the great part.[25] Let those who can come close to imitating her enclosed way of life and her great virtues also imitate her in the simplicity of her prayer. Care must be taken lest someone be tempted to use her *apparent* lack of method as a pretext for giving up all attempts at formal meditation: she herself never abandoned her efforts, however difficult they became.

NOTES

1. Luke 2:19; 2:51.

2. See L. Reypens, "Marie et la Mystique," Du Manoir (ed.), *Maria,* I, 747–63, esp. 749–50.

3. In *Menti nostrae*, September 23, 1950, §47 in NCWC edition.

4. See, for example, A. Brou, S.J., *Ignatian Methods of Prayer,* trans. W. Young (Milwaukee, 1949); St. Francis de Sales, *Introduction to the Devout Life,* II, i–ix; Tanquerey, *The Spiritual Life,* pp. 319–40; Gabriel of St. Mary Magdalen, O.C.D., *Little Catechism of Prayer,* trans. Discalced Carmelite Nuns (Concord, N.H., 1949); and St. Peter of Alcantara, *Treatise on Prayer and Meditation,* trans. D. Devas (Westminster, 1949).

5. Strictly speaking, vocal prayer, if we think of what we are doing and saying, includes mental prayer. See St. Teresa of Avila, *Way of Perfection,* XXIV.

6. Of course the intellect is not really idle during this conversational part; we merely mean that the dominant feature of this second section is found in acts of the will.

7. See St. Francis de Sales, *op. cit.,* II, 2.

8. On this point see Gabriel of St. Mary Magdalen, *op. cit.,* pp. 24–26.

9. See L. Reypens, DuManoir, *Maria,* I, 756–63; and V. Hoppenbrouwers, O.Carm., "The Blessed Mother Teaches Us to Pray," *Analecta Ordinis Carmelitarum XVI* (1951), pp. 253–65. On the term contemplation, see chap. XIII, esp. note 3.

10. When we go before God in prayer, we should always approach in union with Mary, asking her to accompany us and to commend our prayers to God. This practice is most pleasing to God because of the humility contained in it, for we realize our unworthiness, we realize that our own offerings and prayers by themselves are too poor, and hence we depend on Mary's help to compensate for our deficiencies.

11. See Gabriel of St. Mary Magdalen, *St. John of the Cross,* trans. a Benedictine of Stanbrook Abbey (Westminster, 1952), pp. 93–94.

12. "Counsels and Reminiscences," in *St. Thérèse of Lisieux, An Autobiography,* p. 313.

13. St. Teresa of Avila (in *The Way of Perfection,* XXX) reports the case of a nun whose prayer consisted largely in just such a vocal recitation of the *Our Father* — and she was given the grace of pure contemplation in it.

14. Although, strictly speaking, mental prayer can be made in any position, it is important that the posture be such as to manifest reverence to God to whom we are speaking. Body and soul interact; hence a careless posture, or one lacking in respect in any way, hinders prayer. That posture will be best which is both reverent and which experience has shown us is helpful to our prayer. Many persons will find it good to kneel for part of the meditation and to sit for part. If one sits, he should not do so in a slovenly, irreverent way, though he need not be stiff. See Brou, *Ignatian Methods of Prayer,* pp. 175–77.

15. Some writers speak of all meditation as *discursive* up to the time that the soul enters on infused contemplation (of which we shall speak in the next chapter).

16. On detachment, see chap. XV.

17. See Tanquerey, *The Spiritual Life,* §§ 1374 and 1296.

18. Ps. 8:2. The psalms provide many a point from which the prayer of simplicity may begin.

19. Although it is not necessary for us constantly to keep in mind the Sacred Humanity of Christ in every meditation, yet we must not consider it an imperfection (as the Quietists did) to think of His Humanity. It is true that for certain temporary phases in the development of mystical prayer (see the next chapter) it may be impossible to think explicitly of the Sacred Humanity. But such a disability is only temporary. In the highest phases of the unitive way, the soul is ever in the company of both the Divine and the Human nature: see St. Teresa, *Interior Castle,* VI, vii. On the consciousness of the presence of Mary in mystical prayer, see the articles by Reypens and by Hoppenbrouwers listed above in note 9, and especially Venerable Michael of St. Augustine, "The Mariform and Marian Life in Mary, for Mary," McGinnis (ed.), *Life with Mary,* pp. 19–23, 26–27. See also G. Bélorgey, *The Practice of Mental Prayer* (Westminster, 1952), pp. 105–07, 131, 134–35.

20. St. Teresa, *Way of Perfection*, XXVIII.

21. On this prayer in general, see A. Poulain, S.J., *The Graces of Interior Prayer*, trans. L. Smith (5th impression, London, 1950), pp. 8–51.

22. The beginnings of methodical prayer appear in the twelfth century, though the suggestions given in books of that day are very general. Special impetus to its development was provided in the need for reform at the time of the decay of religious spirit occasioned by the Hundred Years War, the Great Schism, and the pagan humanism. St. Ignatius deserves special credit for popularizing and making practical this methodical prayer. See P. Pourrat, *Christian Spirituality*, trans. W. Mitchell (New York, 1927), III, 1–23; and A. Brou, *op. cit.*, pp. 1–11, esp. p. 11.

23. See T. V. Moore, O.S.B., *Prayer* (Westminster, Md., 1951), p. 68. Dom Moore has entered the Carthusian Order since writing this work.

24. A. Combes, *The Spirituality of St. Thérèse*, p. 110.

25. Gabriel of St. Mary Magdalen, *St. John of the Cross*, p. 97.

XIII ... *Mystical Rose*

MENTAL PRAYER is a great means to progress in the love of God. It paves the way for this growth in love especially by disposing us to receive an increase in faith, for it seeks to make ever more and more real to us the truths of the Creed. Without mental prayer, the spiritual landscape becomes desolate, and external works wither up for lack of an inner life to nourish them. Beyond the forms of mental prayer that were described in the preceding chapter lies a much higher form of prayer called contemplation. It was in contemplation that Mary united herself so intimately in spirit with her Son in all the mysteries of His life, from the early years of her own life to the consummation on Calvary. And even after Calvary her life of contemplation continued, until one day it changed into the absolute clarity of the direct vision of her Son and her Creator in Heaven.

In order that we may more easily learn something about contemplation, we must understand that a soul, in its ascent to the highest kind of perfection to which it can attain in the present life, passes through three ways or stages in the course of its spiritual development. The first is the purgative way, the way of beginners, in which the soul meditates by the means described in the preceding chapter, and labors at the first steps in its purification. The passage from the purgative way to the second way, the illuminative way, is made through what St. John of the Cross calls the "night of the senses." [1] There is both an active and a passive aspect to this night: the active part consists in the preliminary work that the soul itself does by its own *activity*, with the aid of the more usual graces, in trying to free itself from attachments to things of the sensory order, and to advance toward God. The *pas-*

123

sive phase is the completion of the work by the action of God Himself.[2]

It is during the passive night of the senses that the soul is introduced to infused contemplation, a new and much higher form of prayer. Infused contemplation is a simple, loving gaze at God, which is not the fruit of human activity, not even of a human activity aided by grace, but of a special inspiration of the Holy Spirit. After the night of sense comes the dawn of the illuminative way, a time of great blessings, in which, under the strong influence of the Gifts of the Holy Spirit, the virtues of the soul are made more solid, and contemplation becomes well developed. The soul is still, however, in need of purification: hence a second night is required, the "night of the spirit." Like the first night, this night of the spirit has both an active and a passive side. The passive part of this second night is far more terrible than the first passive night; in the second, the spiritual faculties are purified by God's action, so that the soul will be prepared for the higher contemplation and union with God which mark the unitive way.[3]

These are the three ways: purgative, illuminative, and unitive, with two nights — that of sense and that of spirit — forming the transition between them.

The prayer of simplicity, which we discussed in the last chapter, may develop to the extent that it merges with the edge of the passive night of the senses, forming a bridge into the initial stage of infused contemplation.[4] In some persons that passage is made so gradually[5] that the soul in which it takes place is not conscious of the change, but in others the change is well defined, and can be identified by certain characteristic signs, of which St. John of the Cross has provided the classic description. According to this description, there are three signs that a soul is passing from the purgative way to the illuminative way, from meditation to infused contemplation.[6]

The first sign is a great aridity, which takes from the soul all sensible consolation in the things of God, and does not permit it to find pleasure in created things.[7] St. John of the Cross says of a soul in this state that God " . . . allows it not to find attraction or sweetness in anything whatsoever." [8] This lack of sensible pleasure results in great weariness in the soul — even in the practice of virtue. As a result, temptation is very burdensome, sacrifices terrify it, and it suffers from even slight causes. The fact that the soul finds pleasure neither in the things of God nor in created things shows that we are not dealing with the common sort of aridity in prayer which is often caused by deliberate sins and imperfections. For although a person who is imperfect and sinful may and usually does find aridity and lack of pleasure in the things of God, he does not simultaneously lack pleasure in all created things.

The second sign is the fact that the soul has an awareness of God which returns persistently in spite of distractions. [9] This consciousness of God is indistinct and obscure but nonetheless very real. At the same time, the soul has great need for more intimate union with God and fears that it is not serving Him well. If this second sign is joined to the first sign, we see further proof that the aridity of the first sign is no ordinary aridity, for in ordinary aridity a soul usually will tend to forget God in the midst of many distractions; but in this night, the thought of God is persistent, so as to appear again after distractions without being sought. This persistent reappearance of the awareness of God, coupled with the soul's desire for Him and fear that it is not serving Him, makes it quite clear that we are not dealing with a mere case of lukewarmness.

Finally, the third sign is an inability to carry on discursive meditation. [10] Abbot Bélorgey gives us a good description of strongly developed cases of this third sign:

> The mind is as if bound; its imagination will not move, its memory is blurred and it seems empty of understanding. At times this emptiness cannot even comprehend a book. At best the soul tries to correspond with the obscure and indistinct awareness of God. . . . Its aridity continues as usual. But outside of prayer there is little trouble carrying on with one's duties; though sometimes study is difficult. [11]

All three of the above-mentioned signs must be present at the same time before a spiritual director can justifiably conclude that a soul is in the transition to the illuminative way.

The forces at work in producing these signs are not too difficult to find: God is taking the soul away from its old form of prayer, in which it had formerly found sensible consolations.[12] Hence, since it cannot succeed in its accustomed prayer, it lacks the sensible consolation it once found therein, without yet having found the higher pleasure of contemplation. This same lack of sensible consolation tends to make the soul think it is no longer serving God well, but rather is falling back. This impression is heightened by the action of the Holy Spirit in the soul, making it fear sin and desire to be more closely united with God and to serve Him ever better and better. The persistent thought of God is produced by the very contemplation that God is infusing into the soul, while the lack of pleasure in any created thing comes from the action of the Holy Spirit which shows it so plainly how vain all earthly things are.

As we have already noted, this transition to infused contemplation may take place so gradually in some souls that the person himself is not aware of it. In such souls, the prayer of simplicity melts gradually into the newer infused contemplation, for fragments of infused light of the sort that produce the infused contemplation appear little by little, in gradually increasing measure, in the last stages of the prayer of simplicity.

The very nature of the prayer of simplicity makes it a ready background for the infused light. As we saw in the preceding chapter, the prayer of simplicity involves a very simple, loving gaze at God or at divine things. A loving gaze at God is also found in infused contemplation, but the gaze in the prayer of simplicity is active — that is, it is the work of the soul itself, aided, of course, by the more usual sort of graces, while the gaze of infused contemplation is passive — that is, it is produced in the soul by God Himself. As more and more of the infused light is mingled with the prayer of simplicity, the soul becomes less active and more passive; hence the gaze lasts longer, since it is, to an ever-increasing extent, produced passively in the soul by infused light. We must not imagine, however, that this contemplation, even when it is well developed, is so prolonged as to be absolutely continuous for even as much as a half-hour: it is interrupted, and distractions are possible,[13] but the thought of God returns persistently. Again, when we say that the contemplation of this night is passive, it must not be thought that the soul is absolutely passive, for it does collaborate in holding itself quiet and attentive to God.[14]

The prayer of simplicity may deal with almost any subject that is suitable for lower forms of meditation, and there may be a rather distinct mental image present — but as more and more infused light enters, the tendency of the object of the prayer to be restricted to the Divinity itself increases; and, if an image was formerly present, it now becomes vague and indistinct and gives way to a mere loving attentiveness to God and awareness of Him in a vague, obscure, and general way.[15] This awareness is faint at first, and its very vagueness and dimness emphasize the need of the three above-mentioned signs: they serve to show that the soul is not merely blank, doing nothing. They also indicate that it is time to abandon attempts to force the soul to meditate in the old ways.

When the soul arrives at the vague, general, loving attentiveness to God and awareness of Him, in the presence of the three signs, whether strongly marked or not, it has reached the state of obscure, hidden, arid, infused contemplation in the first passive night. It should then content itself with mere loving attentiveness to God, not trying to reason, nor to make any special acts of will unless God should move it to some act. For any reasoning or forced acts would disturb the contemplation that God is infusing into it. A soul at this time must also refrain from seeking sensible sweetness, and must beware of the devil, who may offer it just such consolations in order to induce it to block the divine infusion by reverting to its old ways.[16] For although sensible consolations were useful in connection with meditation, to return to them during the onset of infused contemplation would be to interfere with the change that God is working in the soul. Although contemplation itself, when it first comes to the soul, seems to be arid and dark,[17] yet it is really a great light — but the soul is not yet able to discern that fact.

If God so wills, the contemplation will develop further, and be perceived by the soul in a pleasant, clear way; then the soul has but to let itself be held, and to follow the divine action.[18] On the other hand, He may permit the transitional arid night to remain for days or years. And in addition to the suffering caused by the aridity, many souls also are assailed by very strong temptations, especially against chastity and patience. Or there may be sickness, fatigue, and various sorts of crosses arising from external conditions. But not all souls receive these additional sufferings, and some have them only to a rather slight degree.

There are higher forms of contemplation in the illuminative way, which follows after the first night. The most characteristic prayer of the illuminative way is the prayer of quiet, in which the presence of God is felt experimentally, and with great pleasure.[19] The soul seems to be immersed in God, saturated with Him, so that it has an obscure but very perceptibly real contact with Him — as real as that of a hand laid on the table. The feeling seems first to fill the soul itself, and then to overflow on the body. At the same time, the soul feels as it were bound, so that it is impeded more or less from producing the interior acts that it ordinarily would make at will during prayer.[20] In fact, the person may fear to move at all, lest it hinder this wondrous pleasure.[21] Yet distractions in the intellect and in the imagination are not only possible but are not rare during the prayer of quiet, for the divine action is holding captive only the will, not the other faculties.[22]

At first the prayer of quiet usually appears only occasionally, and for but a few moments at a time — perhaps for the length of a *Hail Mary*. In some, this great grace appears abruptly, and when they are not expecting it. They are suddenly seized with an unusual recollection which they cannot help noticing. The divine seems to penetrate them. They remain motionless — and then, as suddenly as it came, it vanishes. But in others these graces appear to come gradually. The intensity of the prayer also varies from time to time.

After the first appearance of this grace, it may not be experienced again for a long time — even for a period of years; such interruptions may be due to the infidelities of the soul receiving it. In other cases the prayer does not suffer such prolonged interruptions: it becomes more and more frequent, and the soul reaches a state in which quietude is habitual. This sweetness may last for a long period, and may come even outside the time of prayer: any mention of God may be enough to invite it.[23]

After the illuminative way there follows the more terrible — and much more rare — purgation of the second passive night, the night of the spirit. This leads into the unitive way, with its higher forms of contemplation, in which not only the will but all the faculties are taken captive by the divine action.

There are some souls, such as St. Thérèse, in whom contemplation seldom appears in a sweet form: most of their contemplation is in an arid form.[24] St. Thérèse must have liked to think that Mary herself walked in this largely (if not entirely) arid way. This thought emerges in her poem, "Why I Love You, O Mary":

> I know that at Nazareth, Virgin full of graces,
> You lived in great poverty, not wishing anything more;
> No raptures, no miracles, no ecstasies
> Embellished your life, O Queen of the elect.
> The number of little ones is very great upon the earth.
> They can, without trembling, lift up their eyes to you.
> It pleases you to walk along the common way,
> Incomparable Mother, to guide them to the heavens.

Whatever may be the truth as to the aridity or sweetness of Mary's contemplation, it is certain that she passed far beyond the level accessible to any other saint.[25]

All authors agree that infused contemplation is something that a soul cannot procure for itself, not even with the help of the usual actual graces. It is received only when God Himself chooses to give it. When it is given, it comes by a special inspiration of the Holy Spirit, received through the Gifts of the Holy Spirit. But is this infused contemplation normal? It is not normal in the sense of being found in many persons. That much is clear. But is it part of the theoretically normal development for souls? The answer is hotly disputed. The view of such theologians as Gabriel of St. Mary Magdalen and Garrigou-Lagrange[26] seems far more probable: that it is theoretically normal, and that therefore every soul may legitimately desire to attain it. But in such a desire two points are to be observed: first, it should not be desired as an end in itself, but as a means of union with God; and, second, it is best that the soul refrain from desiring the arid or the sweet forms as such: that decision should be completely surrendered to God through the hands of Mary.

Is it possible to arrive at sanctity without infused contemplation? Again, as Fr. Gabriel and Garrigou-Lagrange think, the answer seems to be *No*. But there are authors who insist that a soul may develop in other ways, by other paths, and so come even to great sanctity without infused contemplation. Such is the opinion of G. Bélorgey,[27] A. Poulain,[28] A. Tanquerey,[29] and some others. It is true that St. Teresa of Avila states that some persons arrive at sanctity without contemplation.[30] But, as Fr. Gabriel well shows, she has in mind contemplation of an *experimentally felt, sweet* kind.[31] She does not seem to think of the arid forms. Some saints, as we have already said, seem to have received most, if not all, of their contemplation in hidden or arid forms.[32]

It is good for us to keep this ideal of contemplation before our eyes, even in the knowledge that the majority of souls will never attain it. Actually a considerable number of souls do reach it: it is known to occur not only in monasteries, but even among simple lay persons in rural districts, and among working girls in large cities. The very knowledge of its possibility is a useful stimulus to generosity. It is also good to know the direction in which meditation aims, for the light which that knowledge sheds on the normal course of development. For all of us can hope that meditation will gradually become simplified for us, moving toward contemplation, even if we do not reach it.

It is with reluctance that we have refrained from the mention of Mary's role during the description of contemplation. This procedure was suggested by the fact that there are still problems on the role of Mary in contemplation which theologians have not completely solved. Some things are quite clear. We know that Mary herself is undoubtedly the great model of contemplative souls, for her contemplation reached to heights far beyond the reach of the ordinary saints. We know that it is through her that even the graces of contemplation are given to souls, for she is the Mediatrix of *all* graces, without exception. It is likewise clear that even souls whose spirituality is not of the more intimate Marian form often enjoy her association during the illuminative and unitive ways, as well as in the purgative way.[33] In fact, in souls whose every act is guided and moved by the Holy Spirit in the unitive way, their very love of Mary is produced in them by the action of the Holy Spirit.[34] But souls especially devoted to Mary report particular kinds of favors in which Mary's presence is felt in a remarkable way. Thus St. Thérèse reports an experience in which,

> It was as if a veil had been thrown over me hiding all the things of earth. . . . I seemed to be entirely hidden beneath the veil of the Blessed Virgin. . . . I remained in this state for an entire week.[35]

And again the same saint, during the terrible dark night in which she spent the last part of her life, when she was asked: "Have they succeeded in hiding the Blessed Mother, too?" answered:

> No, the Blessed Virgin will never be hidden from me, for I love her too much for that to happen.[36]

But the really difficult problem concerns the consciousness of the presence of Mary at the very moment in which infused contemplation is being given to a soul.[37] A considerable number of Marian souls have reported just such an experience: but the information they have given is, for the most part, so scant that it is difficult to construct a complete theological explanation.[38]

Whatever the answer to the above-mentioned problems may be, it is certain that if we are faithful to Mary, she will make our meditation more fruitful and our progress more rapid. Furthermore, although the grace of contemplation is rare, yet a most faithful practice of the perfect devotion to Mary (which we shall explain in chapter XVIII) will give to all a better chance of reaching it, for Mary makes the path through the dark night of sense much easier and more rapid.[39]

NOTES

1. The interpretation in St. John of the Cross's writings on certain of these matters, chiefly on the position and the normality of infused contemplation, is disputed. We shall sketch the chief features of the dispute at the end of this chapter. We follow the interpretation of such theologians as Fr. Gabriel of St. Mary Magdalen, O.C.D., one of the leading modern Carmelite commentators on St. John, and Fr. Garrigou-Lagrange, O.P.

2. Actually, the night of the senses does not complete the purgation of the sensory part, for the deeper roots of disorders lie in the spiritual part. Hence the first night begins the purification of the sensory part, and the second night completes it, in purifying the spirit. See St. John of the Cross, *Dark Night of the Soul,* II, iii (I, 402–4).

3. Unfortunately, the term "contemplation," without the adjective "infused," is used in quite a variety of ways by different authors. For example, St. Ignatius Loyola at times uses it as synonomous with meditation, even certain forms of beginners' meditation. See A. Brou, S.J., *Ignatian Methods of Prayer,* pp. 130–45, esp. note A, pp. 143–44. St. Peter of Alcantara has a somewhat different use; see his *Treatise on Prayer and Meditation,* pp. 112–18. Needless to say, neither of these authors restricts the term to infused contemplation. It is important, then, in reading any author who uses the term without the adjective "infused" to determine what sense he gives to the word contemplation. Some authors also speak of "active" or "acquired" contemplation. On this, see note 4 below.

4. The term "acquired contemplation" is sometimes used as synonomous with the term "prayer of simplicity," and sometimes to designate the initial infused contemplation of the first night. Gabriel combines both uses of the term. Garrigou-Lagrange does not approve the term "acquired contemplation." This fluctuation in terminology is confusing, and one must be extremely careful in reading any author to note what meaning he attaches to his terms.

5. See Garrigou-Lagrange, *The Three Ages of the Interior Life,* II, 328–30.

6. Judgment on the presence of the three signs must be left to an experienced director. On these signs, see: St. John of the Cross, *Ascent of Mount Carmel,* I, xiii–xiv (I, 114–27), and *Dark Night,* I, ix–x (I, 373–81). See also: Gabriel of St. Mary Magdalen, *St. John of the Cross,* pp. 132–39; Garrigou-Lagrange, (*op. cit.*), II, 43–53; Poulain, *The Graces of Interior Prayer,* pp. 201 ff.; Bélorgey, *The Practice of Mental Prayer,* pp. 105–19.

7. The aridity and other features are more intense in some souls than in others. In general, the higher God plans to lead the soul, the more intense they will be. Certain trials and temptations, especially against chastity and patience, often come in this first night. See Garrigou-Lagrange, *The Three Ages of the Interior Life,* II, 59–61.

8. St. John of the Cross, *Dark Night of the Soul,* I, ix, 2 (I, 373).

9. In *Ascent of Mount Carmel,* II, xiii, St. John of the Cross gives the three signs in a somewhat different form from that which we are following (we follow his *Dark Night,* I, ix–x). Commentators consider the two sets as substantially identical. The chief difference is that the second sign above is replaced, in the *Ascent,* by: "The third and surest sign is that the soul takes pleasure in being alone, and waits with loving attentiveness upon God, without making any particular meditation, in inward peace and quietness and rest, and without acts and exercises of the faculties — memory, understanding, and will — at least without discursive acts . . . the soul is alone, with an attentiveness and a knowledge, general and loving, as we said, but without any particular understanding, and adverting not to what it is contemplating" (I, 116). Gabriel of St. Mary Magdalen (*op. cit.,* p. 54) says of the difference: "Both denote the presence of the same contemplative love, but whereas the sign in the *Night* shows it still inchoate, that of the *Ascent* considers it as already formed."

10. See Garrigou-Lagrange, *op. cit.,* II, 58 (quoting from *Ascent,* II, xv) : " 'The beginning contemplative is not yet so far removed from discursive meditation that he cannot return occasionally to its practice,' when he is no longer under the special influence of the Holy Ghost, which facilitates recollection." See also II, 56; Gabriel of St. Mary Magdalen, *op. cit.,* p. 139; *Ascent,* II, xv, 1; *Dark Night,* I, ix, 9. See also note 16 below.

11. Bélorgey, *op. cit.,* pp. 110–11.

12. See Garrigou-Lagrange, *op. cit.,* II, 47–53.

13. On distractions in contemplation, see *Ascent,* II, xiii, 3, and Garrigou-Lagrange, *op. cit.,* II, 50, n. 30, and pp. 344–45.

14. See Gabriel of St. Mary Magdalen, *op. cit.,* pp. 119–22, 143–44, 169–71; and Bélorgey, *op. cit.,* pp. 126–27.

15. There are many differences between the prayer of simplicity and infused contemplation: in the prayer of simplicity the gaze is not so prolonged, it is maintained by our own efforts (with the help of the more usual graces), and it can deal with a wide variety of subjects and may be associated with a rather distinct mental image. But in arid infused contemplation the gaze is confined to a vague general awareness; it is not the result of the soul's own efforts (though there is some slight co-operation in holding the soul attentive), but it is produced by a special inspiration of the Holy Spirit, and it

lasts longer. In addition, the prayer of simplicity is often associated with sensible consolations — while the first well developed instance of this infused prayer is normally arid, and commonly hidden from the one who receives it.

16. See St. John of the Cross, *Living Flame*, III, lxiii–lxiv. Sensible consolations are useful in accord with the principles given in chap. X until the night comes. Then they are harmful, and one must not accept them. In this connection, we must note that the onset of this purgative aridity is apt to be intermittent (see *Ascent*, II, xv, 1, and *Dark Night*, I, ix, 9); that is, the soul on some occasions has infused contemplation, but on other occasions must return to meditation. When the infused light is not there, the sensible consolations may be useful. See also note 10 above.

17. See *Ascent*, II, xiii, 7. Note also *Dark Night*, I, ix, 6 (I, 375–76) : " . . . although *at first* the spirit *feels no sweetness* . . . it feels that it is deriving strength and energy to act from the substance which this inward food gives it, the which food is the beginning of a contemplation that is dark and arid to the senses . . . and ordinarily together with the aridity . . . it gives the soul an inclination and desire to be alone and in quietness, without being able to think of any particular thing or having the desire to do so. If those souls . . . knew how to be quiet at this time . . . they would delicately experience this inward refreshment. . . . So delicate is this refreshment that ordinarily, if a man have desire or care to experience it, he experiences it not." [*Emphasis added.*]

18. See Gabriel of St. Mary Magdalen, *St. John of the Cross*, p. 121.

19. See Poulain, *op. cit.*, pp. 220–34; St. Teresa of Avila, *Autobiography*, XIV–XV (I, 83–96); *Way of Perfection*, XXXI (II, 126–34); *Interior Castle*, IV, ii (II, 236–39); Bélorgey, *op. cit.*, pp. 120–58; and Garrigou-Lagrange, *op. cit.*, II, 300–3.

20. This phenomenon is called ligature. In regard to it, during prayer the soul should not force any acts, though it may make those acts for which it feels a facility; outside of prayer the soul should use its freedom. On ligature see Poulain, *op. cit.*, pp. 178–99, and Bélorgey, *op. cit.*, pp. 125–26.

21. Slight and brief movement does not cause the prayer to leave, but much movement would drive out the prayer. See Poulain, *op. cit.*, pp. 167–69.

22. Although the will alone is held captive, yet the other faculties are not excluded entirely: they should still be united to God. See Poulain, *op. cit.*, pp. 130–31. On distractions, see St. Teresa of Avila, *Way of Perfection* XXXI (II, 130), and *Autobiography*, XIV (I, 84).

23. On the distinction of this prayer from the prayer of simplicity, see Poulain, *op. cit.*, pp. 222–30, and pp. 64–199 (esp. 64–65, 90–91, and 114). See also St. Teresa of Avila, *Interior Castle*, IV, ii.

24. See Gabriel of St. Mary Magdalen, *op. cit.*, pp. 95 and 97; and Garrigou-Lagrange, *op. cit.*, II, 634–37.

25. See L. Reypens, "Marie et la Mystique," Du Manoir, *Maria*, I, 747–63.

26. To the casual reader, these two authors will seem to be at opposite poles. While there is great difference in their use of terms, there is actually

only a rather small difference in their meaning. See the comparison given in *The Three Ages of the Interior Life*, II, 349, n.28, and 548, n.3.

27. Bélorgey, *op. cit.*, pp. 99–101.

28. Poulain, *op. cit.*, pp. 522 ff.

29. Tanquerey, *The Spiritual Life*, pp. 731–37. Tanquerey, in opposition to the school of Gabriel of St. Mary Magdalen and Garrigou-Lagrange, holds that the first night comes at the beginning of the "mystic unitive way," not at the beginning of the illuminative way. He recognizes that St. John of the Cross (*Dark Night*, I, viii) states that the night of sense comes to beginners (i.e., at the end of the purgative way, according to our view). But Tanquerey thinks that St. John's term "beginners" designates beginners in the mystical forms of prayer, or what he calls the mystical unitive way (for Tanquerey also speaks of the "simple unitive way" in which is found the prayer of simplicity). Garrigou-Lagrange answers this argument (*op. cit.*, II, 42, n.8) by showing that the list of faults which St. John of the Cross (*Dark Night*, II, i–vii) ascribes to his "beginners" would not fit anything but a very watered-down version of the unitive way.

30. St. Teresa, *Way of Perfection*, XVII.

31. Gabriel of St. Mary Magdalen, *op. cit.*, p. 111.

32. See note 24 above.

33. See St. Teresa of Avila, *Interior Castle*, VI, vii; and Bélorgey, *op. cit.*, pp. 134–35.

34. See chap. XIX.

35. *Novissima Verba*, trans. Carmelite Nuns of New York (New York, 1952), p. 42.

36. *Ibid.*, p. 35.

37. There is even a problem in reference to the thought of the Sacred Humanity of Christ during the arid night. See Gabriel of St. Mary Magdalen, *The Spiritual Director*, trans. a Benedictine of Stanbrook Abbey (Westminster, 1951), pp. 109–14. See also note 19, chap. XII above.

38. See V. Hoppenbrouwers, O.Carm., "The Blessed Mother Teaches Us to Pray," *Analecta Ordinis Carmelitarum*, XVI (1951), II, 259–65; L. Reypens, "Marie et la Mystique," Du Manoir, *Maria*, I, 760–63; Ven. Michael of St. Augustine, "The Mariform and Marian Life, in Mary, for Mary," McGinnis (ed.), *Life with Mary*; and Bélorgey, *op. cit.*, p. 107. See also Marie-Eugène de l'Enfant-Jésus, O.C.D., "La decouverte de la Sainte Vierge," *Marie* (Nicolet, P.Q.), November–December, 1952, pp. 70–72; and Jean de Jésus-Hostie, O.C.D., "Notre-Dame des nuits," *ibid.*, pp. 77–79.

39. See Garrigou-Lagrange, *Christian Perfection and Contemplation*, pp. 386–87.

XIV ... *Why the Cross?*

THE SAYINGS of Our Lord on the subject of mortification are many and forceful. "And he who does not carry his cross and follow me, cannot be my disciple" ... "And he who does not take up his cross, and follow me, is not worthy of me," are only two among them.[1] We do not like to read these texts; they are unpleasant to human nature. But they are inescapable: Christianity without the cross is inconceivable. He who follows Christ must take up the cross. Mary accepted the cross most perfectly of all the followers of Christ. We have already seen in detail her perfect union with Him on Calvary; equally perfect was her union with Him in all the hardships of His life before Calvary. In this chapter we shall discover, with her help, the chief reasons for the necessity of the cross.

We have stressed the fact that the very essence of the Christian life is love. We presented humility as a peculiarly necessary prerequisite for that love, for humility is concerned with emptying us of the disordered self in us, so that there may be room for God who is love. Now humility accomplishes this emptying especially in our attitudes toward ourselves and others. It reveals our true position and makes us take the proper reaction to it. An appreciation of our true position also shows the need of mortification. For mortification also deals with this matter of the emptying of self.

The first reason for mortification is the fact of original sin. For even though original sin is removed by baptism, some of its consequences — our weakness and inclination to evil — are not. Hence we must face the fact that we have tendencies to evil. We are composed of body and soul, matter and spirit. We live in a material world, surrounded by things of sense. It is not surpris-

136

ing that the demands of the senses war against those of the spirit. This tendency of the lower nature to get out of hand makes it difficult for the intellect to see truth fairly (recall again the introduction to this book). The will naturally finds it easier to let us go downhill than to plod its way upward. All these things alone make obvious the need for strong corrective measures.

We may well compare our lower nature to a piece of spring steel: in order to straighten it, it is not sufficient merely to push it into a straight position. If we do no more than that, it will jump back to its natural bent. We frequently have to push it far in the opposite direction. In the case of the metal, we might finally be able to make it remain straight. In our own case, the warfare is never over. Now, just as we must regularly push the spring far in the opposite direction, so also we must often deny the senses even lawful things, if we are to keep them under control. If we attempt to walk on the edge of a cliff for long, we shall probably fall over sooner or later. So also, if we hold to the mere minimum at all times, we shall sooner or later fall into sin. Further, it is not merely the tendency of the senses to disorder that we must fear: our very mind, the higher part, also tends to the disorder of pride and to other vices as well.

In short, every part of our being is in need of corrective and precautionary measures. These needs would exist even if we were living in a world of innocent people who never tempted us to get out of line in any respect. But the truth is, the spirit of the world in which we live is frontally opposed to the spirit of Christ. This fact increases the need of mortification. And the forces of the devil provide a constant threat that we dare not ignore; to drop our armaments before such an enemy would be real folly.

These reasons are all valid even for one who has never committed sin. They apply with a new force to those who have committed sin (and we all have: only by a special privilege such as was given to Mary could anyone for his whole life avoid all sin, even venial sin.)[2] Hence we have a great need of penance to counteract the further disorder brought about by our sins. For the weakening effects of original sin are heightened by personal sin. There is a saying: God forgives, man forgives, but nature never forgives. This means that there are certain natural laws whose operation is not suspended by our repentance and pardon. All sins leave us weaker, and more inclined to the same or even worse sins. No amount of venial sins can add up to a mortal sin: yet they do *dispose* us to mortal sin. Every time we commit any sin, our resistance to that sin is weakened for the future. It is obvious that here is a new tendency to disorder which mortification must correct.[3]

The disorder left in our soul by sin involves not only a weakness of will toward good, but also a darkness of mind. We find it hard to see things in their true light, in relation to God and eternity. We naturally gravitate toward believing that this world is the only world, that it can and should be a paradise in which we "shall be as gods." Hence there is need of the sobering influence of mortification to help banish such illusions. God is indeed good to us when He sprinkles our path with difficulties that keep us in our right senses.

We may note in passing that although we ought to use and prize indulgences, they do not at all obviate the need for mortification to correct the disorders of original and personal sins.

We have seen two reasons for the need of mortification: the weakness and tendency to disorder left by original sin and by our own personal sins. Such tendency to disorder would call for mortification even if God had destined us for a merely natural end. But the loftiness of the end for which He has destined us — the supernatural end of union with Him in the face-to-face vision of heaven — reveals another reason for mortification. For since we are destined to such an intimate union with God in Heaven, it is obvious that a high degree of purity is required. Every part of our being — not only our senses but even our higher faculties — stands in need of purification. We have two choices in this matter. We must either accomplish the purification in this life, when it can still merit for us an even greater glory in Heaven, or we must suffer it without any merit in Purgatory.

In the preceding chapter we spoke of the dark night of the senses and the dark night of the spirit. We can, as was said, accomplish part of our purification actively, that is, by mortification with the help of the more usual graces. But there is a point beyond which we cannot advance unless God Himself intervenes and, by what is called a passive purification, finishes the work for us. Hence the need of the two nights. The first of the two nights purifies the sensory part of man and leads into initial infused contemplation. The second of the nights purifies the spiritual side of man and leads him into the unitive way. Few in this life reach the first passive night. Still fewer reach the second. But the work must be done somewhere. If it is not done in this life with merit, it will be done in Purgatory, without merit. Here, then, we have a powerful incentive to work hard on mortification, for it brings such great rewards not only in the next life, but even in this life; while to neglect mortification not only loses advantages for us, but even puts us in danger of losing our final goal altogether.[4]

The fourth and greatest reason for mortification is a reason of love. Just as in the treatment of humility we saw that we ought to be glad to accept humiliations precisely because Jesus and Mary chose them, so for the same reason we can now say that we ought to be glad to accept mortification and suffering, because it is *par excellence* the way of Jesus and Mary: it is the road of the cross. The motive of love also presents the duty of mortification as one of reparation. For once a man who loves God realizes how shamefully both he and others have offended and are offending God, he cannot do other than wish to make reparation to the outraged Heart of Christ. Especially in our own day is there great need for reparation, when the sins of individuals and nations have risen to a pitch seldom if ever equaled in all past history. In his classic encyclical on the Sacred Heart, *Miserentissimus Redemptor,* Pope Pius XI speaks of his own times thus:

> Surely these things are so sad that one might say that through events of this sort even now there are foretold and portended

those "beginnings of sorrows" which "the man of sin . . . who . . . is lifted up above all that is called God or that is worshipped" is to bring. . . .

And so the thought comes upon us, even though our mind is unwilling, that the times are now approaching closer of which Our Lord prophesied: "And because iniquity hath abounded, the charity of many shall grow cold." [5]

In offering our reparation to the Heart of Christ, let us not forget to offer it up through the hands of Mary, so that she may purify it of the stains of self which so readily creep into even our best works, and that she may join it to her own priceless reparation. Thus Pope Pius XI, in the official prayer of reparation, wrote:

> . . . we offer it in union with the acts of atonement of Thy Virgin Mother and of all the Saints and of the pious faithful on earth. . . . O loving Jesus, through the intercession of the Blessed Virgin Mary our model in reparation, deign to receive the voluntary offering we make of this act of expiation. . . . [6]

We owe reparation to the Sacred Heart of Christ because of the pain that sin has caused Him. But Mary shared in His sufferings, for sin was not only the cause of the Passion of Christ, but also of the Com-passion of Mary. Hence it is strictly and literally true to say that every sin of ours has wounded not only the Sacred Heart of her Son, but also her own Immaculate Heart. Therefore, while offering our reparation to His Heart through her, we should not forget to offer reparation to her own Heart as well, for the pain that we have caused her. With this in mind, Saint Pius X, even *before* Fatima, granted indulgences to encourage exercises of reparation to Mary. [7]

When we speak of making reparation, not only for our own sins, but for those of others as well, one may object, "But I have more than I can do to atone for my own sins; it would be pride for me to presume to make reparation for the sins of others." In a certain sense this complaint is valid. But remember: we are not alone: our poor reparation is to be joined to the infinite reparation made by Jesus on Calvary and re-presented in the Mass, and to the reparation that Mary made with Him. In this way we can, without presumption, attempt to repair for the sins of others. Therefore, in that same prayer of reparation, Pope Pius XI encourages us to say:

> . . . we humbly ask Thy pardon and declare our readiness to atone by voluntary expiation not only for our own personal offences, but also for the sins of those who, straying far from the path of salvation, refuse . . . to follow Thee . . . or . . . have cast off the sweet yoke of Thy law. We are now resolved to expiate each and every deplorable outrage committed against Thee. . . . [8]

The right attitude to mortification requires a delicate balance. Various fanatical groups within the Church, both in the past and present, have distorted the balance. In general, they tend to make mortification an end in itself, to be pursued blindly, out of pride in their ability to "take it" and without obedience to proper authority. They forget that mortification is a means to love. They forget that great penances with little love do not have great value (lack of obedience points to pride, not love, as a motive). They forget the law of gradual progress, imposing on everyone without discretion the heroic penances of the saints.

But it is possible to learn something even from those who are in error. For very often such persons err precisely because they have realized some part of the truth so forcefully that they are blinded to all the other elements that should be included. The truth the fanatical groups have seen is that most of us are far from being generous with God. We rightly condemn the errors of fanatics, but we could profitably learn from them the lesson of generosity. It is well to say that we must take prudent precautions, must follow a good director, must advance gradually, must make all subserve the end of love — these things are all true and must be kept constantly in mind. But we must also remember that although great love can make small penances worth much, we must ask ourselves: Are we sure we have the great love? If we had as much love as we are apt to imagine, we would probably find some middle position between our tiny, rare mortifications and the excesses we rightly condemn. And we would tend to grow in generosity. How can we hope to attain with only slight effort the high degree of detachment which we ought to have in order to make room in our hearts for great love? We tend to bargain with God, to ask, "How much do I have to give? I will give this and that, and then I can be free from paying attention to Him for the rest of the time." We are like the child who prayed: "O Lord, I give you all I am and all I have." He read this out of his prayer book. But then, with the simple perception of a child, he realized what it meant, and he hurriedly added, " — that is, all except my little white rabbit."

Although we do not mention our white rabbits in our offerings to God, we do have them. We recite many acts of offering whose words are generous. We think we mean them (do they sometimes flatter our pride?). But God accepts what He sees in our heart, rather than what He hears from our lips. If our lips speak of great love to God, He will not believe them if our hearts and our actions give the lie to our words. Generosity in mortification is one of the most concrete proofs of genuine love.

Finally, we may reduce all reasons for mortification to love. We mortify ourselves because love dictates that we expiate past offenses, we mortify ourselves because intense love naturally chooses hard things to prove its strength to the one loved, we mortify ourselves to make ourselves grow in the capacity to love God still more. Giant penances with little love are worth but little, while small penances, if really performed with great love, are worth much. Hence Garrigou-Lagrange says of those who practice a total consecration to Mary:

> Mary, wonderful to relate, makes the cross easier and, at the same time, more meritorious, because she obtains for us a greater charity which is the principle of merit, and because, by offering our acts to the Lord, she increases their value. By reason of her pre-eminent charity, Mary merited more while performing the easiest acts than all the martyrs in their tortures.[9]

NOTES

1. Luke 14:27; Matt. 10:38. [*Confraternity version.*]

2. We must distinguish between fully deliberate venial sins and semi-deliberate venial sins. It is a defined doctrine that no one, without a special privilege, can avoid all venial sins for a lifetime — but this definition is amply safeguarded if we state that one cannot avoid all venial sins of frailty and surprise for a lifetime. It is possible to hope to obtain the grace to avoid all fully deliberate sins. And of course it is clear that anyone can always avoid any given single sins if he co-operates with the grace given him. Fully deliberate venial sins are a great obstacle to our progress. But venial sins of frailty and surprise are not such an obstacle. See chap. IX on this distinction.

3. St. Augustine has this in mind when he writes, speaking to God: "For You have ordered it, and it is true, that every disordered soul is its own punishment" (*Confessions*, I, xii, 19).

4. On this point see Garrigou-Lagrange, *Christian Perfection and Contemplation*, pp. 356–57, 399–400. Notice *ibidem* that there are equivalents to the two nights, e.g., in the case of infants who die after baptism.

5. Pope Pius XI, *Miserentissimus Redemptor* (May 6, 1928), *AAS* 20:175 and 176. The internal quotations are from Matt. 24:8, II Thess. 2:3–4, and Matt. 24:12, respectively.

6. *AAS* 20:185.

7. He granted plenary indulgence for special devotions on the first Saturday in honor of the Immaculate Virgin, in a spirit of reparation for the blasphemies uttered against her. Confession, Holy Communion, and prayers for the intention of the Holy Father are required. This indulgence is still in force. June 13, 1912, *AAS* 4:623.

8. *AAS* 20:184. See also chap. XX.

9. Garrigou-Lagrange, *op. cit.,* p. 387.

XV ... *Following after the Cross with Mary*

In the preceding chapter we recognized the necessity for mortification. Now we must look into some special principles and considerations relating to the actual practice of mortification, for errors and misunderstandings are common in this sphere.

All mortification falls into one of two large classes: it is either *providential* or *self-imposed.* In other words, some mortifications come our way without our seeking them, while others we take on of our own accord.

Providential mortification embraces the difficulties that are inflicted on us by our state in life, and also the less predictable things that may emerge in any state of life. All these may be called providential in the sense that none of them happens without at least the permission of God, for His Providence affects absolutely everything that happens: He either positively orders or sends it or He merely permits it to happen. Since these providential mortifications are, as it were, chosen especially for us by the hand of God, it is important that we accept them. St. Francis de Sales writes understandingly on this subject:

> Be ready then, Philothea, to suffer many great afflictions for Our Lord. . . . But so long as His divine Providence does not send you such painful and such great afflictions and does not demand of you your eyes, at least give Him your hair — I mean bear patiently the little injuries, the little inconveniences, the losses of trifling importance, which befall you daily; for by means of these little occasions made use of with love and dilection, you will entirely win His heart, and make it wholly yours. These little daily acts of charity, this headache, this toothache, this inflammation, this ill-humour of a husband or a wife, this breaking of a glass, this contempt, or this pouting, this loss of

gloves, of a ring, of a handkerchief, this little inconvenience of going to bed betimes and of rising early to pray, to communicate, this little feeling of shame at doing certain acts of devotion in public — in a word, all these little sufferings, when accepted and embraced with love, are extremely pleasing to the goodness of God, who for a *glass of water* has promised the sea of perfect happiness to His faithful. And because these opportunities occur every moment, to make good use of them is a great means of heaping up much spiritual riches.[1]

Many other examples, some of them peculiar to our own times, could be added to those given by St. Francis. Almost anyone may at times be called upon to endure the discomforts of crowded busses, trains, and other public conveyances, to be patient with other drivers in crowded traffic, to submit humbly to an irritable boss. Then there are the difficulties proper to various walks of life. For example, doctors and nurses need to learn to see Christ even in unpleasant or repulsive patients; clerks in stores must be courteous to unreasonable customers who are "always right"; students sometimes have to endure boring teachers dispensing equally boring subjects; assembly-line workers submit to a monotony more fitted for machines than for men.

The value of these, as of other forms of mortification, depends on the love we invest in them. Hence we should aim not merely to bear troubles, but to embrace them joyfully out of love of God, and to thank Him for the opportunity of serving Him.[2] But even then, if we want our mortifications to have really great value, we should ask Mary to unite them to her own sufferings and to those of her Divine Son, and to offer them up for us.

Some will be more generous in accepting this providential form of mortification than others. Little love wishes to give little: great love wishes to give much. For an example of how a saint profited by this sort of mortification, read the *Autobiography* of St. Thérèse of the Child Jesus.

Unless we are at least sincerely trying to make good use of this providential form of mortification, our self-imposed mortifications will not be very acceptable to God. The truth is, it is usually easier to assume the ordinary sort of mortifications than to make the most of providential mortifications. Still, the fact that self-imposed mortification is easier (except in the case of heroic penances) does not mean that we should neglect it for the providential. Both kinds are needed for our development; love itself urges that we practice both. In fact, self-imposed penances serve very well by training us to contradict our own will and inclinations, and to accept providential mortifications with love.

How far should one go in this matter of self-imposed mortification? The answer will depend upon how great our past sins have been and how disorderly our actual inclinations are, and how much providential mortification we are already suffering. Three principal factors, then, should be considered in our individual plan of mortification: our need, our ability, and the generosity of our love. Our need is great indeed. As for the past, we have reparation to make for our many sins; as for the rest, we set up the goal of a complete emptying of self, absolute detachment from self and from things of earth. Our ability is limited, and we must obey the law of gradual progress (see again chapter IX). The rate of our progress is controlled by our ability and our love. Little love will incline one to move slowly: great love will approach closer to the limits of its ability. Great prudence should be coupled with great generosity. In practice, one should not take any radical step without the approval of his director.

There are two extremes one must avoid. On the one hand, he must not inflict such severe penances as may jeopardize his health; on the other he must also beware of favoring and pampering himself, constantly alleging health as a dispensation from mortification. Relatively few persons are inclined to over-severe penances, though some will vacillate from one extreme to the other. St. Francis de Sales displays his usual lucid, well-balanced prudence in writing on this problem; we strongly recommend a careful reading of chapter 23, Book III, of his *Introduction to the Devout Life*.

St. John of the Cross gives us a practical piece of advice on our choice and use of mortifications. After pointing out that the natural man, who is led by his desires, is following a blind guide, he adds what some may find a surprising comment:

> For this reason one must greatly lament the ignorance of certain men, who burden themselves with extraordinary penances and with other voluntary practices, and think that this practice or that will suffice to bring them to the union of Divine Wisdom: but such is not the case if they endeavour not diligently to mortify their desires. If they were careful to bestow half of that labour on this, they would profit more in a month than they profit by all the other practices in many years.[3]

Elsewhere St. John speaks of those who practice mortification in the wrong way as doing no more than "the penance of beasts." [4] He means that although there are many reasons and justifications for mortification, it is necessary to choose and carry out our penances in such a way as to obtain detachment. But a deeper comprehension of the teaching of St. John on desires is worth our study. At the same time we can examine his principles on the closely related topic of the right use of pleasure, and add a few comments on the purification of memory.

St. John stresses the evils of the wrong kind of desires. But, since he does not explain for us which desires are harmful, we must now examine that question for ourselves.

Which things, then, should we desire? First of all, we must greatly desire the glory of God — the goal of every creature. Closely allied with that glory is our own eternal salvation [5] and that of our neighbor; all else must be subordinated to these desires. There are various means to attain the glory of God and our salvation. Some, like virtue or grace, have value in themselves, because they really make us blessed. We should, of course, desire them. Below these true spiritual goods are temporal things, the goods of the world. Now we can use these temporal things either for our salvation or for our ruin. Hence St. John would have us be indifferent to temporal things insofar as they are of indifferent value for salvation.

A number of distinctions need to be made on how we should desire and use spiritual goods and means to spiritual goods. Our general guide is this: seek out and fulfill the will of God *insofar as it is made known* in any way — by the commandments, by the counsels, by orders of lawful superiors, by special inspirations,[6] by various providential arrangements of events, or a combination of manifestations.

God's will may be clear in some aspects of a problem and not in others; or He may give us an indication of His will, but then, in order to try us, He may change it before we can complete the proposed task. Thus, the patriarch Abraham was told by God to sacrifice his son Isaac, but was ordered to stop before actually doing so. In a somewhat similar way God may give a young man a vocation to the priesthood; it may seem that it is God's will that he sanctify himself through offering Mass and administering the sacraments. Yet it may please God to change all that, to send a crippling illness, so that before or even after ordination that man may find that God wills his sanctification through a lifetime of suffering as a shut-in. Or again, God may give to a priest, through his superiors, the order to conduct a drive to build an orphanage. Now certainly God wills the works of charity. Yet, for a greater good, God may wish to permit this campaign to fail in whole or in part, or to be carried on by other means. Such reverses also come to lay persons. Thus God may give to a young man a special aptitude for surgery, and even allow him to finish medical school, with the hope of serving Christ in the sick. Yet God may permit an auto accident resulting in the loss of a hand or an arm. Another may feel himself called to the work of a lay apostle, for example, in the field of social work or in writing. But failure and rejection of his efforts may come in an unending stream. Another may feel that God is calling him to enter a monastery, but when his father is disabled by a stroke, he sees that God wants him to become the financial support of the family.

In all these cases the person involved should work diligently in the direction indicated by the will of God, but be so disposed as to accept lovingly and readily whatever change or outcome may be subsequently indicated. He should desire only that he may carry out the will of God perfectly, by whatever means, and at whatever time He wills.

At other times God may make use of our desires in order to show us His will. This is very commonly true in what is called our dominant spiritual attraction. Although the basic laws of the spiritual life are the same for all, there are many possible variations in means and in kinds of emphasis. For example, if St. Thomas Aquinas had tried to force himself into the kind of spirituality practiced so well by St. Francis of Assisi, he would have been opposing God's will. For God wanted St. Thomas to grow and serve Him in a life filled with intense theological study and writing. But St. Francis served God while avoiding these things, and it would have been a mistake for him to have tried to make himself into the scholarly type. We could compare many other pairs of saints — for example, St. Francis de Sales as contrasted with St. Benedict Joseph Labre. God wills to manifest His goodness in a wonderful variety of ways, and it is to our spiritual advantage to find the type of attraction He wills for us. In this matter our spiritual desires are likely to point toward the will of God rather than in the opposite direction.

With regard to merely temporal advantages, such as pleasures, honors, riches, or health, indifference (lack of desire) has a wider field. For these things are of indifferent value for salvation: a man may use them well, or may use them to his own destruction. Now we need not be unable even to feel the attraction of pleasures and other temporal things. But we should refrain from desiring them, from letting them be a factor in our decisions. Of course we need to *use* certain temporal things to a certain extent as means to go to God. But it is one thing to *use* them prudently (considering also their relative advantages and disadvantages as means), but it is another thing to allow the merely temporal attraction to influence us or to make us desire them. In other words, in merely temporal goods we should try to follow the advice of St. Paul, who urges us to use this world as though not using it.

St. John's principles on desire also advise us to practice abandonment to God's will in the things that His Providence sends us, desiring only that His will be done. Therefore we should lovingly accept whatever results He is pleased to give our labors. But we should accept with equal love the things that He sends without making use of our instrumentality, such as sickness, health, poverty, wealth, success, failure.[7]

Of course it is not always positively wrong to desire even temporal things. There are many desires that are not sinful though they are less than perfect. But he who wishes to advance rapidly and far will follow the advice of St. John of the Cross.

Now, we might ask, why this special emphasis on avoiding the wrong sort of desire? There are many reasons. St. Augustine says well: "You have made us for Yourself, and our hearts are restless until they rest in You."[8] Desire is a form of love, and restless desire competes with love of God. Our disordered self-love prompts us constantly to be desiring something, and, since anticipation is, in earthly things, greater than realization, we desire to desire, enjoying the pursuit more than the attainment. If we pull our desires and attachments loose from one thing, they quickly and silently fasten onto something else. We might say that we are attached to attachment: our self-love will give up one thing only to seize quickly on something else. We so often seem to think: just this one thing more, and I can "live happily ever after." But it is an ever-receding mirage. In view of this, it will be worth while to study in detail three specific reasons for the danger of desire.

First of all, St. Augustine tells us that love is like a weight carrying us to the object of our love.[9] Creatures tend to pull us to their own level and to hold our *thoughts* [10] and *love* there (see "attachment"). There are various levels of creatures, all of which are good in themselves, but they must be used carefully. At the lowest level are things of sense: these, though they are not spiritual goods, do have a lower sort of good in themselves, and may even be helpful spiritually if properly *used*.[11] But God is above the level of things of sense. The more enmeshed in things of sense we are, the less our freedom to go to Him. But we must say the same of creatures higher than those of sense.[12] Thus, the things of the intellect (for example, study), though higher than sense, may hold us down to a level that is too low — if we are attached to them or desire them inordinately. Even visions and revelations, though above the merely intellectual and human level, are below God. Hence attachment to them is harmful.[13]

The second danger is that disordered desire and attachment make it hard for us to hear the inspirations and guidance that Mary may send us.[14] We may think that we want to be guided by her wishes, but this will not be true if our desires make us blind and deaf. For if we have a strong pull of desire in one direction, we cannot easily perceive the delicate voice of inspiration calling us to the other direction. The reason is fundamentally the same as that which we saw in the Introduction: what we think and what we do tend to harmonize. If we engage in desire of the wrong things, it is difficult for the thought even to occur to us that we ought to move in the opposite direction. We cannot expect to hear the voice of reason, grace, or the Holy Spirit when our desires shout something else in a louder voice. Therefore, if we are led by desires, we are unintelligently following a blind guide. St. Francis de Sales compares a soul full of desires to a hunting dog in spring. For in spring there are so many scents around that the dog can hardly find the scent of the game (by the game he means the love of God). Therefore he says:

> . . . those souls that ever abound in desires, designs and projects, never desire holy celestial love as they ought, nor can perceive the delightful strain and scent of the divine beloved. . . . He who aspires to heavenly love, must sedulously reserve for it his leisure, his spirit, and his affections.[15]

The third danger is this: desires block our progress in habitual recollection and mental prayer and these are essential means to any great progress in love. All forms of prayer aim to raise our minds and hearts to God. But, Our Lord warns, "Where thy treasure is, there is thy heart also." [16] Therefore, if our minds and hearts (wills) are enmeshed in lower things, it is hard to raise them to God in prayer. For it is as though a weight were holding our thoughts and love down, so that they cannot rise easily. In addition, it is obvious that many desires furnish abundant material for distractions. On the contrary, if we do what we can to free our souls of useless desires and other obstacles, we will grow in prayer and thereby in love. When a soul has worked sufficiently at its own purification, God will surely intervene and complete the work by passive purification [17] and will even grant infused contemplation. Thus St. John of the Cross says:

> When in this way the soul voids itself of all things . . . it is impossible . . . that God should fail to perform His own part by communicating Himself to the soul, at least secretly and in silence. It is more impossible than that the sun should fail to shine in a serene and unclouded sky. . . . God, like the sun, is above our souls and ready to communicate Himself to them.[18]

On the other hand, if one seems to advance in mental prayer without growth in mortification, he is in danger. As St. Jane de Chantal says,

> A person to whom God gives graces at prayer should give good heed to accompany them with true mortification and humility . . . : if they do not, the graces will not last, or are nothing but illusions.[19]

St. John of the Cross has much more to say of the harmfulness of desires,[20] but now we must move on to a closely related subject: that of the correct use of pleasure.

There is a great difference between the problem of desire and that of pleasure. In the case of pleasure, we may find a certain partially redeeming feature that is not present in the case of desire. For God created pleasure to be a help to us in our advance toward Him; that is, if we use creatures and their pleasures properly, as means to God, we may find some assistance in them. As St. John of the Cross says, even things of sense can be helpful: "For there are souls who are greatly moved by objects of sense to seek God." [21] But although creatures may help us toward God when we are *actually using* them, they cannot help us when we merely desire them. It is as though they have a certain helping power in them: this power can be made to assist us when the creatures are *present* (being used), but not when they are *absent* and merely desired.

St. John of the Cross suggests an excellent means of determining when our use of sense objects is helpful or harmful to us (with proper modification the same principle could be adapted to other classes of created things):

> I wish, therefore, to propose a test here whereby it may be seen when those delights of the senses aforementioned are profitable, and when they are not. And it is that, whensoever a person hears music and other things, and sees pleasant things, and is conscious of sweet perfumes, or tastes things that are delicious or feels soft touches, if his thought and the affection of his will are at once centered upon God, and if that thought of God gives him more pleasure than the movement of sense which causes it, and save for that he finds no pleasure in the said movement, this is a sign that he is receiving benefit therefrom, and that this thing of sense is a help to his spirit.[22]

Thus we have the correct criterion for the use of pleasure. Pleasure is intended to be a means to an end. It should aid us toward God and help us to do His will, but should not keep our *thoughts* and *love* fixed on itself. God created pleasure in order to insure that certain things be accomplished. For example, God put pleasure into eating to insure that creatures would eat sufficiently [23] for life and health.[24] Therefore we use pleasure rightly when we use it to the extent that it helps us toward God — and leave it alone otherwise. It is part of God's plan that much of our satisfaction should be merely incidental to our work and ordinary activities: it is like an oil that makes the machinery run smoothly.[25] If we ever seek pleasure *merely* for its own sake, we are in disorder, and are following a blind guide. At times we do seek pleasure *directly,* but still as a means. (Pleasure incidental to work is sought *indirectly.*) For we need a certain amount of relaxation and recreation.[26] To take it properly, without any inordinate desire or attachment, is an act of virtue.[27] To take less recreation than we really need is a fault — a fault, be it added, to which few are prone.[28] But for the sake of the few who might go to excess in mortifying pleasures, we quote from Fr. Gabriel of St. Mary Magdalen, O.C.D., an eminent commentator on St. John of the Cross:

> The principle of the necessity of complete detachment is absolute, but in its application the individual must take account of human weaknesses and needs. The man who would banish from his life every alleviation and recreation would soon fall into a physical and moral weariness which would be detrimental to the spiritual life itself.[29]

But most of us need to be discouraged from a more or less constant search for pleasure, a pursuit we may carry on without realizing it. St. Thomas says that recreation is like salt on food: a little goes a long way.[30]

Desire looks forward to a good thing to come; pleasure enjoys a present good, and memory tends to dwell on past goods. Hence, St. John of the Cross tells us, we must also take care to avoid lost motion in memory.[31] For to think lovingly over past pleasures is apt to be merely a case of attachment to creatures. Memory is not likely to have the restless character of desire, but there is little chance that it will have the compensating features that are found in the actual use of creatures. Hence we need to guard against mere idle memories that serve no good purpose. They may occupy our minds and wills with creatures to the detriment of recollection and love of God.

The proper attitude to creatures could be rather well summed up in these words of St. Thérèse: "Let creatures touch us only in passing." [82] If our contact with them is only *in passing,* we will deal with them only when they are *present.* Thus we will avoid the disorders of desire, which looks to the *future,* and of memory, which looks to the *past.* But even in the present, the contact will be light and detached, it will be made *in passing.*

At first sight these principles on desire, pleasure, and memory may seem to rob life of much of its freedom of spirit and joy; but experience shows that this fear is vain. The saints, who put these principles into practice, were joyful. We read of St. Thérèse that when she was absent from recreation period the others would say: "There will be no laughing today — Soeur Thérèse is not here." [33] Similarly, St. John of the Cross insists that the only persons who can really enjoy things are those who are detached from them. [34] St. Paul shows the same sort of attitude when, in enumerating the fruits of the Holy Spirit, he lists joy and peace, but not sourness and disquietude. [35] And we must not forget that Our Lord Himself and His Mother were able to join in the celebration at Cana, so much so that He was willing, at her request, to provide more wine by a miracle.

God is the best of fathers. He takes no pleasure in seeing His children suffer, but He knows that present suffering makes it possible for Him to confer unimaginable, unending happiness on them at the end of this brief life. Hence He sends suffering as a great treasure to His friends, as a means of increasing their likeness to His well-beloved Son and His Mother. But even in this life, God sends a deeper kind of peace and even joy into the midst of providentially-permitted sufferings and self-imposed mortification. For God has so arranged His world that those who spend themselves in a relentless pursuit of pleasure find that it escapes them; while solid joy comes to those who seek the kingdom of God and His justice.

In this connection we may note that this principle of renouncement is the way of happiness not only for priests and religious, but also for married persons. If two persons enter marriage, each with the idea of enjoying as much selfish pleasure as possible, and conceding no more than necessary to the other partner, that marriage will certainly be miserable. But if each mate proposes to work more to please the other than for his or her own satisfaction, happiness is fairly certain for both. And if the partners who live in such a spirit of self-sacrifice will raise it to the supernatural level, they will find that this true form of love of neighbor is a great aid to growth in the love of God. The sacrifices necessary for the welfare of the children can be similarly elevated so as to bear great fruit in the spiritual life.

Mortification presents no problem for some: they have little if any appreciation for its necessity and act accordingly. But others are convinced of its need, and, in addition, may belong to a religious community in which the rule prescribes certain practices. Those who realize that they have a duty to mortify themselves are sometimes turned into spiritual cripples and hypochondriacs by fear for their health. In fact, self-love easily deceives them, unconsciously, into counterfeiting incapacities to avoid facing mortification. St. Teresa of Avila warns us:

> For this body of ours has one fault: the more you indulge it, the more things it discovers to be essential to it. ... if once the devil begins to frighten us about losing our health, we shall never get anywhere.[36]

This does not mean that we should ignore all thought of health,[37] or adopt the extreme physical penances of some of the saints, but there is a prudent, generous position that is right for each one at any given time. A good director is almost indispensable in finding that position for us. But the mortification of desire, attachments, and pleasures can easily be carried out in such a way as not to endanger health. Mortification is particularly beneficial to mental health. As the outstanding priest-psychiatrist Thomas Verner Moore, O.Cart., M.D., says, one who really carries out the renunciation called for by St. John of the Cross " . . . will be fairly confident of one thing: he will never suffer mental shipwreck in the storm of life." [38]

Now to add just a few observations. First of all, we must remember that attachments and disordered desires and pleasures easily develop even in the legitimate use of creatures, even in our work. For whenever we have enjoyable dealings with creatures, we tend to develop a desire for more of the same stimulation. This is a psychological law. The fact that we act with a good intention does not cancel out this danger. Hence St. Francis de Sales says:

> If the heart that aims after Divine love be deeply engaged in terrene and temporal affairs, it will bud late and with difficulty: but if it will have only so much to do with the world as its condition requires, you shall see it bloom timely in love. . . .[39]

We must be realistic about this matter of detachment. It is idle to tell ourselves that we are detached from creatures and their pleasures if we renounce hardly any of them. It is not enough to say: "I am detached from them." If one really is, he will *actually* give up much; the extent will depend on the circumstances of his whole life situation.

We easily become *preoccupied* even with things that are good, for our motives tend to be complex. A man may assure himself, for example, that he is doing some work purely for the glory of God, but a large part of the driving force may really be a certain pride that he takes in accomplishment, a self-satisfaction. Then there arises great eagerness or perhaps impetuosity in action — tendencies not under the influence of grace, and consequently at least imperfect.[40] A similar merely natural (i.e., unsanctified) eagerness may dominate our legitimate recreation.[41] We may think we are using recreation as a means to go to God. But we easily deceive ourselves, and our "good faith" will not prevent some harm from being done. As Thomas Merton says, "The laws of human psychology are not suspended by formalistic acts of pure intention." [42] We should also remember that although we may have begun an action with a really pure intention, we can easily slip into a merely natural behavior during the course of the act.[43]

In mortification itself we need to watch our motives, for a certain secret pride can easily enter, in which we are driven, at least to some extent, by the desire to show ourselves that we are generous, or that we are not soft. It would be a mistake, however, to curtail mortification to little or nothing out of fear of some open or hidden pride.[44] As a defense against such pride, we will call on the help of our Mother Mary. She will teach us how little of any good work is really ours, that when we have done all these things, we are still unprofitable servants. Furthermore, we must realize that our mortifications, to have really great value, must be offered to the Eternal Father in union with the immense, priceless sufferings of Jesus and His blessed Mother. It is on such values that we rest our trust, rather than on our own trifling efforts.

Finally, we must remind ourselves again that all these things have to be done in accord with the general law of gradual progress.[45]

An ungenerous soul will be inclined to measure too carefully: it will often be puzzled as to how far to go. For it has many strong pulls and attachments that distract it so that it cannot readily hear the voice of the inspirations that Mary will obtain for it. But a generous soul is less inclined to measure. It approaches more nearly to what St. Louis de Montfort calls Mary's "universal mortification," [46] by which she, with her Divine Son, could say: "My meat is to do the will of him that sent me." [47] In ungenerous souls there is an attraction of creatures that pulls them constantly downward: in Mary, however, the love of God drew her ever upward, until one day it carried off her soul to God, so that now, where her treasure is, there is her heart also.[48]

A note on the mortifications of St. Thérèse

The "little way" of St. Thérèse is sometimes so presented as to leave the impression that little if any self-imposed mortification is necessary. It is true that we find quite a contrast between her life and the giant works of some other saints. Actually there is no contradiction here: all mortification must be so carried out as to serve the four purposes outlined above, paying special attention to the counsels of St. John of the Cross and St. Francis de Sales on uprooting desires and attachments. St. Thérèse accomplished this to a heroic degree by denying herself in *everything*. She could say in all truth, "God will do all I wish in Heaven, because *I have never done my own will on earth.*" [49] This suppression of desire and attachment is a great mortification, and largely self-imposed. But she also took on much additional mortification. And we must not forget the great austerities that were a normal part of the Carmelite rule under which she lived. Anyone attempting to follow exactly in her footsteps would not find a path of thornless roses. The "little way" is a work of spiritual genius, but it must be properly understood. [50]

NOTES

1. St. Francis de Sales, *Introduction to the Devout Life, III*, xxxv (pp. 196–97).

2. We all tend to go to extremes. The pendulum does not readily come to rest in dead center, but seeks to swing to the opposite side. Similarly, though it is more difficult at the start to accept difficult things joyfully, yet, after the start has been made, it is much more easy to accept them with joy than merely to tolerate them.

3. St. John of the Cross, *Ascent of Mt. Carmel*, I, viii, 4 (I, 42–43).

4. *Dark Night of the Soul*, I, vi, 2 (I, 365).

5. See chap. IX for a more complete treatment of the desire for salvation.

6. For a more complete discussion of inspirations, see chaps. XVIII and XIX.

7. The teaching of St. John of the Cross on desires is essentially the same as the doctrine of St. Francis de Sales on obedience to the signified will of God and abandonment to the will of good pleasure of God. On this see St. Francis, *Treatise on the Love of God*, VIII and IX, and X, iv–v (pp. 325–409, 418–25); see also V. Lehodey, O.C.R., *Holy Abandonment*, trans. A. J. Luddy (Dublin, 1951), esp. pp. 40–53. Compare also St. Thérèse's "Love alone draws me. I wish for neither suffering nor death, yet both are precious to me and I have long called upon them as the messengers of joy . . . now the spirit of self-abandonment is my sole guide — I have no other compass. I am no longer able to ask eagerly for anything save the perfect accomplishment of God's designs on my soul." — *St. Thérèse of Lisieux, An Autobiography*, chap. 8 (p. 146, Kenedy ed.).

8. St. Augustine, *Confessions*, I, i. See also Thomas Merton, *The Ascent to Truth* (New York, 1951), chap. I, and St. Augustine, *De Diversis Quaestionibus LXXXIII*, XXXVI, i.

9. *Confessions*, XIII, ix, 10. See *ST*, I, q.16, a.1; I–II, q.28, a.1.

10. Note the relation to habitual recollection.

11. See *Ascent of Mount Carmel*, III, xxiv, 4 (I, 283–84): "For there are souls who are greatly moved by objects of sense to seek God. But much caution must be observed herein. . . . "

12. Let no one be so foolish as to say: "Mary is, after all, a creature. We must not pay too much attention to her lest she keep us from God." The answer is found by recalling that our relations with creatures are profitable insofar as they correspond to God's plans for our use of them. Now God has placed Mary in the position of His constant companion and co-operator throughout all the work of salvation. She is most closely united to him in earning and distributing all graces. Hence we need her aid constantly and she most effectively promotes our union with God. See St. Louis de Montfort, *True Devotion to the Blessed Virgin Mary*, §75.

13. For a fuller treatment see chap. XXI. We must also note a special danger in creatures that are higher than those of sense: we are less likely to suspect the danger in them, and so fall into it more easily. Even the study of theology can involve undue attachment.

14. By actual graces or through the Gifts of the Holy Spirit. See chaps. XVIII and XIX.

15. St. Francis de Sales, *Treatise on the Love of God*, XII, iii (pp. 536, 537).

16. Matt. 6:21.

17. See chap. XIII.

18. *Living Flame of Love*, III, xlvi–xlvii (III, 185).

19. St. Jane Frances Frémyot de Chantal, *Exhortations, Conferences and Instructions* (Westminster, 1947), p. 261.

20. See *Ascent of Mount Carmel*, I.

21. *Ibid.*, III, xxiv, 4 (I, 283–84).

22. *Ibid.*, III, xxiv, 5 (I, 284).

23. Some who mortify themselves in other respects make eating a sort of compensation for the sacrifice of other things (unconsciously, of course).

24. See St. Thomas, *Contra Gentiles*, III, 26; "Pleasure exists for the sake of obtaining a certain result, and not vice versa" (" . . . *est delectatio propter operationem, et non e converso. . . .* ")

25. Even here we must watch for disorderly affections, for every pleasurable experience tends to build up desires for more.

26. See *ST*, II–II, q.168, a.2–4. In a.2, St. Thomas observes that there are three chief conditions on the manner of pleasure: 1. Pleasure must not be sought in any forbidden, shameful, or harmful thing; 2. We must not completely give up our composure (*gravitas animae* — do not give up all recollection); 3. The pleasure should be regulated according to person, time, place, and other circumstances.

27. *ST*, II–II, q.168, a.2.c.

28. It is not strictly required to have a formal recreation period, unless one belongs to an order in which the rule prescribes it.

29. Gabriel of St. Mary Magdalen, *St. John of the Cross*, p. 30, note 10.

30. *ST*, II–II, q.168, a.4.c.

31. *Ascent of Mount Carmel*, III, i–xv.

32. *Collected Letters of Saint Thérèse of Lisieux*, trans. F. J. Sheed (New York, 1949), 74, p. 114.

33. From the *Summarium* of her cause: quoted in: *St. Thérèse of Lisieux, An Autobiography*, pp. 326–27, n.2 (Kenedy ed.). See *ibid.*, p. 305, the

words of a Carmelite who as a novice had been under St. Thérèse: "Our dear Mistress used to say that during recreation more than at any other time we should find opportunities for practicing virtue. 'If your desire is to draw great profit, do not go with the idea of enjoying yourself, but rather with the intention of entertaining others and practicing self-denial.'" The result was great joy both for St. Thérèse and the others, even though she seems to have made her pleasure largely indirect even in recreation.

34. *Ascent of Mount Carmel*, III, xx (I, 272). See esp. §2.

35. Gal. 5:22–23.

36. *Way of Perfection*, XI and X (II, 47 and 46). See *ibid.*, X (II, 45).

37. See St. Francis de Sales, *Introduction to the Devout Life*, III, xxiii.

38. *Prayer*, p. 147. See our note 23, p. 122.

39. *Treatise on the Love of God*, XII, iii (pp. 536–37).

40. See Garrigou-Lagrange, *The Love of God and the Cross of Jesus*, I, 310–14.

41. See St. Francis de Sales, *Introduction to the Devout Life*, I, xxiii.

42. Thomas Merton, *Ascent to Truth*, p. 166. See St. John of the Cross, *Ascent of Mount Carmel*, III, xxiv, esp. §4.

43. Thus on a given day a priest might start to study a problem of theology for pure motives, but, in the process of study, he may be carried away by merely natural curiosity and eagerness. Natural activity is not evil, but it must be subjected perfectly to grace.

44. See St. Francis de Sales, *Introduction to the Devout Life*, III, v (p. 126).

45. See *Ascent of Mount Carmel*, I, ii, 1. There are very useful practical rules for mortification given in St. Louis de Montfort, *The Love of Eternal Wisdom*, trans. the Montfort Fathers in England (Bristol, 1949), IV, xvi, pp. 100–4; also, by the same saint, *A Circular Letter to the Friends of the Cross* (Bay Shore, N.Y., 1950), esp. §§42–62 (pp. 37–52).

46. St. Louis de Montfort, *True Devotion to the Blessed Virgin Mary*, §34 (p. 23).

47. John 4:34.

48. See Matt. 6:21: "For where thy treasure is, there is thy heart also." See also chap. VI on Mary's death from love.

49. Quoted in *Autobiography*, p. 329 (Kenedy ed.).

50. See A. Combes, *St. Thérèse and Suffering*, trans. P. Hallett (New York, 1951).

XVI ... *Renewing Calvary with Mary*

THE GREATEST of all the means to grace are the Mass and the sacraments. If we use them well, they allow us to come under the full force of the torrents of grace that were earned for us in the Redemption. As we have seen, Mary's role is not merely that of one of many means to grace, as though she were competing with other channels for our attention: no, *all* graces come through her, even the graces of the Mass and the sacraments.[1]

To understand the relation of Mary to the Mass, we need to review certain dogmatic facts that we have already studied.[2] Mary was present on Calvary, not just as a mere spectator, not even in the same way in which St. John was present. Although John surely suffered at the sight of his suffering Master, and joined in the dispositions of the Heart of Christ, yet he shared only in the subjective redemption, the distribution of grace, not in the once-for-all atonement and earning of all grace. But Mary participated in the sacrifice of Calvary in a very special way.

In a sacrifice, there are two aspects or elements: the external sign, and the interior dispositions. The external sign of the sacrifice of Calvary was the bloody death of Christ. The interior dispositions expressed by the external sign were those of the Heart of Christ: love, adoration, contrition, thanksgiving, supplication. Instead of merely expressing in words to God: "I love you, I thank you, I wish to offer reparation for sin, I beg for all graces for humanity," the Son of God expressed these acts of His Heart much more eloquently by an action: His terrible death. Now Mary joined in both the external sign and in the interior dispositions. She did not, of course, physically die with Him, but she did suffer intensely with Him, and she literally furnished the flesh in which He could suffer and die. In these ways she was

162

intimately united to His death. No less intimate was the union of the dispositions of her heart with His. Though it cost her untold agony, she gladly extended the *fiat* of Nazareth to Calvary, joining in the offering of her Son to the Eternal Father. But there is still more. She did all this not merely as a private person, but as a sacred person, designated by the Eternal Father to share in the offering, so that what the Father accepted as He looked down upon Calvary was *a joint work* of Mother and Son, the New Adam and the New Eve. Of course His offering alone would have abundantly sufficed without her, but it was part of the generous design of God that she should be associated in the work of the Redemption, in the atonement and earning of all graces.

The Council of Trent teaches us that the Mass is the renewal, the re-presentation of Calvary, except that the manner of offering is changed from the bloody manner of Calvary to the unbloody manner of the Mass.[3] If, then, we add the above teaching on Mary's immediate co-operation on Calvary to this statement of the Council, the most elementary logic yields a wonderful conclusion: Mary must co-operate in the Mass in a way parallel to her co-operation on Calvary!

Theologians are only beginning to realize this possibility. Of course those few who deny the immediate co-operation on Calvary[4] will be logically forced to deny this conclusion as well; since, however, the vast majority of theologians accept the immediate co-operation on Calvary, it seems logical that they should also accept this deduction, and a considerable number have. One of the most recent and distinguished theologians to uphold this position is Cardinal Lercaro, Archbishop of Bologna, who, at the Mariological Congress held in Rome in 1950, at the time of the solemn definition of the Assumption, developed this theme at some length. Among other things he said:

Now the Virgin remains ever the Mother of Christ, and her will continues to be intimately united to the will of her Son. Therefore, just as on Calvary, in a union of will, she offered with Jesus the life of her Son, so also at the altar, still in union of will, she offers Jesus in mystical immolation. For she is present at the altar as at Calvary, in the same role! [5]

Now Cardinal Lercaro did not imply that Mary is a priest in the usual or sacramental sense of the word.[6] Nor did he mean that she is present in the Sacred Host, or is physically present on the altar. But she is spiritually present, in a "union of will" with the will of her Son, and she is physically present in Heaven, where Christ ever shows His wounds to the Father. It is there that the Mass celebrated here below is accepted. The acts of the will of Christ Himself are not multiplied with each Mass. The external sign, the mystical immolation, is multiplied with each Mass. But His dispositions of heart are not only *like* those He had on the Cross: they are the *same* dispositions *still continuing* without interruption.[7] For death does not change the attitude of one's heart toward God: it makes it permanent for eternity. Similarly, Mary's love of God and willingness to offer her Son have not diminished, nor have they suffered any interruption since that day. It is true her sorrow has been "turned into joy," [8] but that is true also of her Son, as He Himself foretold. Neither the Son nor the Mother suffers any more nor do they make new satisfaction or earn new merit. Rather, the Mass applies the merits and satisfactions once earned on Calvary. But they were earned as a joint work, the work of Jesus and Mary, as we have seen.

Another excellent theologian, R. P. Poupon, expresses the truth this way:

Could Mary, the Mother inseparable from the Son, be absent from the eucharistic sacrifice? — Since her Assumption, she lives body and soul in the glory of God; there also, Jesus, by the wounds of His Passion, represents to the Trinity the death He underwent on the cross; without ceasing, He offers the loving acceptance that He made of that bloody death. There, more perfectly than on Calvary, Mary unites herself to the priestly activity of her Son, and, as in a brilliant mirror, she sees the unique sacrifice of Calvary reproduced on all the altars of here below, and she assists at it with an incomparable wisdom. In that mysterious union of heaven and earth, Mary continues her *fiat* of adoration, of entire subjection, that she made to the will of the Father; she offers the divine Lamb, who, in the Host, bears the sin of the world. . . . [9]

This view that Mary co-operates in the Mass as she once did on Calvary seems to be implied in the principle of *consortium,* emphasized so many times by so many Popes.[10] According to this principle, God, having once begun to associate Mary with Him in the work of redemption, does not repent of His action, but continues to keep her forever associated with Him in this work. Pope Pius XII deduced even the fact of the Assumption from this association.[11] But even earlier, before his election, he stated this principle of association in an especially appropriate form:

> After all, the application of the merits of Christ constitutes, together with their acquisition, a single complete work: that of salvation. It was fitting that Mary should co-operate equally *in the two phases* of the same work; the unity of the divine plan demands it.[12] [*Emphasis added.*]

Now if Mary had shared in Calvary, but did not share in the renewal of Calvary, we could hardly say that she would be co-operating "equally in the two phases" as "the unity of the divine plan demands." Would it not be strange to have Mary associated with her Son in all *except* the Mass?

It is not at all surprising, then, that the Church, in the official prayers before Mass, urges each priest to say:

> O Mother of piety and mercy, most blessed Virgin Mary, I, a miserable and unworthy sinner, flee to you with my whole heart and soul, and I beg of your devotedness that *just as you stood by your most sweet Son hanging on the Cross, so also you may be pleased graciously to stand beside me,* a miserable sinner, and all priests who are offering here and in the entire Holy Church,

so that, with the help of your grace, we may be able to offer a worthy and acceptable host in the sight of the supreme and undivided Trinity. Amen. [*Emphasis added.*]

For the priest, who at Mass is so thoroughly another Christ that when he says, in the first person, "This is my body. . . . This is my blood," the bread and wine become the body and blood of Christ — this priest is taught by the Church to ask that Mary stand beside him, even as she stood beside Christ on Calvary.

It is obvious, then, that Mary can help us wonderfully to unite with the Mass. Now, according to the encyclical *Mediator Dei,* the faithful who assist at Mass join in the offering in two ways: ". . . they not only offer the Sacrifice by the hands of the priest, but also, to a certain extent, in union with him." [13] The Holy Father continues, explaining more clearly what he means by each of these two ways. First he tells us:

> . . . the faithful offer the Sacrifice by the hands of the priest from the fact that the minister at the altar in offering a Sacrifice in the name of all His members represents Christ, the Head of the Mystical Body. [14]

The first manner of participation, therefore, is in virtue of the fact that the people are members of the Mystical Body of Christ. But Mary is the spiritual mother of that Mystical Body, [15] and the physical mother of the Head of that Body, Christ. Hence it is through her that the faithful are enabled to share in this first manner of joining in the sacrifice.

The second way in which the faithful join in the Mass

> . . . is based on the fact that the people unite their hearts in praise, impetration, expiation, and thanksgiving with the prayers or intention of the priest, even of the High Priest Himself, so that in one and the same offering of the Victim and according to a visible sacerdotal rite, they may be presented to God the Father. It is obviously necessary that the external sacrificial rite should, of its very nature, signify the internal worship of the heart. [16]

It is clear that the most important part of this second manner of participation depends on the union of dispositions of the faithful with those of Christ. Now Mary is most closely united to His Heart. Hence, the more closely one is united to her, the more closely he is joined to the Heart of Christ. Let us, therefore, earnestly beg her to help us to unite with her Son, and ask her to make us share in the matchless dispositions with which she once assisted at Calvary, and with which she still assists at each Mass.

But this participation in the attitudes of the Heart of Christ ought to extend beyond the time of the Mass itself. Of this the same Holy Father says:

> . . . it is necessary that the people add something else, namely, the offering of themselves as a victim. This offering, in fact, is not confined merely to the liturgical Sacrifice.[17]

For it would be vain to express many fine sentiments toward God and not to *live them out* in our daily lives. Thus the Mass is extended, gathering up, in a way, the spiritual offerings of the previous day, and also looking forward and offering in anticipation the spiritual sacrifices of the day that is beginning. If we give ourselves completely into Mary's hands, she will help us to carry out this program of the sanctification of our whole lives. But it is not enough merely to say in words that we give ourselves to her: we must live out this gift. The more thoroughly we actually live under her influence, the more completely she will form us in the image of her Son, the true High Priest and Victim. Hence a thoroughgoing consecration to Mary, such as that which we intend to discuss in chapter XVIII, is a most powerful means of uniting with the Mass through Mary.

The Church provides us with many a reminder of the close association of Mary with the Mass. First of all, she does this in the official prayer before Mass, from which we have already quoted. This prayer most aptly suggests the correct attitude, a spirit of union with Mary who played so important a part in the first Calvary.

The Mass itself begins. The priest bends low before the altar, proclaiming his sinfulness to God, and "to Blessed Mary ever Virgin, Blessed Michael the Archangel, Blessed John the Baptist, the Holy Apostles Peter and Paul, and all the saints." He then begs for pardon, asking the intercession of all the saints, but in the first place of "Blessed Mary ever Virgin." Thus we have a reminder of Mary in the introduction to the Mass.

The first of the principal parts of the Mass is at hand. Having offered the Host and the Chalice, the priest bows in the middle of the altar and prays:

> Receive, O Holy Trinity, this oblation, which we offer You in memory of the passion, resurrection, and ascension of Jesus Christ, Our Lord: and in honor of Blessed Mary ever Virgin. . . .

We approach the most solemn part of the Mass, the twofold Consecration. Shortly before pronouncing the awesome words of Consecration, the priest recalls the fellowship he and the people have with the saints:

> We join in union with, and venerate the memory of: in the first place, the glorious ever Virgin Mary, Mother of God and of Our Lord Jesus Christ; but also, the blessed Apostles and Martyrs. . . .

The Consecration itself is complete. A few prayers are said immediately after it, terminating in the Lord's Prayer. The server has answered: "But deliver us from evil." The priest adds his *Amen* silently, and continues, making an extension of the last petition:

> Deliver us, we beg, O Lord, from all evils: past, present, and to come: and by the intercession of the Blessed and Glorious ever Virgin Mother of God, Mary, with your Blessed Apostles Peter and Paul, and Andrew, and all the saints, graciously grant peace in our days. . . .

Before the Communion of the people, the *Confiteor* is repeated, with its double invocation of Mary. Finally, in the official prayers of thanksgiving after Mass, the Church inserts a beautiful prayer asking Mary to be with us to supply for our inability to make a worthy thanksgiving, asking her to offer her own love and adoration to her Son in our behalf (we shall examine this prayer in the next chapter).

Thus we see that before and after the Mass, and constantly throughout it — before and after each of the principal parts — the liturgy puts Mary before our eyes. And it is not strange: the Mass is, as we have seen, the repetition of Calvary, in which Mary took an important part.

Now no one will deny that objectively, in itself, it is best to use the missal at Mass. For the missal should be a help both to a union of dispositions of heart and to a closer external participation in the sacred rite. But we may ask: Are there any conditions in which it is good to recite the Rosary during Mass? Some writers, without examining the principles involved, have jumped to a negative conclusion. The Holy See, however, does not share that attitude. Let us cite another passage from the encyclical on the liturgy, the *Mediator Dei:*

> Many of the faithful are unable to use the "Roman Missal" even though it is written in the vernacular; nor are all capable of understanding correctly the liturgical rites and formulas. So varied and diverse are men's talents and characters that it is impossible for all to be moved and attracted to the same extent by community prayers, hymns and liturgical services. Moreover, *the needs and inclinations of all are not the same, nor are they always constant in the same individual.* Who then would say, on account of such a prejudice, that all these Christians cannot participate in the Mass nor share its fruits? On the contrary, they can *adopt some other method* which proves *easier for certain people,* for instance they can lovingly *meditate on the mysteries of Jesus Christ* or perform *other exercises of piety* or *recite prayers* which, though they differ from the sacred rites, are still essentially in harmony with them.[18] [*Emphasis added.*]

We cannot avoid noticing the broad attitude of the Holy Father. Some cannot profit from the missal at all, others cannot profit from it at certain times. Therefore, he says, let them meditate on the mysteries of Jesus Christ, or recite some prayers that are in harmony with the Mass. It is entirely obvious that the Rosary is just such a method, for it is a most excellent way of meditating on the mysteries of Jesus Christ, and the vocal prayers of the Rosary are surely in harmony with the Mass. For the people assisting at Mass ought, as we have seen, to unite their dispositions with those of Christ Himself on the altar: certainly the *Our Father,* which He Himself composed, is in perfect harmony with His dispositions. Nor is the *Hail Mary* out of harmony with His Heart: the first half contains the first heaven-sent announcement of the mystery of the Redemption, which was consummated on Calvary and is renewed in the Mass. The remainder of the *Hail Mary* is a beautiful prayer of petition and an acknowledgment of sinfulness — and both attitudes enter intimately into the principal ends of sacrifice.

From these principles and the text of the *Mediator Dei* we conclude that the use of the missal is *objectively* the best way of assisting at Mass, and its use is to be encouraged. In our zeal for liturgical reform, however, we must not assume that it is the best method for every person on every day, and that all other methods, such as the Rosary, are to be rejected. The cardinal rule is this: *Whatever helps one best to unite with Christ offering Himself on the altar is the best means for that person on that day.* Certainly, for some persons on some days, and for others on all or nearly all days, the Rosary will be the best method. Pope Leo XIII did not hesitate, in the decree by which he established October devotions, to order that the Rosary be said daily either *during Mass* in the morning, or later in the day before the Blessed Sacrament exposed.[19] Clearly, then, to attempt to exclude the Rosary from the Mass is to ignore sound principles and the teachings of Pope Leo XIII and Pope Pius XII.

Whatever means of assisting at Mass grace leads us to choose at any particular time, let us remember to use it in close union with Mary. For the Mass is the renewal of Calvary, that joint offering of the supreme sacrifice in which Mary was so closely associated with the great High Priest, her Son.

NOTES

1. See again chap. V.

2. In chaps. I–V, esp. IV.

3. See H. Denzinger, C. Bannwart, I. Umberg, S.J., *Enchiridion Symbolorum* (21st–23rd ed.; Friburg, 1937), §940.

4. See Appendix III C.

5. G. Lercaro, "La Missione della Vergine nell'Economia Eucaristica," p. 50, *in Alma Socia Christi*, VI, 1 (Academia Mariana, Rome, 1952), pp. 38–56 (esp. pp. 46–52). When he wrote this article, Archbishop Lercaro held the See of Ravenna. Since then he has been promoted to the See of Bologna, and, in January, 1953, was created a Cardinal. See also A. Lhoumeau, *La Vie spirituelle à l'École du Bⁿ L.-M. Grignion de Montfort* (5th ed.; Tours, 1926), pp. 479–82. See esp. p. 480: "It [the Mass] is none other than the Sacrifice of Calvary renewed. Therefore the Mother of Jesus ought to co-operate in it just as she did at the immolation of her Son on the Cross." See also J. M. Hupperts, S.M.M., *La Sainte Messe en union avec Notre-Dame* (Secrétariat de Marie–Médiatrice, Louvain, 1932), pp. 9–10; and J. M. Alonso, C.M.F., "De B. M. Virginis actuali mediatione in Eucharistia," in *Ephemerides Mariologicae* II (1952), fasc. 2–3, pp. 202–3. See also the reference to R. P. Poupon in note 9 below.

6. In 1872 a work appeared by Msgr. Van den Berghe, *Marie et le Sacerdoce*. The author received a letter of congratulation for it from Pope Pius IX on August 25, 1873. Pope Pius IX also approved the title *Virgo Sacerdos*. On May 9, 1906, Saint Pius X gave an indulgence of 300 days to a prayer in which Mary was called *Virgo Sacerdos*. Therefore the doctrine that Mary in some sense is a priest is not false. For she has the dignity or grace of the priesthood in an eminent, though not a sacramental, form. The ordinary faithful share in a sense in the priesthood of Christ through incorporation with Him. She by her unique *consortium* had a special kind of share. But the Holy See wishes that the doctrine and devotion to the Virgin Priestess be suppressed for prudential reasons for the present, to avoid great misunderstandings. For the history of the case, see: M. P. Pourrat, P.S.S., "Marie et le Sacerdoce," Du Manoir, *Maria*, I, 801–24; and Basilio de San Pablo, C.P., "Los Problemas del Sacerdocio y del Sacrificio de Maria," *Alma Socia Christi*, IV, 141–220. See also D. Bertetto, S.D.B., "De Marialis Sacerdotii Natura," *Ephemerides Mariologicae*, II (1952), 4, pp. 401–7; and G. de Broglie, S.J., "Autour du Sacerdoce Marial," *Marianum*, XV (1953), 2, pp. 214–16.

7. See Garrigou-Lagrange, *De Eucharistia* (Turin, 1946), p. 292.

8. John 16:20.

9. R. P. Poupon, *Le Poème de la parfaite consécration à Marie* (Librairie du Sacré-Coeur, Lyon, 1947), p. 513. Pope Pius XII has sent a letter of congratulation to Fr. Poupon and this letter is printed in an English abridgment of the same work: *To Jesus Through Mary* (Cork, 1951), p. 7.

10. See the many passages quoted in chaps. III and VI.

11. See chap. VI.

12. Quoted in *AER* 121 (November, 1949), p. 360. See also Appendix III, B 6, text 1.

13. NCWC translation, §92.

14. *Ibid.*, §93.

15. See chap. II.

16. *Mediator Dei* (NCWC translation), §93.

17. *Ibid.*, §§98–99.

18. *Ibid.*, §108.

19. The original order was issued September 1, 1883 (*ASS* 16: 113–18, esp. 117), and was reissued on August 20, 1885 (*ASS* 18:95–96), and August 26, 1886 (*ASS* 19:92–93). In addition, the Sacred Congregation of Rites was asked whether the Holy Father ordered the Rosary *during* Mass or *after* Mass. On January 16, 1886 (*ASS* 19:48), the Sacred Congregation replied that the Rosary was to be said during Mass, not after Mass. This decree still remains in force, as the *Ordo* reminds us each year.

XVII... *Mary Welcomes Her Son in Us*

WE HAVE SEEN that a close union with Mary helps us to join most perfectly in offering to the Eternal Father the great gift of the renewal of Calvary which is the Mass. In the same Mass, God's gift comes to us, the gift of the Body and Blood of His Son in Holy Communion. In order to receive Him most fittingly, and to gain the greatest fruit from that reception, let us ask the help of Mary who shared in earning all these graces for us. But now, in order to deepen our understanding of what we need to do in receiving Holy Communion, we are going to examine a few special principles.

We are all familiar with the teaching that morally good actions, when the proper conditions for merit are present, earn for us an increase of sanctifying grace. For practical purposes this increase means an increase of the love of God, for the two rise and fall together. Hence it is obvious that we can grow in the love of God by performing meritorious actions.[1] Now the question may be raised regarding these meritorious actions: When do we receive the increase in love that is earned by a meritorious act? It is clear that if the act is performed generously, fervently, the increase is both earned and obtained immediately. But can we say the same if the act is performed in a weak or remiss fashion, or if it is somewhat deficient in generosity? Now, although we cannot really measure virtues in mathematical units, yet, for the sake of clarity, let us use the following loose comparison: Suppose a man has five degrees of love of God, but acts as though he had only two degrees. Will he obtain the increase *at once?* or will the actual increase be delayed until later? Some theologians think he will obtain the increase at once, but others, St. Thomas Aquinas among them, disagree. St. Thomas says:

. . . by every meritorious act, man earns an increase of grace, just as he earns the consummation of grace, which is eternal life. But just as eternal life is not given at once, but at the proper time, so neither is grace at once increased, but at the proper time, that is, when one is sufficiently disposed for an increase of grace.[2]

It is obvious that this principle is of the greatest importance for spiritual growth. It opens up the possibility that a man living a good life, but doing his good works only in a remiss fashion, might not receive the increases in grace for a long time. Now since the grace we already possess at the time of a good action is one of the notable factors that determine how much additional grace we may derive from that action, it is clear that remiss actions may bring our rate of progress almost, if not entirely, to a halt. Let us use again the (strictly speaking) inapplicable but convenient numbers. Suppose a man having five degrees of love lives a life almost entirely devoid of fervor for twenty years. Although he may earn many increases of grace, to be received sometime later,[3] he is obtaining but slight *actual* increase. If he had acted fervently, each increase would have been received at once, and therefore each subsequent fervent action would have a value proportioned to the increased capital of grace. By acting fervently, he might have risen to, let us say, two hundred degrees after the twenty years. But, since he almost always acts remissly, he has grown only from five to seven degrees. It is clear that our growth may be enormously more rapid if we are fervent than if we are remiss.

And now another difficulty raises its head: Does this principle of disposition apply also to growth through the sacraments? St. Thomas does not ask or answer the question, and modern theologians are divided.[4]

Those who maintain that the principle does not apply to the sacraments are moved by the fact that the Council of Trent tells us that the sacraments produce grace *ex opere operato,*[5] that is, from the mere fact that the sacred rite is duly performed by the proper minister (even though the minister be unworthy) provided that the recipient does not put an obstacle in the way of the grace. Hence, it is argued, if we state that the increase in grace is delayed, we violate the principle laid down by the Council, and reduce the sacraments to the same level as that of any good work.

How can the theologians who hold that the reception of grace is delayed in those whose dispositions are insufficient be in agreement with the Council? The difficulty is not insuperable, for, even though the reception of the grace is postponed, yet it is still true that the sacrament has the *ex opere operato* effect of giving that grace to the recipient. He will obtain the grace, and obtain it by virtue of the sacrament — but it is only sometime later that he will actually receive it. Furthermore, did not the Council state that grace is produced only in those who put no obstacle in the way? Now it is clear that mortal sin is an obstacle such as to nullify completely the effects of those sacraments that require the state of grace for their reception. Lack of contrition nullifies the effects of the sacrament of penance. May we not say that lack of dispositions in a smaller way is capable of merely postponing the reception of grace? Thus it seems that this group also is safely within the wording laid down by the Council.

Which of these two views is the correct one? We do not know, but, in practice, the answer is not needed, for both answers amount to almost the same thing. For even those who hold that the sacraments do confer grace immediately even on the remiss will admit that the measure of grace given is exceedingly slight. Hence someone might receive Holy Communion daily for a period of years, but almost always carelessly, as a mere matter of routine. His spiritual growth will be, according to both schools, but slight. Holy Communion received fervently is a marvelous means of growth, for the grace given is proportioned chiefly to the graces already possessed, and to the fervor of the one who receives. If each day we received fervently, we would greatly increase our capital of grace, so that on the next day, our increase would be much greater. This multiplication, in practically a geometric series, can go on indefinitely.

Something like the principle of gravity applies in the spiritual life: the closer a falling object approaches to the ground, the greater its increases in speed. So also our rate of growth should be ever more and more rapid.[6] Hence it is staggering to imagine the increase of grace in Mary's soul with each Holy Communion she received from the hands of St. John during the time before her own Assumption.[7]

When we speak of receiving Holy Communion fervently, we do not mean that emotion must necessarily be present. This point has already been covered sufficiently in chapter X. But there is also a danger that someone may misunderstand this teaching on emotion: it must not be taken to mean that one can receive in a merely routine fashion, making no very special effort, and still gain all possible profit from each Holy Communion. No, there is a fervor of the will which is non-emotional. It consists in doing our very best, in trying to shake off the fog that so easily comes in the morning, in arousing ourselves to a realization of what we are doing: in other words, in putting genuine, vigorous effort into what we are doing.

In receiving any of the sacraments let us call on Mary to help us to receive them well, in the dispositions that will bring us the greatest profit. Let us not forget that even the graces of the sacraments come through her, that she shared in earning all of them for us. But it is especially in our thanksgiving after Holy Communion, the greatest of the sacraments, that her help is of priceless worth.

When Our Lord was born, He, unlike other children, was able to choose all the circumstances of His birth. For, insofar as He is God, He planned in advance to be born in the stable in Bethlehem. We notice that He deliberately chose the worst of almost everything — His surroundings were poorer than those into which even poor children were ordinarily born. He wished to impress forcibly upon us that earthly things are of small account: if they were really worth while He would have provided them for Himself and His Mother. Although He wanted *almost* all things poor, however, He did make up for the general poverty in another way: what more than made up to Him for the squalor was the fervor of the love of His Mother.

There can be a great deal of similarity to Bethlehem in our reception of Holy Communion. The hearts of even the fervent are little, if any, better than a stable for Him. For even the best of us have sometimes sinned, and most of us are by no means free from all attachment to earthly things, or even to venial sin. Now since the slightest moral stain is immeasurably worse than any physical squalor, it may be literally true that our hearts are poorer places than the stable. But the more closely we are united to Mary, by our generosity in giving to her everything we are and have, the more closely we can duplicate the beauty of the scene at Bethlehem. We can invite Mary to come and help us welcome her Son.[8] And if we have given everything we are and have to her,[9] we thereby enter as it were into a partnership with her: we have a kind of claim on her merits. In the proportion in which we have done this, she will offer her own spotless merits and love along with our poor prayers.

Therefore, in addition to using suitable prepared prayers of thanksgiving (those which the Church puts in the missal for the use of the priest after Mass are most suitable), we should also pray informally in our own words. And specifically in this informal prayer we should ask Mary to offer her love to make up for the poverty of our love, to adore Jesus with us and for us, since we are unworthy, to help us to realize who it is that we have received. We ask her to help us thank Him for the priceless privilege of Mass and Holy Communion, for giving us the true faith, for the forgiveness of our sins, for various other favors we have received — including the great gift that God has made to us of Mary herself! We call on her to aid us in expressing sorrow for our past sins, for our present poor state. We ask her help in obtaining every grace that we need for ourselves and for those for whom we ought to pray: grace to overcome all temptations, especially the temptations of the coming day, grace for the duties of our state of life, the grace of final perseverance and a happy death, and also the graces we need most to serve God well. Indeed, we probably do not know all the things we actually need, but we ask Mary to obtain for us what she knows we need. It is an aid to our memory to group our prayers around love and the four ends of sacrifice: adoration, contrition, thanksgiving, supplication (A C T S). These four should, of course, culminate in and be motivated by love.

But we should not do all the talking during our thanksgiving. We should also listen. Not that we expect Our Lord to appear or to speak audibly — no, but He may wish to send us graces of light, to lead us to see better what He wants of us,[10] to remind us of some failing, or to urge us on to some good work.

By way of summary let us read one of the prayers contained in the official thanksgiving after Mass in the missal — a prayer that expresses the same thoughts about asking Mary's help as those we have just explained:

> O Mary, Virgin and Mother most holy, behold, I have received your dearly beloved Son, whom you conceived in your immaculate womb, brought forth, fed, and pressed in most sweet embraces. Behold, humbly and lovingly I give back to you Him at whose sight you were glad, and filled with all delights. I offer Him to be clasped in your arms, loved by your heart and offered to the Most Holy Trinity in supreme worship, for your honor and glory, and for my needs and those of the whole world. Therefore I ask you, most devoted Mother, obtain for me the forgiveness of all my sins, abundant grace to serve Him more faithfully hereafter, and then that final grace, that with you I may be able to praise Him throughout all ages of ages. Amen.

NOTES

1. Love of God is an infused virtue, that is, God, as it were, pours it into us. We cannot directly increase the infused virtue of ourselves, but can dispose ourselves (with the help of grace) for an increase, and can earn an increase by merit, obtain an increase by prayer, the Sacraments, etc.

2. *ST,* I–II, q.114, a.8, ad 3; see also II–II, q.24, a.6,c and ad 1.

3. For a discussion of the time when the increase is actually granted see Garrigou-Lagrange, *The Three Ages of the Interior Life,* I, 136, n. 19.

4. See, for example, A. M. Lepicier, O.S.M., *De Gratia* (Paris, 1907),

p. 428, on the affirmative, and Garrigou-Lagrange, *op. cit.*, I, 141–43, on the negative.

5. Denzinger, Bannwart, Umberg, *Enchiridion Symbolorum,* §§849, 851.

6. See *ST,* I–II, q.35, a.6.

7. For an excellent development of this thought, see Garrigou-Lagrange, *The Mother of the Saviour,* pp. 118–23.

8. See again the section on the presence of Mary in chap. X.

9. The method of doing this is described in chap. XVIII.

10. On how to recognize true inspirations, see chaps. XVIII and XIX.

XVIII... *St. Louis de Montfort's Consecration to Mary*

I<small>N</small> THE FIRST GROUP of chapters we saw the solid dogmatic foundations on which our devotion to Mary ought to rest. We saw that God, though He had and has no need of Mary, had yet freely chosen to associate her most intimately with His Son in every stage of the Redemption, from beginning to end, both in the history of the world as a whole, and in the entire life of each individual human being. We noted that we can do nothing more perfect than to imitate the ways of God. Hence it is clear that the more thoroughly we employ Mary in our spiritual life, the more precise is our conformity to the plan of God.

If we compare the designs of God to a complex lock, having many elements harmoniously combined, we may compare the method we are about to consider to the intricate key to such a lock, a key that faithfully follows every notch in the structure of the lock. But just as the plans of God, though they are in a way complex, yet partake of that simplicity which is His very nature, so the consecration we are to study likewise appears at first sight to be complex, but is actually simplicity itself. By it we give to Mary the same place in our personal spiritual life that God gives her in the whole work of redemption: we give all to Jesus through Mary.

This chapter is captioned "St. Louis de Montfort's Consecration to Mary." This is correct in as much as that saint is one of the chief proponents of the method. Yet he himself makes clear in his book on "True Devotion" [1] that many had both taught and made such a consecration before his day. More names could be added to those listed by St. Louis. Furthermore, as we shall see in a later chapter, the act of consecration to the Sacred Heart of Jesus, if properly understood, as St. Margaret Mary understood it, really means the same as the consecration of St. Louis. So also does the consecration of the Legion of Mary, which is expressly borrowed from St. Louis.

We have all recited various prayers marked "An Act of Consecration." It is easy to recite these prayers in a way that means little, implying hardly more than a gesture of honor to Our Lord, or to Mary, or to some saint. Some understand an act of consecration to mean that they place themselves under the protection of a certain saint. The act of consecration which we are about to consider is more than a pious gesture. It takes the word "consecrate" in a very literal and strict sense; it means to give oneself *entirely* and *permanently* to the service of Jesus through Mary.

St. Louis de Montfort loves to describe this consecration as "slavery" to Jesus through Mary. This description is very helpful in bringing us to realize that by it we propose to live in the closest dependence on Mary our Queen, considering ourselves as her property, so that our body and soul and our possessions, even our spiritual goods, belong to her and cannot be used or disposed of except according to her will. Some souls shrink from the concept of slavery as being contrary to the freedom of the sons of God. But we must not forget that we are all, by very nature, the slaves of God: "The earth is the Lord's and the fullness thereof: the world, and all they that dwell therein." [2] St. Paul opens many of his epistles with the words, "Paul, the slave of Jesus Christ." Mary herself, when the archangel told her that she was to be the Mother of God, replied: "Behold the slave girl of the Lord" ("slave girl" being the more accurate translation of the Greek, as we saw in chapter II). Mary, as Queen of all, shares in the dominion of Christ the King, so that by very nature all belong to her also.

But by this consecration we add a new title to our slavery: we do not merely acknowledge our natural condition, but we make ourselves slaves by *love,* proposing to serve Jesus and Mary, not in a spirit of constraint, but in the generosity of love, thereby giving ourselves all the more perfectly, in a more perfect spirit of dependence, surrendering even the proprietorship that we might have lawfully reserved over our spiritual goods. Those who are the slaves of men serve without wages. The slaves of Jesus and Mary know well that they will receive an abundant reward, but it is love rather than the thought of reward that moves them to serve their King and Queen.[3]

This concept of slavery not only does not contradict the fact that we are children of God and Mary, it perfects the notion of spiritual childhood. St. Paul says well:

> . . . as long as the heir is a child, he differs in no way from a slave . . . but he is under guardians and stewards until the time set by his father.[4]

A human child, even though he may have been the heir to a great fortune, lives in dependence on parents or guardians until he comes of age: he cannot even dispose of the wealth he may possess. Similarly, by this consecration, we propose to live in complete childlike dependence on God our Father and Mary our Mother, leaving to them — for her will is perfectly in accord with His — the disposal of all that we are and have. We accept this dependence for time and for eternity: God will never cease to be our Father, nor will Mary ever fail to be our Mother.

There are two phases to this consecration. The first phase consists in the act of consecration itself, by which we actually make a gift for once and all of everything that we are *able* and *free* to give to Mary for her Son. The second phase consists in the actual living out of all the implications of the original gift. Thus it can be seen that the two phases are really integral parts of one and the same thing.

As to the first phase, the gift itself, we have said that by it we give over to Mary for Jesus everything that we are able and free to give, not only what we now have, but all we shall acquire in the future as well. We have both spiritual and temporal assets. Our spiritual assets include chiefly four kinds of goods: 1. Condign merit (a right to a reward based on justice, as was explained in chapter III); 2. Congruous merit (merit looking toward a reward from the friendship or the generosity of God rather than from His justice); 3. The impetratory power of prayer or good works; 4. The satisfactory power of prayer and good works.

The first type, condign merit, is by nature so personal that we cannot dispose of it at all: only Our Lord Himself, in virtue of the fact that He is the New Adam, was able to give such merits to us. Hence we cannot give this sort of merit to Mary to use as she wills. But we can give it to her to preserve for us, lest it be lost, and, what is equally important, to cleanse it from the stains of self which creep imperceptibly into even our best actions, for our good works easily become unacceptable to God because of these stains. But Mary, in presenting all our works to God, will join them to her own priceless merits. Thus she cleanses, and multiplies, and preserves our condign merits for us.

The case is different with congruous merit: we are able to spend it at will, to make someone else benefit by it if we wish. Hence, by this consecration, we give to Mary the right to dispose of our congruous merit for whatever end she wishes, such as the conversion of a sinner, the release of a soul in purgatory, or any other purpose, according to her good pleasure.

The power of impetration depends upon the words of Christ: "Ask and you shall receive." [5] In virtue of His promise, we have a right to expect that our prayers, made under the proper conditions and in the proper way, will be heard, but by this consecration we surrender to Mary the disposal of this power in our prayers and good works. This consecration does not forbid us to pray for any legitimate intention, nor does it dispense us from praying according to the demands and suggestions of charity for relatives and others toward whom we have obligations; but we have always at least the implied condition in our every prayer, "if Mary wishes it so." If she wishes to spend some of the value of our prayers for purposes other than those for which we have asked, we give her that right. Furthermore, we will often pray without even suggesting a purpose for our prayers, leaving it entirely up to Mary what purpose should be served with them.

To have the power of satisfying for sin, a good work must be in some way afflictive or laborious: [6] all good works are, at least to some extent, laborious for our fallen nature. By virtue of this consecration, we allow Mary to spend this satisfactory value of our good works for whatever intention she wishes.

To sum up, we give to Mary the right to dispose of all that we are able and free to give her of our spiritual goods. This includes congruous merit, impetration, and satisfaction. But condign merit is given to her not to spend, but to cleanse, multiply, and preserve from loss.

As for temporal assets, we give to Mary the possession and ownership of our body and all its faculties. We also give her the ownership of all our temporal goods. Not that we can put Mary's name on our bank account, but we agree to use our bodies and our possessions exclusively for her service. This is a complete acknowledgment of her rights as Queen.[7] What this means in practice is to be considered under the second phase of the consecration: that of living out the gifts we have made.[8]

We now come to the second phase, the application of this consecration to daily life. It is obvious that we should try to perform all our actions in a spirit of union with Mary. One of the most helpful means to accomplish this is to cultivate an habitual, loving consciousness of Mary's presence.[9] Of course, it is not possible for a person in any walk of life to keep the thought of Mary explicitly before him at all times: it will often recede into the background, or even disappear for a time. But we can think of her often, and try never to let the thought of her be far from us. It will help if we speak often to her in an informal conversational way, telling her what we are doing, what is going on around us, asking her help, thanking her for everything. The development of this frequent and habitual awareness of Mary can come only slowly and gradually: it requires much prayer and persevering effort over a long period of time.

Our consecration also calls upon us to try to keep in mind our dependence on Mary. It is especially easy and fitting to recall this dependence when we pray. Whenever we make any prayers, we ought to make them through Mary. This does not mean that we may not speak directly to Our Lord, or to the saints: it means that we always ask the aid of the intercession of Mary in obtaining whatever we wish. It is not strictly required that all of our prayers contain an explicit invocation of Mary: our general intention of always praying through Mary will suffice on those occasions when we do not explicitly call on her help. But we ought to aim to be as conscious of this dependence as we can, and we should often express it in our prayers. This dependence will also appear in the fact that in every prayer we have the proviso (at least implicit or understood) that what we ask is subject to the approval of Mary, since we have given to her the right to dispose of all our spiritual goods.

We must not misunderstand this point. It would be incorrect to think that we should not pray for really worth-while intentions — the advance of the glory and kingdom of God, our own salvation and that of relatives, friends, benefactors and even enemies. We also pray for the souls in purgatory. To omit these petitions would be laziness and an evil sort of indifference. Mary loves our dear ones even more than we do, and she recognizes the obligations under which we lie to pray for them. Their needs will not be less well cared for because of this dependence on Mary: rather, we and our relatives and friends will be cared for, not out of our own skimpy spiritual assets, but out of the limitless treasures of the Mediatrix of all graces. In regard to prayer for particular intentions, we should note, however, that many persons pray for mere trifles with little or no relation to salvation — e.g., for victory in a football game. Not only those who make this consecration, but everyone in general, would do well to pay less attention to such ephemeral things when there are so many great intentions that need prayers.[10]

The spirit of dependence on Mary ought to grow in us as we advance, for we should come to realize more and more clearly how inadequate we are in spite of our best efforts, how tainted with self are our purest acts. Then we will beg Mary over and over to "pool" (so to speak) our poor contribution with her own merits and sufferings and with those of her Divine Son. Relying on this partnership we can have the greatest confidence.

We agree also to try to be increasingly responsive to the inspirations we will receive through Mary. For it is through her that we receive both actual and habitual graces, and the inspirations of the Gifts of the Holy Spirit. In this matter we must not make the mistake of thinking that we have bound ourselves always to take the most perfect course we can think of, to do every good work that comes to mind, or every penance we might imagine: the heroic virtue of the saints would be required for that. Mary expects us to grow, and to grow gradually. The general law of gradual progress applies here as elsewhere. What Mary expects of us will increase as we grow.

But how are we to know what Mary wants us to do? If we consider our lives as a whole, it is obvious that she wants us to obey all laws and commands of legitimate authority. She also wants us to be faithful in carrying out the duties of our state in life. She wants us to practice generous abandonment to the will of God in the things that His good pleasure sends us (as we saw in chapter XV). But, in addition, she wants an ever increasing generosity, which not only avoids sin, but which constantly strives to exert itself to the limits imposed by prudence and our strength in avoiding even imperfection. Thus, in any given deliberate choice, if we have several courses open to us — let us say: good, better and best — we must at least choose *good,* but should try more and more often, according to our stage of growth, to choose the *better* and the *best.* But to try to choose the thing *best in itself* at *all* times, would not be the *best for us* in our imperfect state. Not that we do not have the strength for these things considered *one at a time,* but a constant policy of taking *all* would demand heroic endurance (some of the saints actually did such things). At the same time we must note carefully that to hold ourselves constantly down to the minimum would be contrary to our consecration, and to choose a lesser good out of laziness, mere whim of pleasure, or contempt for spiritual good would involve venial sin.[11]

But there are times in our lives when there are no laws or commands or other obvious indications to make immediately clear what our Mother wishes of us. At such times we should simply ask Mary to guide us, and try to reason out what she would do in such a situation. Especially when some thought or suggestion presents itself to our mind, we should ask ourselves: Is that likely to be sent by Mary? or is it more likely from self or the devil? Often an idea or plan seems to us to be reasonable, but when we ask if it could have come from Mary, the mask falls off, and we see it at once for what it is. But in all these things we must beware of letting mere imagination give the answer. Nor should we wait expectantly for some feeling or emotion to strike us, and, when it does, conclude that it is an inspiration from Mary.

When we receive any inspiration for our guidance, it will come from one of two directions: by way of the more ordinary sort of actual graces, or by way of the Gifts of the Holy Spirit. We shall consider the Gifts in the next chapter; here we shall look at some general features of inspirations. St. Francis de Sales, in his *Treatise on the Love of God,* gives us a good description of how God's inspirations work and how we are to conduct ourselves toward them.[12]

> Inspiration is a heavenly ray which brings into our hearts a light full of heat, by which it makes us see the good and inflames us with a desire to pursue it.[13]

We note the two elements in St. Francis' definition: inspiration gives us a light to see what ought to be done, and a help to the will to carry it out. Now if an inspiration is presented to us, we must take care to identify the source of the inspiration, for movements similar in appearance come from nature and from the devil, who may transform himself into an angel of light,[14] and urge us even to genuinely good things, but in such a way as to produce more evil than good. The first point to note is well stated by St. Francis: "We are to proportion our attention to the

importance of what we undertake." [15] Some matters are of such
little moment as to require practically no consideration; others
of greater moment deserve more thought. St. Francis gives us
three marks of genuine inspiration: [16] 1. Are they in harmony
with our vocation? or do they lead us to perseverance in some
good course already adopted? — or, on the contrary, do they lead
to inconstancy, to many starts with no follow-through? 2. Are
they conducive to peace and gentleness of heart? Divine inspirations seldom cause any upset, except in the case of one who is
tepid or in sin, to prod his conscience to extricate himself from
that condition. Or do they cause disquiet and solicitude? Divine
inspirations may cause some disturbance at their first appearance,
but peace soon follows.[17] 3. Are they in accord with obedience?
This last point is of cardinal importance. According to St. Francis,
"In obedience all is secure, outside of it all is to be suspected." [18]
In other words, any decision that deals with an important matter
or with a general policy that will affect many small things should
be submitted to the proper authority, be that an ecclesiastical
superior and/or a spiritual director. Many additional considerations can be found in other writers. Especially valuable is the
detailed treatment given by St. Ignatius of Loyola of "Rules for
perceiving . . . the different movements which are caused in the
soul" and "Rules for the . . . discernment of spirits" in his
Spiritual Exercises.[19]

St. Louis de Montfort compares Mary to a mould.[20] There
are two ways to make a statue or image, says St. Louis. One way
is by chiseling it out of a block of stone, one stroke at a time. In
this method very great skill is needed, as great damage might
come from one slip. The other is to have a perfect mould, and
pour molten material into it. Mary is the mould in which Christ
was formed. So also we could be quickly formed to the image of her
Son, by docility to the inspirations which come through her, both
by actual graces and by the gifts of the Holy Spirit, whose spouse
she is. But in order to achieve this, the material must be molten
and pliable: hard material forced into even a perfect mould will
not yield to change. This means that great docility is required;

and docility itself requires much humility, detachment, mortification, and habitual recollection.[21] But grace is necessary even for
obtaining these dispositions; and all these graces can be obtained
much more readily if we are faithful to Mary.

We have already stressed the fact that this consecration does
not result in any loss to ourselves or to our relatives and others
dear to us: all are cared for out of Mary's vast treasures. But
what is to be said of one who, before making this consecration,
has already contracted particular obligations to offer specific
prayers for specific intentions? The general principle is that we
are not required to do anything about obligations already contracted at the time we made this consecration. Such commitments
may be allowed to stand as they are.

Some of these obligations, however, are such that we are free
to change them: that is, obligations not imposed by law nor by
any similar strict sanction may be transferred and placed under
this new method. To take a concrete example, some persons have
made the excellent Heroic Act for the souls in Purgatory, giving
over to them the satisfactory value of all their good actions. Such
a one has two options: he may merely let the Heroic Act stand
without change; or he may decide that since it is an obligation
that he may retract without sin,[22] he wishes to withdraw the
previous gift *so as to give it anew,* and give it in a way which will
really be of even more help to the Souls in Purgatory than it was
before. In other words, he retracts the offering of his satisfactions,
includes them in the consecration, and then asks Mary to take
care of the Poor Souls. She, being Queen of Purgatory, loves the
souls there far more than we do, and will, out of her limitless
resources, help them far more than they could have been helped
by our own satisfactions alone.

Obligations that we are not free to retract remain unchanged.
For Mary respects the obligations that a changed *state of life,*
e.g., entry into a religious order, may impose on us even after
making the consecration.

The question of the application of the Mass presents a few
special problems. We do not refer to the case of one who merely

assists at Mass; whatever spiritual values he may obtain are covered by this consecration, just as are other good works. We consider here the case of the priest who offers Mass. It is a matter of divine law that the priest who offers the Mass must determine the intention for which it is applied.[23] Hence in no case may the celebrant *directly* allow Mary to determine the purpose for which the Mass is to be applied. He himself must make that determination.[24] When he is bound by a stipend or other means, such as the command of a religious superior, he must simply make the application as directed. But whenever he is offering a Mass of which he is free to dispose, he may, if he wishes (though he is not obliged to do so by this consecration), *indirectly* allow Mary to determine it. For he is permitted to offer Mass "for a special intention" when someone so requests. This means that the priest determines the application of the Mass as being for the intention which the giver of the stipend has in mind. The priest himself thus determines the application, even though, as is usually the case, he does not ask what purpose the donor has in mind. He may do similarly with regard to Mary, unless, as was said, he is bound by stipend or other obligation; he may offer a Mass for the intention or intentions for which Mary wishes to have it offered. In view of the above-mentioned provision of divine law, however, he is not strictly obliged to allow Mary to determine it thus *indirectly* even when he is free to do so.

What of a person who has made this consecration and now wishes to have a Mass offered for a definite purpose — e.g., for the soul of his father? In view of the provision of divine law mentioned above, he has a choice: he may merely request a Mass for his father, making no mention of Mary; or he may ask the priest to say a Mass for the intention for which Mary wishes it said, and then turn to Mary and ask that it be for his father — and he may be entirely confident that Mary will grant the request. Of course, someone who is merely transmitting Mass offerings given by other persons is not free to use this second method: he must comply with the request of the donors, without making any modification whatsoever.

Does this method interfere with devotion to other saints? Definitely not. Our chief reason for embracing this method is that it is so perfectly in line with God's own plan of using Mary as a *universal* helper in all His dealings with us. Similarly, it is part of God's plan that we should use the intercession of other saints *on occasion,* but their function is not universal as Mary's is. Furthermore, just as we must still always employ the intercession of Mary though we may speak directly to God, so also the saints obtain through Mary all the favors they ask, for she is Mediatrix of *all* graces. They will obtain favors for us in this way whether or not we ask them to, but it is fitting that we should at times make this explicit in our prayers. Hence devotion to various other saints — our own personal patrons, those of our parish, our school, our community, our profession — is to be encouraged.

Nor does this interfere with devotion to the Sacred Heart of Jesus. All that we give to Mary is given to her that He may find it more acceptable coming through her pure hands than through our stained hands. She keeps nothing for herself, but transmits it all to Him.

Some persons, once they realize all the implications of this consecration, ask: Is this not going too far? is this theologically sound? [25] We can only point out again that it is merely following the pattern traced for us by God Himself. But if some are still unable to follow the reasoning we have used, they have abundant assurance that this method is not only safe but is to be recommended highly, when they learn that *every Pope* (six in all) since the time the book *True Devotion to the Blessed Virgin Mary* was first examined by Rome, has not merely approved but recommended it.[26] Saint Pius X practiced this devotion himself, and in addition granted the Apostolic Blessing to all who would even read St. Louis' book, a distinction enjoyed by few books!

To sum up, then, by this consecration we give to Jesus through Mary all that we are able and free to give. We give our strict merits to purify, increase, and preserve; all our other spiritual treasures to dispose of as she pleases — our entire being and all that we have, to be used according to her inspirations. We try to carry out the implications of this gift in every action, striving to live always in Mary's presence, to do all in union with her, in dependence on her, constantly seeking to discover what Mary would wish us to do in this case, what she would do. We ask her permission for everything. But especially — and this is very important — we learn to rely more on the support of Mary than on our own "goodness." Not that we are excused from doing our best, but that we should come to realize more and more clearly our own inadequacy, and ask Mary not only to purify our own slight offerings, but to unite them to her own tremendous merits, and to the Heart and Wounds of her Son: on such treasures we rely, rather than on what we give.

If we do our best to live out all the implications of this consecration, then we are really complying with the suggestion of Saint Pius X:

> For who does not know that there is no more certain and easy way than Mary to unite all with Christ and to attain through Him the perfect adoption of sons, that we may be holy and immaculate in the sight of God? [27]

NOTES

1. St. Louis de Montfort, *True Devotion to the Blessed Virgin Mary,* §§159–63.
2. Ps. 23:1. See also *True Devotion,* §§68–77.
3. On the relation of love and reward in our motivation, see chap. IX.
4. Gal. 4:1–2. [*Confraternity version.*]
5. John 16:24.
6. See *ST,* Suppl. q.15, a.1.c. St. Thomas says that even prayer made with spiritual pleasure is satisfactory, because although there is pleasure for the spirit, there is affliction for the lower nature in it: Suppl. q.15, a.3.ad 1. Even in satisfactory works, however, we must remember that the most important thing is the love with which they are performed. See also Tanquerey, *The Spiritual Life,* §§736–50.
7. See chap. VII.
8. This consecration does not bind under pain of sin unless we have made it a vow — a step never to be taken without permission of our spiritual director.
9. See the remarks on habitual recollection in chap. XII and the section on the presence of Mary in chap. X, especially the references in note 15 to chap. X (McGinnis, *Life with Mary,* pp. 35–37 is especially helpful). Many

practical suggestions for living out the consecration will also be found in Gabriel Denis, S.M.M., *The Reign of Jesus Through Mary* (Bay Shore, N.Y., 1949); and E. Neubert, S.M., *My Ideal, Jesus Son of Mary* (Kirkwood, Mo., 1947).

10. See also the treatment of desires in chap. XV. We must, however, note that there is less danger that inordination or attachment will creep in when we pray that others may have temporal blessings as a means to spiritual goods than if we made the same prayer for ourselves. For if, for the good of a neighbor's soul, we provide even material goods for him, we practice the works of mercy. See also St. Teresa of Avila, *Way of Perfection,* I (II, 4–5): "Let us not pray for worldly things, my sisters. It makes me laugh, and yet it makes me sad, when I hear of the things which people come here to beg us to pray to God for; we are to ask His Majesty to give them money and to provide them with incomes — I wish that some of these people would entreat God to enable them to trample all such things beneath their feet. Their intentions are quite good, and I do as they ask because I see that they are really devout people, though I do not myself believe that God ever hears me when I pray for such things. The world is on fire. Men try to condemn Christ once again, as it were. . . . They would raze His Church to the ground — and are we to waste our time upon things which, if God were to grant them, would perhaps bring one soul less to Heaven? No, my sisters, this is no time to treat with God for things of little importance."

11. On venial sin creeping into imperfections, see chap. IX.

12. St. Francis de Sales, *Treatise on the Love of God,* VIII, x–xiv (pp. 349–64).

13. *Ibid.,* VIII, x (p. 349).

14. As we saw in chap. X.

15. St. Francis de Sales, *op. cit.,* VIII, xiv (p. 362).

16. *Ibid.,* chaps. xi–xiii.

17. Compare III Kings 19:11–13: "And he said to him: Go forth, and stand upon the mount before the Lord: and behold the Lord passeth, and a great and strong wind before the Lord overthrowing the mountains, and breaking the rocks in pieces: the Lord is not in the wind, and after the wind an earthquake: the Lord is not in the earthquake. And after the earthquake a fire: the Lord is not in the fire, and after the fire a whistling of gentle air. And when Elias heard it, he covered his face with his mantle, and coming forth stood at the entering in of the cave: and behold, a voice. . . ."

18. St. Francis de Sales, *op. cit.,* VIII, xiii (p. 360).

19. See also *The Spiritual Doctrine of Father Louis Lallemant* (Westminster, 1946), pp. 176–79; De Guibert, *The Theology of the Spiritual Life,* pp. 137–41; Parente, *Spiritual Direction,* pp. 51–53; and Garrigou-Lagrange, *The Three Ages of the Interior Life,* II, 241–48.

20. St. Louis de Montfort, *True Devotion to the Blessed Virgin Mary,* §§219–21.

21. See Garrigou-Lagrange, *op. cit.,* II, 233–34.

22. Unless, of course, he has made it a vow, which is not usual.

23. A threefold fruit is given to mankind through each Mass: 1. The general fruit, which goes directly to all the faithful, living and dead, and

indirectly, to those outside the Church for their conversion; 2. The special fruit, which is given to those for whom the celebrant specially applies the Mass; 3. The most special fruit, which is for the celebrant himself. In the passage above, we speak of the special fruit: from the fact that the priest has received from Christ the power to offer Mass, it is his function to determine the application of this special fruit. See Tanquerey, *Synopsis Theologiae Dogmaticae* (23rd ed.; Paris, 1934), III, §796.

24. See H. Noldin, S.J., A. Schmitt, S.J., *Summa Theologiae Moralis* (25th ed.; Oeniponte, 1938), III, §179, 3 b.

25. See the quotations from the Popes opposite the title page of the Montfort Fathers edition.

26. For a thorough theological study of this consecration, see A. Lhoumeau, *La Vie spirituelle à l'École du B⁰ L.-M. Grignion de Montfort;* and R. P. Poupon, *Le Poème de la parfaite consécration à Marie.*

27. *Ad diem illum* (Feb. 2, 1904), *ASS* 36:451.

XIX ... *Spouse of the Holy Spirit*

WHEN the Word was made flesh in Mary's womb through the overshadowing of the Holy Spirit, Mary, in a spiritual and entirely unique sense, became His Spouse. From the very beginning of her life, Mary had always been solicitous to fulfill His every wish, never grieving Him in the slightest degree. She was led by this Divine Spirit from grace to grace, to heights of sanctity far beyond the ken of any other creature.

Ordinary souls, if they are to advance far in the spiritual life, must also be led by the same Holy Spirit through His Gifts, which they receive through Mary. It is largely the failure to utilize the great potentialities of guidance and strength offered by the Holy Spirit which accounts for the fact that so many souls, although they make frequent use of the Mass and the Sacraments, are slow in reaching perfection— if indeed they ever reach it at all in this life.

Every soul in the state of grace possesses these wonderful Gifts of the Holy Spirit in a greater or lesser degree. They are given to us along with sanctifying grace, and grow in us as we grow in grace and in love of God. The Gifts are permanent, infused dispositions that perfect the infused virtues, and make the soul capable of being readily enlightened, guided, and moved by the Holy Spirit Himself, through special inspirations and movements.[1]

Now since these Gifts are so important, what can we do in order that the Gifts may bear their full fruit in us? In order to answer this question, we must learn something of the nature and operation of the Gifts. It is wise for us to approach the question by first considering the fact that in our every action it is possible for us to act in one of three manners: the animal manner, the human manner, and the superhuman manner.[2]

An animal is completely dominated by natural impulses, instincts, and desires. When it is hungry, it will inevitably seek food. When it is thirsty, it will inevitably seek a drink. When any urge whatsoever comes upon it, it will not fail to try to satisfy that urge. Human beings sometimes act in the same way: their *sole* reason for doing a thing is the fact that a whim or desire for the object in question has just touched them. They would consider themselves fools not to try to satisfy that desire if they can easily do so; their reaction to any natural urge is as predictable as that of an animal. It is obvious that to act on this low animal level is unworthy of a human being, and will result in nothing but degradation. Such a man walks in the dark, led by blind impulse.

Above the animal level is the human level. Man is a *rational* animal; hence, he acts in a way worthy of his natural position when he acts according to the dictates of his *reason*. A man who lives by reason will, of course, often grant the desired satisfaction to natural urges. He will eat, he will drink, he will rest and do other things when his lower nature calls for them. In so doing, however, he will not act with the blind regularity of an animal: he will let reason moderate all these actions, so that sometimes when his appetite calls for food, he will refuse to satisfy it, on the ground that it is not the proper time, or because the amount or kind of food desired is unsuitable for his own well-being. The rational man will also decide to do or not to do certain things because he sees them to be opposed to some law.

The reasonable but merely natural activities of the rational man may be elevated greatly by being placed under the influence of grace and the supernatural virtues. A soul in the state of grace is the temple of the Holy Spirit, as St. Paul says;[3] it shares in the very nature of God,[4] and so is, in a way, divinized. When it acts, utilizing the infused virtues and under the movements of actual graces, it can perform actions of great worth. Despite this fact, St. Thomas says that a soul fitted out with the infused virtues, and receiving various actual graces, still lacks something that is needed not only for higher perfection, but even for salvation itself![5]

The basis for this surprising statement is that our destiny is to reach the beatific vision, in which we are to live the life of God Himself, a divine life, sharing in His nature. Grace and the infused virtues do elevate our activities in a certain way, so as to direct them to a supernatural object, the knowledge and love of God. Something is still lacking, however, for a man working with actual graces and the infused virtues is still operating only in a *human manner,* whereas, to reach the goal of sharing in the life of the Blessed Trinity in heaven, a soul needs to be able to work in a *superhuman manner.*[6]

What does it mean to say that by virtue of the Gifts a man is able to work in a *superhuman manner?* It means that the Holy Spirit gives to man's will a strength and movement that are more than human, so that he is made capable even of heroic things. And it also means that the Holy Spirit gives wonderful light to a man's *intellect,* so that he can understand and penetrate truths, and reach conclusions and decisions in a way otherwise beyond his reach: the Holy Spirit dispenses the intellect from the need of reasoning.

In order to grasp what it means to be dispensed from the need of reasoning, we must recall that when our minds work in the ordinary, human way, in an effort to penetrate or understand a truth, or to reach a conclusion, we use a step-by-step process called discursive reason. For example, here is a man who has committed a serious sin. He may reason: "Since I have sinned I must not only repent and go to Confession, but I must also make reparation. What reparation shall I make? Shall I fast? or give alms? or shall I do both? How much money can I afford to give? What fasting would my health permit?" And so he may continue, moving step by step from one idea to another, until finally, with the help of grace, he understands what is right for him, considering all circumstances, and makes his decision.

This repentant sinner reached his decision by a relatively slow and laborious process of many steps. Through the Gifts of the Holy Spirit, however, he might have been given the same understanding, the same conclusion *at once without any steps of reasoning,* by a sort of intuition. The Holy Spirit could supply him with the resultant understanding ready-made, as it were. For by the Gifts, the Holy Spirit Himself leads man. Man acting in the animal manner has blind impulse for his guide; man acting in the human manner has reason for his guide (with perhaps the help of the infused virtues and actual graces); man acting in the superhuman manner has the Holy Spirit Himself as his guide. It is obvious that with such a guide, the soul can be led to levels far higher than those to which reason would have brought it.

This guidance of the Holy Spirit is superior to reason, beyond reason. Does this mean that a man acts irrationally, as though seized by a blind impulse? By no means. Unhappily, the language often used in describing the workings of the Gifts could give the impression of irrationality. We often see the terms "instinct" and "impulse" used in discussions of the Gifts. Such terms are good enough in the Latin from which they are taken, but are unfortunate in English. For by the Gifts, a man is led in an *intelligent* manner: the Holy Spirit sends light to his intellect whenever any movement is given to the will.[7] The Holy Spirit does not send mere blind impulses. When a man is guided by reason, he is using his intelligence, and when the Holy Spirit guides him, his intelligence is also called into service. Under the influence of the Holy Spirit, however, a man does not have to work in a step-by-step process of deduction in order to reach an understanding or a decision: the action of the Holy Spirit dispenses him from that.

It would be misleading, however, to give the impression that every inspiration of the Holy Spirit is concerned with leading a man to make a decision about some external action: the action of the Holy Spirit also shows us the insignificance of created things and our own nothingness before the infinite Majesty of God. It shows us how to find God in creatures, helps us to penetrate the revealed truths,[8] and even brings that wonderful, simple loving gaze at God and knowledge of Him which we call infused contemplation. In addition the Holy Spirit gives us a true child-like spirit towards God our Father, bringing with it a filial fear of offending Him, great confidence in Him, and devotedness to His service and to all that pertains to it. Finally, in order that nothing may hinder our advance, He gives us a strength and courage that can joyfully surmount all obstacles. Thus these Gifts perfect all virtues, but especially the greatest virtues — faith, hope, and love.[9]

When we read that the Holy Spirit, through these Gifts, shows a man what to do, and moves his will towards it, we may conclude that the divine light always leaves a soul *certain* of what is to be done. Such, however, is not always the case: many times the Holy Spirit will show a soul that a thing is good, give the will a desire for it, but yet leave the person not quite convinced that he should carry out this course of action. By leaving a man in this uncertainty, the Holy Spirit leads him to consult his director and/or whatever other superior is competent in the matter in question. For the general rule remains, even for one who is guided through the Gifts: *Any decision involving an important matter, or a general policy that will embrace many small matters, should be submitted to one's director and/or other competent superior.*[10] This keeps a soul in proper subjection to the human authorities to whom He has given power. There are times when the Holy Spirit will give certitude to the soul. When He does so, it does not dispense that person from due subjection to superiors. Of course, there are certain small matters about which there is ordinarily no need of any consultation — for instance, if an inspiration to pray for light should come while one is studying. It is obvious that such an inspiration may be accepted, unless, of course, it is repeated with such frequency as to interfere with work. Even in important matters it may sometimes be impossible to avoid a decision and also impossible to seek advice; in that event, the guidance of the Holy Spirit can supply for lack of consultation.

Another special characteristic of inspirations sent through the Gifts is that even though they may give us a rather strong conviction that we ought to do a certain thing, they do not show us clearly the motives for doing so. In other words, motivation tends to be vague or hazy. Although we perceive in some way that the thing is good, we cannot explain the reasons for our desire. Hence we have another justification for submitting any matters of consequence to a director or superior.

The one who examines an alleged inspiration of the Holy Spirit should be guided by sound theological rules,[11] especially those of St. Francis de Sales, described in the preceding chapter. In the present situation as well, one may not act if a superior refuses permission. If the superior is wrong, it is God's place to deal with him; the person receiving the inspiration must not presume to disobey (we assume, of course, that the order of the superior is not in contradiction to the moral law).

Despite the fact that all souls in the state of grace have received these Gifts, their influence is usually perceived little if at all by souls still in the purgative way. But the Gifts do function during even this period. Sometimes (but more rarely) they operate in a very obvious way, so that their influence is clear; but their influence is usually a latent one. In this latent form they facilitate and promote the goods being accomplished for the great part in a human manner, with the aid of actual graces. In the fullest development of the Gifts, the soul is *passive,* so that its co-operation is largely a matter of giving consent to being guided and moved in this way; when the Gifts are not operating, a soul is thoroughly *active.* Therefore, when the Gifts work in a latent way, the soul is in an intermediate status — partly active, partly passive.[12] For example, a soul in the gradual transition from the last stage of the prayer of simplicity to initial infused contemplation, is in this active-passive status, for in it more and more of the divine light, from the Gifts, mingles with the human activity of the soul.[13] The person who receives this latent form of help from the Gifts will probably not realize that it is being given, since it merely aids and advances him in activities that are for the great part being carried on at the more ordinary level, with the aid of actual graces. Again, for example, if a man is deliberating, using the infused virtue of prudence, an inspiration from the Gift of Counsel might add a sudden light to his mind, or it might put before him a thought from the Gospels. This sort of aid could blend in so well with the process of rational deliberation as to pass unnoticed.

Why is it that the influence of the Gifts is relatively slight in most souls? [14] It is not only that in souls in the purgative way these Gifts have not reached their higher degrees, for they grow with grace; but we ourselves, by our deficiencies, bind the action of these Gifts, so that we are not very docile to the Holy Spirit. This unfortunate condition is the result of affection to venial sin,[15] and of our deficiency in humility, recollection, detachment, and mortification. For as we saw in the chapters on mortification, our desires and our love of creatures exert strong pulls on us, tending to draw not only our will but even our judgment in the direction of earthly things. The special inspirations of the Gifts find us unresponsive: when we are listening to so loud a voice from creatures, we cannot hear the delicate whisperings of the Holy Spirit. We are like a compass needle, which cannot respond to the pull of the north when it is in the midst of the gross attraction of many nearby powerlines.

As a soul advances, it may be compared to a sailing vessel with oars, whose sails are being gradually unfurled: the more open they are, the more readily they will catch and move under even a delicate breeze. Then the vessel proceeds much more easily and swiftly than when it had to depend on the labor of the oarsmen. In the rare heights of the unitive way, a soul may be dominated in all things by the Holy Spirit through these Gifts without losing its freedom. Such was Mary herself, as St. John of the Cross says so well:

> . . . God alone moves the faculties of these souls to do those works which are meet, according to the will and ordinance of God, and they cannot be moved to do others. . . . Such were those of the most glorious Virgin, Our Lady, who, being raised to this high estate from the beginning, had never the form of any creature imprinted in her soul, neither was moved by such, but was invariably guided by the Holy Spirit.[16]

What a contrast between the soul of Mary, whose every movement was directed by the Holy Spirit, and the lives of those who follow only their own blind desires!

It was through Mary's "mighty prayers," as Pope Pius XII

says,[17] that the Holy Spirit was given to the newborn Church on Pentecost. It is still through her that He is given to souls today. Those who give and consecrate themselves to her, the Spouse of the Holy Spirit, not merely in word, but in deed, will learn by experience the truth of that which St. Louis de Montfort describes:

> When the Holy Ghost, her Spouse, has found Mary in a soul, He flies there. He enters there in His fulness; He communicates Himself to that soul abundantly, and to the full extent to which it makes room for His Spouse.[18]

It was in and through Mary that the Holy Spirit formed the Sacred Humanity, the Heart of Christ. So also it is in and through her, the "mould of God," [19] that He will form us to the likeness of Christ.

A special feature of this likeness to Christ is a higher, more intimate kind of love for Mary. For in the human soul of Christ, the Holy Spirit produced a wonderful love for His Mother, and the closest union with her.[20] In souls especially dear to Mary, the same Spirit of Christ produces a truly Christlike love for the Mother of Christ, so that these souls live most intimately as her children in her presence. Without this special favor, souls may enjoy a certain closeness to Mary, but by the action of the Holy Spirit, this loving filial union with Mary is raised to a wonderful new plane, so as to be carried on in a manner above that which is merely human.[21] Venerable Michael of St. Augustine says of this:

> Is it any wonder, therefore, if the Spirit of Jesus, which in the hearts of the children of God cries Abba, Father[22] . . . also cries from those same hearts, Ave, Mater . . . ? [23]

NOTES

1. We must distinguish the Gifts themselves from the inspirations. The Gifts are the permanent dispositions in a soul rendering it receptive to the inspirations.

2. On the Gifts, see John of St. Thomas, *The Gifts of the Holy Ghost*, trans. Dominic Hughes, O.P. (New York, 1951); Tanquerey, *The Spiritual Life*, §§1307–57; *The Spiritual Doctrine of Father Louis Lallemant*, pp. 108–79; P. Philippe, O.P., *Doctrina Mystica S. Thomae* (Rome, 1952), pp. 1–104; Garrigou-Lagrange, *The Three Ages of the Interior Life*, I, 66–82,

90–96, and II, 223–40. See also M. M. Amabel du Coeur de Jésus, *To Love and To Suffer,* trans. a Discalced Carmelite (Westminster, 1953).

3. I Cor. 3:17.

4. II Peter 1:4: ". . . by whom he hath given us most great and precious promises, that by these you may be made partakers of the divine nature. . . . "

5. *ST,* I–II, q.68, a.2. See Pope Leo XIII, *Divinum illud munus* (May 9, 1897), *ASS* 29:654: "More than this, the just man, that is, a man living the life of divine grace, and acting by fitting virtues as by faculties, definitely needs those sevenfold gifts which are properly called the Gifts of the Holy Spirit."

6. See *ST,* I–II, q.68, a.l.

7. See Philippe, *op. cit.,* p. 39.

8. The action of the Gifts does not give such penetration of mysteries that no mystery remains.

9. On the action of the individual Gifts, see references given above in note 2, esp. *The Spiritual Doctrine of Father Louis Lallemant,* pp. 129–66, and Tanquerey, *The Spiritual Life,* §§1321–52.

10. See *Lallemant,* pp. 110–11, and Garrigou-Lagrange, *op. cit.,* II, 236–37.

11. See *Lallemant,* pp. 173–79; Garrigou-Lagrange, *op. cit.,* II, 241–48; and especially, in the *Spiritual Exercises* of St. Ignatius Loyola, Rules for perceiving . . . the different movements which are caused in the soul" and "Rules for the . . . greater discernment of Spirits."

12. See Garrigou-Lagrange, *op. cit.,* II, 225, 333–34.

13. See chap. XIII.

14. See *Lallemant,* pp. 126–28; Garrigou-Lagrange, *op. cit.,* II, 233–36.

15. On dangerous affections, see St. Francis de Sales, *Introduction to the Devout Life,* I, xxii–xxiii.

16. St. John of the Cross, *Ascent of Mount Carmel,* III, ii, 10 (I, 230–31), and *Living Flame of Love,* I, iv; I, ix; and II, xxxiv.

17. Pope Pius XII, *Mystici Corporis* (June 29, 1943), *AAS* 35:248. "She it was, who, by her most mighty prayers, obtained that the Spirit of the Divine Redeemer, already given on the Cross, should be bestowed on the newborn Church on the day of Pentecost, in the company of miraculous gifts."

18. St. Louis de Montfort, *True Devotion to the Blessed Virgin Mary,* §36 (p. 23).

19. See *ibid.,* §§219–21 (pp. 165–66).

20. Since all souls in the unitive way are guided and moved by the Holy Spirit (see St. John of the Cross, cited above, note 16), it is obvious that the soul of Christ was guided and moved in all things by the Divine Spirit. It was, then, this same Spirit who produced in Christ His great love for His Mother.

21. That is, this love is in the superhuman manner, as are all activities produced in a soul by inspirations received through the Gifts of the Holy Spirit.

22. See Gal. 4:6: ". . . God hath sent the Spirit of his Son into our hearts, crying 'Abba, Father.' "

23. Ven. Michael of St. Augustine, O.Carm., "The Mariform and Marian Life in Mary, For Mary," McGinnis (ed.), *Life with Mary,* p. 28.

XX ... Mary and Devotion to the Sacred Heart of Jesus

THERE is an excellent Latin saying: *Corruptio optimi pessima,* "The corruption of the best is the worst." This means not merely that it is a more terrible offense to distort an excellent thing than to distort something less good; it means primarily that the result obtained by distorting an excellent thing is all the worse in proportion to the excellence of the thing that we distort. Now devotion to Mary is indeed an excellent thing. But the very height of its excellence is the measure of the ruin that may result from distorting it. One who carefully observes all the principles explained thus far will be practicing a true and most beneficial devotion to Mary. But it is so easy to slip into a sugary, spineless sentimentality, a refined form of self-seeking (especially by attachment to sensory consolations, as described in chapter X).

One may test himself in various ways to discover if his devotion is genuine. One excellent test is this: Is devotion to Mary really leading us to a more solid devotion to Jesus? For we have shown that the purpose of Mary is to lead us to her Son. If this does not happen, we must suspect that even our devotion to Mary is not genuine. Above all, Mary will lead us, gradually but surely, to a greater attachment to the Blessed Sacrament. For all real love of Our Lord must center in that sacrament. There are only two places in which His Sacred Humanity is present: in Heaven, and on our altars. A devotion that pretends to a great love of Christ and yet does not seek Him where He is, is justly to be suspected.

The relation of Mary to devotion to Our Lord appears in a special way in the case of devotion to the Sacred Heart of Our Lord. This devotion to the Sacred Heart, like the devotion to the Immaculate Heart of Mary, has developed only in relatively recent times. It is true that honor was paid to the Hearts of Jesus and Mary already in the Middle Ages, but then the devotion was the privilege of only a few chosen souls. The flowering and general spread of devotion to the Sacred Heart of Jesus was due especially to two saints of the seventeenth century, St. John Eudes and St. Margaret Mary. St. John is largely responsible for introducing devotion to the Hearts of Jesus and Mary into the liturgy.[1] We note that he joined the Hearts of both Jesus and Mary. We shall see more of the relation of these devotions later, when we examine the contribution made by St. Margaret Mary.

The principle, *corruptio optimi pessima,* applies even more to devotion to the Sacred Heart of Jesus than it does to devotion to Mary: because of the very excellence of devotion to His Heart. The sad consequences of abuses are all too apparent: some persons make devotion to the Sacred Heart consist in little more than in singing sickly, sentimental hymns, or in burning vigil lights before feminine statues of what should be the thoroughly manly Christ. It is clear that we need to re-examine the true nature of devotion to the Sacred Heart. For this purpose we shall use two of the best authorities, the classic encyclical of Pope Pius XI,[2] and the *Autobiography* of St. Margaret Mary.[3]

It is well known that the basic reason for adoring the Heart of Christ is that it is hypostatically united to the Divinity (see chapter VII). And the special reason His Heart is given this honor is that it is the organ of His immense love. But the question is: In what way should this love and honor be given? Early in his encyclical, Pope Pius XI shows us that true devotion to the Sacred Heart consists in two things, which can readily be reduced to one — consecration and reparation:

> But certainly, among the other things which properly belong to the worship of the Sacred Heart, that *consecration* stands out and is notable, by which we, recognizing that we have received all that we are and have from the eternal love of God, dedicate *ourselves and all that we have* to the Divine Heart of Jesus. When Our Savior, impelled not so much by His rights, as by His boundless love for us, had taught that most innocent disciple of His Heart, Margaret Mary, how much He yearned for

this sort of consecration from mankind, she, with her spiritual director, Claude de la Colombière, first made this consecration to Him.... [4] [*Emphasis added.*]

The words of the Holy Father are unmistakably clear: the primary element in devotion to the Sacred Heart is an act of consecration. We learn further that by it we "dedicate ourselves and all that we have to the Divine Heart." We see also that St. Margaret Mary is proposed as the model of those who make this consecration in the best way. We shall see the complete implications of these points later. Now let us note the second element included in this devotion:

> ... if the *first and chief thing in consecration* is the *repayment of the love* of the creature to the love of the Creator, the *second thing at once follows from it,* that, if that Uncreated Love has been neglected by forgetfulness or violated by offenses, compensation should be made in some way for the injustice that has been inflicted: in common language we call this debt one of *reparation....*

> Therefore, to consecration ... there is to be added expiation, by which sins may be completely blotted out, lest the sanctity of Supreme Justice reject our shameless unworthiness, and rebuff our gift as hateful instead of receiving it as pleasing.[5] [*Emphasis added.*]

The second element, then, is reparation. But the Holy Father explicitly tells us that "the second thing" (reparation) "at once follows from it" (consecration). For, once a consecrated soul sees that it has failed in repayment of love to the Heart of Christ, it cannot do other than will to make reparation, for its own defections and those of others as well. The consecration itself demands it, for the self-oblation, which is the heart of consecration, will not be acceptable unless such reparation is made, at least for one's own sins. Left to ourselves, we should probably think that since our debts are so great, it would be presumptuous of us to offer reparation for the sins of others as well. Yet the Holy Father gives us a warrant for doing so. In the official prayer of reparation which he himself prescribed, he wrote:

> . . . we humbly ask Thy pardon and declare our readiness to atone by voluntary expiation not only for our own personal offenses, but also for the sins of those who, straying far from the path of salvation, refuse . . . to follow Thee . . . or, renouncing the vows of their baptism, have cast off the sweet yoke of Thy law. We are now resolved to expiate each and every deplorable outrage committed against Thee. . . .[6]

The Holy Father made another stirring plea for reparation in the encyclical itself. After a vivid description of the evils of his own day,[7] he added:

> For if anyone lovingly meditates on these things which we have mentioned up to now, and has them, as it were, fixed in his very heart, he cannot do otherwise than both shrink from and avoid every sin as the supreme evil, and give himself totally to the will of God. He will strive to repair the wounded honor of the Divine Majesty by constant prayer, by afflictions voluntarily taken on himself, and by patiently bearing those troubles that befall him: he will spend his whole life in this zeal for expiation.[8]

Pope Pius XI has shown us the true nature of devotion to the Sacred Heart. He makes clear that it consists essentially in a consecration, and that reparation is a duty enjoined by the consecration itself. He himself stresses the fact that our consecration and reparation are to be made through Mary:

> May the most gracious Mother of God smile upon and favor these our prayers and undertakings, she, who since she brought forth Jesus the Redeemer for us, nourished Him, and offered Him as a Victim at the Cross, is, and is called the Reparatrix, in virtue of her intimate union with Christ, and an altogether singular grace of His.

O Loving Jesus, through the intercession of the Blessed Virgin Mary, our model in reparation, deign to receive the voluntary offering we make of this act of expiation. . . .[9]

As we have seen, Pope Pius XI pointed to St. Margaret Mary as the one who first made the special consecration requested by Our Lord. We can learn of the precise nature of this consecration from a study of her *Autobiography,* and, in particular, from a careful comparison of two passages. In one of these, the Saint tells us of a written offering which Our Lord requested of her:

On one occasion my Sovereign Sacrificer asked me to make in His favour and *in writing* a will or an entire and unreserved *donation, as I had already done verbally, of all that I should do and suffer,* and of all the prayers and spiritual goods which should be offered for me, either during my life or after my death. . . . and when I presented the testament to this only Love of my soul, He expressed great pleasure, and said that *He wished to dispose of it according to His designs and in favour of whomsoever He pleased.*[10] [*Emphasis added.*]

It is not at all difficult to recognize that the donation of which the saint speaks is identical with the consecration described in chapter XVIII. It is true that only spiritual goods are mentioned, but we may assume that all other goods, and the intention to live in the spirit of the consecration, are included. St. Margaret Mary gives all, and allows Our Lord to dispose of it, to spend it for whatever intention He wills. The only question one might raise is this: Was the gift made through Mary? We noticed in the above-mentioned quotation that the saint says she had already made the same donation *verbally.* Hence we ought to examine carefully the earlier portion of her *Autobiography* in the hope of finding a description of the earlier verbal donation (the written donation was made in the same sense, as the saint indicates). Now there is such a passage, dealing with the early part of her life:

On another occasion He said to me: " . . . I then confided thee to the care of *My Holy Mother, that she might fashion thee according to my designs."* And truly she has always shown herself a good Mother to me, nor has she ever refused me her help. In all my troubles and needs I had recourse to her with the greatest confidence, for it seemed to me that I had nothing to fear under her maternal protection. . . . and *I gave myself to her as her slave,* begging her not to refuse to accept me in this capacity. I spoke to this good Mother quite simply as a child, and henceforth felt for her a truly tender affection.[11] [*Emphasis added.*]

St. Margaret Mary lived slightly earlier than St. Louis de Montfort; hence her expressions could not have come from him. Yet we notice that she uses his favorite word — "slave." She saw clearly that the concept of slavery is not at all inconsistent with treating Mary as our Mother; in the very next sentence, she continues: "I spoke to this good Mother quite simply as a child." [12] She also quotes Our Lord Himself as confiding her to His Mother "that she might fashion thee" — which reminds us of St. Louis de Montfort's description of Mary as the "mould of God."

Is this early consecration through Mary the one St. Margaret Mary referred to as the earlier verbal donation? Though we cannot be absolutely certain, it is at least highly probable. But even if the reference were to something else, it is clear that she who had once consecrated herself as a slave of Mary would not later refuse to continue to go to Jesus through Mary. A beautiful prayer written by St. Margaret Mary, which we shall quote presently, makes this entirely clear.

Therefore, genuine consecration to the Sacred Heart, as taught to St. Margaret Mary by Our Lord Himself, is a *total* one, one made through Mary, and precisely the same as that which we analyzed in chapter XVIII.

But perhaps someone might think that, since the function of Mary is to lead us to her Son, once that is done, we may take leave of Mary. Again we may learn a lesson from St. Margaret Mary.

For in one of the late pages of her *Autobiography,* after she had received many great revelations from the Sacred Heart, she wrote as follows:

> Having by obedience represented all this to Our Lord, I did not fail to recover my health immediately. For the most Blessed Virgin, my good Mother, appearing to me, bestowed upon me many caresses, and, after having conversed with me for a long time, she said: "Take courage, my dear daughter, in the health which I restore to thee at the will of my Divine Son, for thou hast yet a long and painful way to go, always upon the Cross, pierced with nails and thorns and torn with scourges. But fear nothing, *I will not abandon thee and I promise thee my protection." A promise which she has since fully made me realize in the GREAT NEED I HAVE HAD THEREOF.*[13] [*Emphasis added.*]

Or again, on one of the last pages of the *Autobiography,* we read:

> I never spent a retreat in such joy and spiritual delight. I seemed to be in heaven by reason of the great and repeated favours lavished upon me and the intimacy I enjoyed with my Lord Jesus Christ, His most Holy Mother, my good Angel Guardian and my blessed Father St. Francis of Sales.[14]

Finally we may cite part of the prayer which St. Margaret Mary composed, and which she recited frequently:

> O most holy, most amiable and most glorious Virgin, Mother of God, Mistress and Advocate to whom we are all vowed and consecrated, making it our glory *to belong to thee as children, servants and slaves* for time and eternity! behold . . . we throw ourselves at thy feet to renew our vows of fidelity and *servitude to thee,* and to pray thee that *as we belong entirely to thee, thou wouldst offer, dedicate, consecrate and immolate to the Sacred Heart of our adorable Jesus, ourselves and all that we are, all that we shall do and suffer,* without reserving anything for ourselves. We wish to have . . . no other glory except that of be-

longing to Him as slaves and victims of His pure love. . . .
. . . grant, O most charitable Mother, *that He may receive and
accept this consecration . . . through thy mediation.* . . . [15]
[*Emphasis added.*]

Thus it is clear that our need of Mary will never end; she is the
Mediatrix of *all* graces; all descend to us through her. And the
way for us to ascend to the Sacred Heart of Christ is through the
Immaculate Heart of His Mother: *ad Cor Jesu per Cor Mariae!*

It is not surprising that these two Hearts, which were and are
so closely united throughout all the Redemption, should also be
closely united as objects of our devotion.[16] Pope Pius XII has
shown us clearly that, with due subordination, devotion to the
Immaculate Heart of Mary is not only intimately related to devotion to the Sacred Heart of Jesus, but that these devotions are
closely parallel. On that historic day of October 31, 1942, when
he consecrated the world to the Immaculate Heart of Mary, the
Holy Father solemnly pronounced these words:

> To You, to your Immaculate Heart, We, as the common Father
> of the great Christian family, as Vicar of Him to whom was
> given all power in heaven and on earth . . . to You, to your Im-
> maculate Heart . . . we confide, entrust, and consecrate not only
> the Holy Church, the Mystical Body of your Jesus . . . but the
> entire world as well. . . . [17]

And then, at the close of this act of consecration, the Pope clearly
referred to the parallel character of the devotion to these two
Hearts:

> Finally, just as the Church and the whole human race were
> consecrated to the Heart of your Jesus . . . so also, from today
> on let them also be consecrated to You and to your Immaculate
> Heart, O our Mother and Queen of the world. . . . [18]

Let us try to unfold some of the implications contained in this
papal teaching, in order to see what is meant by the statement
that these devotions are both parallel and united.

As we have already seen, the fundamental reason for our adoration of the Sacred Heart of Christ is that it is a Heart hypostatically united to the Divinity itself; in particular, however, we honor His Heart as the organ of His immense love. We do not, of course, adore the Immaculate Heart of Mary, for it is not the Heart of a divine person, but we do honor her Heart because it is so closely united to His Heart in all things, and we honor it as the organ of her inexpressible love for her Son and us.[19]

The great means of devotion to the Sacred Heart of Jesus is consecration. Pope Pius XI urged all to make the consecration to the Sacred Heart of Jesus, and, in pointing to St. Margaret Mary as a model of this consecration, he invited us to make our consecration through Mary. Pope Pius XII, having himself consecrated the Church and the whole world to the Immaculate Heart of Mary, also encouraged each of us to ratify personally the act that he had made in the name of all, by consecrating ourselves individually to the Immaculate Heart.[20]

Pope Pius XI has shown us that reparation to the Sacred Heart of Jesus is a duty flowing from the very nature of consecration. Hence we may ask, Is reparation due also to the Immaculate Heart of Mary?

It is obvious that it is not only permissible but highly proper that we offer reparation to Mary in the sense that we may place in her hands the reparation that we owe to the Sacred Heart of her Son. She will cleanse our offering of the stains that normally cling even to our best actions, and will join it, thus purified, to her own priceless reparation and present it to Him. It is thus that He is most pleased to receive it.

But we may and should offer reparation also to Mary herself.[21] Our very consecration to the Immaculate Heart of Mary calls upon us to make reparation for the offenses that we and others have committed against her. The Church, in inviting us to consecrate ourselves to her Immaculate Heart, implicitly calls upon us for this reparation. But more explicitly, and even before Fatima, Saint Pius X offered a plenary indulgence to all who on the first Saturday of the month would observe special devotions in honor of the Immaculate Virgin in a spirit of reparation for the blasphemies uttered against her.[22]

There is, however, an even more basic reason why each one of us owes reparation to the Immaculate Heart of Mary: every sin of ours caused grief and suffering to her in union with her divine Son. For sin was the cause of that terrible day on Calvary when she, as the New Eve, shared in the torment of the great sacrifice, and, amidst indescribable pain, brought forth spiritually all the members of the Mystical Body of her divine Son. *God willed that Mary should be intimately associated with His Son in bearing the burden of all sin; surely then, her Immaculate Heart, in union with His divine Heart, should receive reparation from us who have caused them such pain.* If anyone causes hurt to even a very ordinary human being, he does not overlook the need to make amends. How much more do we owe to the Hearts of Jesus and Mary! [23]

Early in this chapter we warned against reducing devotion to these two Hearts to mere sentimentality. That is a real danger. Sentimentality is only a caricature of real warmth. But we do insist that this devotion to the Hearts of Jesus and Mary should be marked by a genuine, a solid warmth, not necessarily emotional. In the Gospels Our Lord went to great lengths to prove His enormous love and mercy for us, but not all men have learned those lessons. Hence, through St. Margaret Mary,[24] He has re-taught and re-emphasized the lessons that men should have learned from the Gospels — the burning love and wonderful mercy of His Heart. He wants men to have great confidence in that love and mercy, for confidence is a special characteristic of the warmest love, and greatly promotes it.[25] Devotion to the Sacred Heart is really a devotion to His Love. The association of the Heart of His Mother with His own Heart is intended to lead us more effectively to know and love Him. For her Heart is like His — He created it. And His Heart is like Hers — she formed it. In knowing the one, we come to know the other better. Here, then, is a great means to growth in confident love.

It is natural to keep these two Hearts together in our devotion.

For how can anyone think he really loves the Son who neglects the Mother? They who wish to practice devotion to the Sacred Heart of Jesus in its best form can do no better than imitate the method taught by Our Lord Himself to St. Margaret Mary, the method of a complete consecration offered to Him through the hands of His Mother, a consecration bringing with it a burning zeal for reparation to the Hearts of both Jesus and Mary.

NOTES

1. See *AAS* 1:480.

2. *Miserentissimus Redemptor* (May 8, 1928), *AAS* 20:165–78.

3. *Autobiography of St. Margaret Mary*, trans. Sisters of the Visitation (Walmer Kent, England, 1930).

4. *AAS* 20:167–68.

5. *AAS* 20:169.

6. English text in *AAS* 20:184.

7. In 1928, before Atheistic Communism had swallowed one-third of the world. Yet he used obviously apocalyptic language, saying that the evils of that time brought to mind the Scriptural "beginnings of sorrows" which "the man of sin" is to bring (*AAS* 20:175).

8. *AAS* 20:176.

9. In the conclusion of the encyclical and in the official prayer of reparation (*AAS* 20:178 and 185).

10. *Autobiography*, §84 (p. 97).

11. *Ibid.*, §22 (p. 39).

12. The relation of slavery to childhood is explained more fully in chap. XVIII.

13. *Autobiography*, §60 (pp. 73–74).

14. *Ibid.*, §106 (p. 119).

15. Quoted in P. O'Connell, *The Devotion to the Sacred Heart of Jesus*, (Washington, National Center of the Enthronement, 1951), pp. 119–20. See pp. 100–1. See also F. L. Gauthey, *Vie et Oeuvres de Sainte Marguerite-Marie Alacoque* (Paris, 1920), II, 771, 781–82.

16. On devotion to the Immaculate Heart of Mary, see J. F. Murphy, *Mary's Immaculate Heart* (Milwaukee, 1951).

17. *AAS* 34:318.

18. *AAS* 34:318–19. The Holy Father had in mind the consecration made by Pope Leo XIII, as the footnote on p. 319 of *AAS* 34 makes clear. On the parallel, see also *AAS* 37:50.

19. See *AAS* 37:50.

20. See the indulgenced form of consecration given us by Pope Pius XII in *AAS* 34:345–46.

21. On reparation to the Immaculate Heart of Mary, see T. M. Sparks, O.P., "Reparation to the Immaculate Heart of Mary," *From an Abundant Spring*, The Walter Farrell Memorial Volume of *The Thomist*, pp. 39–56.

22. June 13, 1913; *AAS* 4:623. Confession, Holy Communion, and prayers for the intention of the Holy Father are also required in order to gain the indulgence. It is still in force.

23. In speaking of the need of employing the intercession of Mary in every prayer (in chap. VIII), we stated that every prayer rightly made contains at least an implicit invocation of Mary, since the one who prays well intends at least implicitly to do so according to the economy of salvation established by God. Similarly, anyone who offers reparation for sin, offers reparation at least implicitly to the Heart of Mary itself in union with the Heart of Jesus, for his fundamental intention is to make his offering according to the will of God.

24. The same lesson is re-emphasized in other seemingly genuine apparitions since the day of St. Margaret Mary, esp. in those to Sister Josefa Menéndez, recorded in *The Way of Divine Love* (Westminster, 1950). As to the authenticity of the revelations to Sister Josefa, see note 8, chap. XXI.

25. See the excellent meditation book, Paul de Jaegher, S.J., *The Virtue of Trust* (New York, 1932). See also Sister Josefa Menéndez, *Christ's Appeal for Love*, trans. L. Keppel (Westminster, 1951), esp. pp. 112–16.

XXI . . . *Marian Visions and Revelations*

Dᴜʀɪɴɢ ᴛʜᴇ ᴘᴀsᴛ ᴄᴇɴᴛᴜʀʏ devotion to the Blessed Mother has, by Divine Providence, received fresh impetus from the appearance of Mary herself at a number of places where world-famous shrines have since been erected. The Church has not only approved the accounts of the apparitions, but has shown signal favors to some of these shrines. The most notable honors and privileges have been extended, not only by individual bishops, but even by the Holy See itself to the shrines of Lourdes and Fatima. Pope Pius XI raised the shrine at Lourdes to the dignity of a minor basilica and, through his legate, placed a crown on the statue of Mary there. Pope Leo XIII established a new feast for the Lourdes apparition, and Saint Pius X extended the feast to the universal Church.[1] Although the Fatima apparitions are relatively recent, Pope Pius XII sent a legate to Fatima to place a crown on its statue on May 13, 1946. At the same time, he himself spoke via the Vatican Radio to the crowds assembled there. On September 24, 1951, the same Holy Father sent a letter to Cardinal Tedeschini, appointing him as his personal representative at the special Holy Year solemnities to be held on October 13 at Fatima. In this letter he said:

> We . . . from the first years of our Pontificate, have again and again urged the good faithful of Portugal and the other regions of the earth to go with ever greater confidence and more ardent prayer to the famed image [which] five years ago we decreed should be crowned in a solemn rite. . . .[2]

On the day of the celebration, which was the anniversary of the last of the Fatima apparitions, the Pope again spoke to the pilgrims at Fatima over the Vatican Radio.[3]

But since in certain other places there have been false reports of apparitions, which the Church has either condemned or at least refused to approve, and since much harm has come to souls through misunderstanding of the proper role of visions and revelations in the spiritual life, let us review the fundamental theological principles on private revelations and apparitions.

At the outset we should note that there is a difference between public and private revelation. Public revelation is that which is contained in Scripture and Tradition, and it ceased with the death of the last of the twelve Apostles. As a result, all revelations since that time are considered private, since they do not form a part of the general deposit of the truths of faith. Private revelations, hence, will not supply us with any information or directives that will alter or contradict what is found in public revelation. All the means that we need for salvation are contained in public revelation. Some private revelations of our own times, such as those of Fatima, are directed to all Christians, not only to one individual; still they are technically called private, to distinguish them from that revelation which closed with the death of St. John.

Now although private revelations, if declared genuine by lawful authority, may prove very helpful to the spiritual growth of the original recipient, and may even help to rouse those who merely hear of them, yet we must always keep in mind that visions and revelations are only *means* to an end. They are not the *proximate* means of union with God in this life: the proximate means are faith, hope, and love. In fact, it is not merely possible, but it actually does happen at times, that even the original recipient may fail to profit as he should from private revelations. For, as we have said, growth in holiness is growth in sanctifying grace, in love of God. A person may have received many extraordinary favors, and even the gifts of miracles and prophecy, and yet he may not only not grow, but may even be lost eternally. This is a shocking thought, but Our Lord Himself tells us:

> Many will say to me in that day: Lord, Lord, have we not prophesied in thy name, and cast out devils in thy name, and

worked many miracles in thy name? And then will I profess unto them: I never knew you: depart from me, you that work iniquity.[4]

It is true that ordinarily God gives these extraordinary favors only to very holy persons, but it is not always so, and we dare not make light of the warning from the lips of Our Lord Himself.

St. John of the Cross, a Doctor of the Church and one of the greatest of the mystic theologians, is very severe with persons who desire to be the recipients of visions and revelations.[5] St. John never wearies of repeating that the proximate means of union with God in this life are the three theological virtues of faith, hope, and love. True growth consists in intensified love, which is founded on faith and hope. Now although St. John encourages everyone to aim at infused contemplation (even though relatively few will attain it), he strongly reproves anyone who desires to be the recipient of a vision or revelation. The great St. Teresa of Avila, who herself was deluged with visions, takes a similar stand. She admits that great profit can be had from such things when they are genuine and are received in the proper spirit. Yet she says:

> I will only warn you that, when you learn or hear that God is granting souls these graces, you must never beseech or desire Him to lead you along this road. Even if you think it is a very good one, and to be greatly prized and reverenced, there are certain reasons why such a course is not wise.[6]

She then goes on at length to explain her reasons: First, such a desire shows a lack of humility, in asking for what one cannot have deserved; Second, one thereby leaves himself open to "great peril because the devil has only to see a door left slightly ajar to enter"; Third, the danger of auto-suggestion: "When a person has a great desire for something, he persuades himself that he is seeing or hearing what he desires. . . ."; Fourth, it is presumption for one to want to choose his own path, as only the Lord knows which path is best for us; Fifth, very heavy trials usually go with these favors: could we be sure of being able to bear them? Sixth, "you may well find that the very thing from which you had expected gain will bring you loss." She adds that there are also other reasons, and continues with some very salutary advice to the effect that one can become very holy without this sort of thing:

> There are many saintly people who have never known what it is to receive a favour of this kind, and there are others who receive such favours, although they are not saintly.

In fact, she says, one may even merit more without them in some cases:

> It is true that to have these favours must be the greatest help towards attaining a high degree of perfection in the virtues; but anyone who has attained the virtues at the cost of his own toil has earned much more merit.[7]

We are forced to think again of St. Thérèse of Lisieux: her life was almost totally lacking in such extraordinary favors, so much so that even dryness was usual for her. Yet she rose to untold heights of sanctity.

The dangers of diabolic interference of which St. Teresa of Avila speaks are very grave. Many cases are on record in which the devil appeared in the guise of Our Lord, and even gave true prophecies and urged people on to virtue. The devil is willing to tolerate some real good, so long as he has hope of accomplishing greater evil out of the affair in the long run. To distinguish a vision of divine origin from one that is diabolic is extremely difficult. Even skilled theologians may err in this matter. A large number of cases of alleged visions are probably diabolic.

In view of such dangers, especially the danger of diabolic interference, some who were favored with visions have prayed that God might lead them by the merely normal path, without such extraordinary means. Even in the case of a series of apparitions which have been declared authentic by the proper authorities, some error or diabolic influence may easily creep in. And the visionary himself may, and often does, misinterpret (involuntarily) or interpolate something merely human into the divine message. Thus St. Joan of Arc in prison heard a voice promising her deliverance through a great victory. She thought it meant her release from custody, but the outcome shows it really meant her martyrdom. A very holy Sacred Heart religious, Sister Josefa Menéndez (who died in 1923), had many visions that seem to have been genuine, yet she also frequently experienced attempted diabolic counterfeits.[8]

Because of these facts, the great theologians and saints teach that the visionary himself must not take any great account of or accept any visions or revelations until he has submitted the whole matter to the proper authorities, and first of all to his spiritual director, who should know the proper mode of handling such developments. He must not even carry out any orders given to him in a vision unless the director approves. This was the principle followed by St. Teresa, who had so much experience in visions, and whose spiritual directors included several canonized saints. When she was told in a vision to found a stricter Carmelite community of nuns, she went ahead only after submitting the project to four advisers.[9] The director must examine any such orders in the light of sound theology and reason. Even though Our Lord Himself is appearing to someone, He will not object to this method; in fact, it is the method that He wishes to have followed. This truth is forcefully shown in the *Autobiography* of St. Margaret Mary. Her superior had ordered her not to do some of the things that Our Lord wished. Much troubled, the saint asked Him what she should do, and received this reply:

> Therefore not only do I desire that thou shouldst do what thy Superiors command, but also that thou shouldst do nothing of all that I order thee without their consent. I love obedience, and without it no one can please Me.[10]

It may seem shocking to some that Our Lord Himself wishes an earthly superior to be obeyed in preference to what He Himself commands in a vision. But there is good reason: the authority of the superior comes from Him. Further, if He were to lay down a rule that one should disobey the superior because of a vision, all sorts of false visionaries could claim such authorizations and create endless disorder by what they might think were divine commands directly received. On still another occasion, Our Lord gave this additional teaching to St. Margaret Mary:

> But listen, My daughter, believe not lightly and trust not every spirit, for Satan is enraged and will seek to deceive thee. Therefore do nothing without the approval of those who guide thee; being thus under the authority of obedience, his efforts against thee will be in vain, for he has no power over the obedient.[11]

The implication is clear: those who wish to trust to their own resources and not depend on obedience are such as the devil *does* have power to harm. Hence one is perfectly safe in following the orders of proper authority, even in contradiction to an order given in a vision, while one not acting under obedience is guilty of exposing himself without cause to diabolical deception.

How do these principles apply to those who merely hear of visions, and are not the actual recipients? It is obvious that we must always keep in mind the true place of visions — that although they may be helpful, they are not of the essence of the spiritual life; they are not the proximate means of union with God, and they do not necessarily make us holy. St. John of the Cross warns us that attachments to such things will actually hinder our spiritual progress. In fact, he adds that if our spiritual director seems fond of visions, we ought to give him up! [12]

The danger of diabolic illusion is not only possible, but rather common. This diabolic influence may creep even into a genuine group of visions. Moreover, the seer himself, through no fault of his own, may misunderstand or misinterpret his visions, or even interpolate merely human considerations. This is not at all rare in the history of spirituality. And any prophecies made in these revelations are by their very nature understood to be *conditional*, even though no condition be expressed. Thus, St. Vincent Ferrer went about working miracles and proclaiming that the Last Judgment was near — a conditional prophecy whose realization was averted precisely by the reformation effected through his preaching.[13]

Hence it is clear that our attitude to private revelations must be marked by great caution. Above all, we should adhere closely to whatever directives the authorities of the Church give in any particular case, never daring to act contrary to them. This is true even if we should think that we have better than the usual hearsay reports on an alleged revelation. It is true that the local bishop is not infallible. But let us remember what Our Lord told St. Margaret Mary: "I love obedience, and without it no one can please Me." Even if the Bishop in charge should make a mistake and reject a true vision, we, in following him, are guided by obedience, without which no one can please God.

Before the decision of the Church is announced in the case of an alleged revelation, reports on it are often widely circulated. Provided that such reports are printed with ecclesiastical approval, one may read them. Some persons find that reading such accounts stimulates their devotion. This may be true, but great care is needed to avoid vain curiosity and attachment (recall the principles of chapter XV on attachment). Such persons must be careful not to let their spiritual lives center about private revelations, and must diligently preserve an attitude of submission to the ecclesiastical authorities, for pride in one's own judgment in these cases can easily lead to contempt for authority.

If the content of the alleged revelations consists largely of thoughts on basic truths of faith, as in the revelations given to Sister Josefa (mentioned above), then a book containing these revelations may be very helpful for meditation, but its value will be independent of the authenticity of the alleged revelations.

What is the force of the Church's approval of a private revelation? Such an approval is no more than a declaration that the private revelations are not contrary to public revelation, and that they may be proposed as credible to the pious belief of the faithful. Thus we see that the Church does not give us an absolute guarantee of the divine origin of any private revelation. Even in those approved by the Church, some error (non-heretical) may have crept in because the visionary misunderstood or misinterpreted it or even, unconsciously, embroidered the facts.[14]

Is the acceptance of a private revelation an act of divine faith by which we (who are not the recipients of the vision, but merely those who hear of it) adhere to the truth on the authority of God, as we do in our belief in the Creed? All the theologians answer No: our acceptance is only an act of *human* faith by which we consider these revelations worthy of pious credence. It is not an act of the divine virtue of faith. This is the case even when the Church has approved a private revelation. Hence we can see what is to be thought of those who wish to accept every alleged revelation before the Church decides, and who censure those who wait as lacking in faith! Even after approval these private revelations are not an object of divine faith for those who are not the immediate recipients of the vision, and even if they could become the objects of divine faith for us, we would still have to wait until we were sure that God had really spoken. It is begging the question to ask us to believe that something is true because God has spoken when the prime question is still *whether* He has spoken at all. Theologians dispute about the status of the recipient himself: some hold that he does make an act of divine faith; others (more probably rightly), that his adherence to the revelation is based on a *prophetic light* granted at the time, not on the virtue of faith. Therefore when the light disappears, as it normally does, even the recipient is left with only a moral certitude.[15]

To sum up, then, we must employ great caution in regard to any alleged private revelations, and cling closely to the guidance of the authorities of the Church. Even in the case of revelations that have been approved by the Church, we must diligently shun attachment, and not allow our spiritual lives to be centered about these things. To gain the greatest graces from these means, we must take care not to stop short at the exterior elements of a vision or revelation: we should use these outward elements only insofar as they aid us to amend our lives and to rise to meditation on spiritual things and to union with God and His Blessed Mother.[16]

We have dwelt at some length on the dangers of visions and revelations because so many Catholics today have misunderstood the proper role of these means in the spiritual life. For some make the major part of their devotion to Mary consist in recounting the stories of visions. Such persons are often not content with those visions that have been approved by the Church, but practically demand that we accept every unproved report before the proper authorities have issued any decision at all, and censure those who are reluctant as lacking in faith. Others go so far as contempt for the authorities of the Church, and even when an official condemnation has been issued in a particular case, they will complain, not too quietly, that the bishop is not infallible, that time will show who is right!

On the other hand, through the right attitude we can derive great value from the messages given to us by Our Lady in such genuine apparitions as those at Lourdes and Fatima. What has been her theme there? It is a restatement of the Gospel call: Repent and do penance. If we were to gather together the principal requests she has made, we would find that she asks for penance, for consecration and reparation to her Immaculate Heart and to the Sacred Heart of her Son, for the recitation of the Rosary and the wearing of the Brown Scapular.[17]

The call to penance is basic. Fundamentally, it means that we are asked to keep God's law, and to perform well the duties of our state in life, making good use of the providentially sent opportunities for mortification that come to each of us in his own state.[18] To these, each one, according to his own generosity and ability, will add other self-imposed penances.

Devotion to the Immaculate Heart of Mary did not begin at Fatima, though it received special impetus from the requests which she made there for consecration and reparation. Consecration, if properly understood, is a total dedication to the service of Jesus through Mary. The most complete form of consecration to the Immaculate Heart of Mary is that which we have already examined in chapter XVIII. Reparation to the Sacred Heart of Jesus and the Immaculate Heart of Mary is a duty that is already demanded of us by our very consecration, and the request of Our Lady makes the call still more urgent.[19] To encourage souls in the practice of reparation to his Sacred Heart, Our Lord gave us the great First Friday promise through St. Margaret Mary. According to Sister Lucia, sole survivor of the Fatima children, our Blessed Mother has made a similar pledge, saying:

> I promise to assist at the hour of death with the grace necessary for salvation all those who, with the intention of making reparation to me, will, on the first Saturday of five consecutive months, go to confession, receive Holy Communion, say five decades of the beads, and keep me company for fifteen minutes while meditating on the fifteen mysteries of the rosary.[20]

The Bishop of Leiria, in whose diocese Fatima is situated, published this promise on September 13, 1939.[21]

As to the Rosary and the Brown Scapular, which we shall treat in the next chapter: the one is among the most excellent of all private prayers, and the other, an outward badge of the consecration requested by the Blessed Mother.

If then Our Lady's apparitions stimulate us to carry out this worth-while program, we shall find ourselves growing greatly in love for her divine Son and for her, for if we would carry out these requests in the fullest sense, we will be led to utilize all the interior means that have been suggested in the preceding chapters.

At Lourdes and Fatima the principle, "To Jesus through Mary," is clearly followed, for there we find the highest honor paid to Jesus through Mary. There Mary says again: "Whatsoever he shall say to you, do ye," [22] while He Himself, hidden beneath the sacramental veils, goes about at her prayer to heal sick bodies, and, even more, sick souls.

NOTES

1. Officially recorded in the historical lessons for Matins on the feast of February 11.

2. *AAS* 43:780–81.

3. The text is in *AAS* 43:800–2.

4. Matt. 7:22–23.

5. See Gabriel of St. Mary Magdalen, *Visions and Revelations in the Spiritual Life*, trans. by a Benedictine of Stanbrook Abbey (Westminster, 1950); and Garrigou-Lagrange, *The Three Ages of the Interior Life*, II, 575–88; and Poulain, *The Graces of Interior Prayer*, pp. 299–399.

6. St. Teresa of Avila, *Interior Castle* VI, 9 (II, 319).

7. *Ibid.*, p. 320.

8. See Sister M. Josefa Menéndez, *The Way of Divine Love*. Before his election Pope Pius XII wrote a letter warmly recommending this book as suitable to promote the love of the Sacred Heart, and he has given permission for the same letter to be printed in the present edition. The letter does not, however, constitute a declaration that all her alleged visions are authentic and divine. See chap. XX, n. 24.

9. See her *Autobiography*, 32.

10. *Autobiography of St. Margaret Mary*, §47, p. 62.

11. *Autobiography* §57 (p. 71).

12. See Gabriel of St. Mary Magdalen, *op. cit.*, esp. pp. 90–94, 98.

13. See Tanquerey, *The Spiritual Life*, § 1507 (p. 708).

14. We can now see another reason for prizing Holy Scripture so highly. Since it was written under the inspiration of the Holy Spirit, the dangers of error which threaten private revelations are excluded from it. And, in interpreting it, the Church does more for us, for she gives us infallible interpretations of the public revelation contained in Scripture and Tradition.

15. See Garrigou-Lagrange, *op. cit.*, II, 581.

16. Recall the treatment on attachments and the proper use of created things in chap. XV.

17. See J. A. Pelletier, A.A., *The Sun Danced at Fátima* (Worcester, 1951), pp. 131–36, 163.

18. It is reported that Our Lord Himself gave this interpretation of the call of penance to Sister Lucia. See Roger M. Charest, S.M.M., "Montfort et Fatima," *Marie* (Nicolet, P.Q., September–October, 1952), p. 91.

19. See chaps. XIV and XX on reparation to Mary, and chap. XVIII on consecration to her.

20. Quoted in Pelletier, *op. cit.*, pp. 135. The apparition took place on December 10, 1925. Our Lady had foretold in the earlier apparitions that she would come to ask for First Saturday Holy Communions.

21. See Pelletier, *op. cit.*, pp. 135–36. In a document published with the Imprimatur of the Bishop of Leiria on September 21, 1939, it is explained that the confession may be made within eight days before or after the First Saturday (provided that Holy Communion is received in the state of grace), and that the meditation may be on one or several mysteries, or even on all taken together or separately.

22. John 2:5.

XXII... *Special Devotions in Honor of Mary*

THE EXTERNAL FORMS of devotions that have been devised by the Church and her children to show their love and interior devotion to Mary are so varied, so numerous that merely to list all would require the space of a long chapter.[1] Let us mention merely the chief types and classes.

As we have already seen,[2] Mary's name is put before us many times in the Ordinary of every Mass, not to mention the variable seasonal prayers that regularly include a special invocation of Mary. The calendar of the universal Church includes at present eighteen feasts that are celebrated everywhere, besides an even larger number of feasts that are observed in certain nations, dioceses, or religious orders. In addition, every Saturday is specially dedicated to her honor, and plenary indulgences are offered to arouse special devotion on the first Saturday of each month. The large Divine Office parallels the Mass in its remembrances of Mary and her feasts; and the Little Office is hers in a special way.

Many religious orders, congregations, and societies were either founded expressly for her honor, or are in other ways dedicated to Mary. We must add to these the several confraternities and sodalities, and the Legion of Mary. To various groups belong a large number of Marian scapulars and special medals.

Then there are the special prayers and devotional exercises of a nonliturgical character, such as the Litany of Loreto, the *Memorare,* the *Angelus,* the many Marian hymns, the varied novenas.

Finally, throughout the world there are countless basilicas, churches, chapels, and shrines in her honor. At some of these she herself has appeared to chosen souls.

No matter which of these many forms of devotion we should

select for special consideration, we would be forced by the sheer immensity of the task to omit many of considerable importance. Wherefore, let us single out two of the most important devotions: the Rosary and the Brown Scapular of Our Lady of Mount Carmel. These are among the most universally loved and most valuable devotional practices because of their eminent intrinsic worth. But today we find additional reason for cultivating them in the requests that Our Lady made in such apparitions as those of Lourdes and Fatima. When Lucia at Fatima asked Our Lady who she was, she is reported to have said: "I am the Lady of the Rosary. Continue to say the Rosary every day." [3]

The Rosary

Although certain devotional practices of reciting many *Aves,* and even counting devices of beads were known before the time of St. Dominic, yet it seems clear that we ought to consider him as the author of the Rosary.[4] Many Popes have given this title to St. Dominic, even though they have not presented their statements as a teaching to be imposed authoritatively on the universal Church.[5] For it seems clear that, under the inspiration of Mary, he was accustomed to go into the villages and preach long series of sermons on the mysteries of salvation, during which, in order to implore heavenly aid, and to provide a respite for his hearers, he interrupted his discourse at suitable points, and had his hearers recite some *Paters* and *Aves.*[6] From this practice our present devotion of the Rosary evolved.

St. Dominic was surely led and aided in this work by the interior promptings and graces that Mary obtained for him. But some writers think that she also appeared to him and gave him the Rosary. In the writings of a fifteenth-century Dominican, Alan de la Roche (died 1475) we find this account. It was the year A.D. 1206. St. Dominic had been laboring with great diligence for the previous three years, preaching, disputing, and writing against the Albigensian heresy, but had reaped little fruit from his efforts. Accordingly, he went to a forest at Prouille, and there, giving himself over to many prayers and severe penances, begged for the help of the Queen of Heaven. On the third day Mary appeared to him, praising him for his valiant fight against the heretics, and announcing that she had come to bring him help. She then gave him the Rosary as a mighty weapon, explained its use and efficacy, and told him to go to Toulouse and preach it to others. St. Dominic went as he had been directed, and, with the support of miracles, taught the Rosary with great success.

Many scholars today, including some Dominicans, either reject or seriously question the authenticity of the alleged apparition. The Holy See has shown some signs of favor to it, but has not given any real decision.[7]

But the nature of the Rosary is such that its value does not at all depend on whether or not we accept the story of the Prouille apparition. We can see the unique importance of the Rosary in two ways: by examining the inner source of its power, and by considering the wonderful favors which have been obtained by its use in the past, and which still come to souls today.

The essential prayers of the Rosary are the *Our Father* and the *Hail Mary*, accompanied by some form of meditation on the mysteries of our Redemption. Many saints and scholars have given us lengthy and beautiful commentaries on the beauty of the *Our Father*, but for our purpose, in order to see its great power, we need only to recall that it is a prayer composed by Our Lord Himself. No further recommendation is needed; that fact alone establishes its great power to please the heart of the Father.

The *Hail Mary* contains two parts, the first of which is drawn from inspired Scripture. It opens with the words of the Archangel Gabriel to Mary, and the words of Elizabeth, who, as Scripture tells us,[8] was at that time filled with the Holy Spirit. The second part of the *Hail Mary* is of ecclesiastical origin. It developed chiefly in the fourteenth and fifteenth centuries, though the form was then somewhat fluid, and was not fixed until 1568, when Pope St. Pius V ordered the present form to be used in the Breviary.[9]

As to meditation on the mysteries, it is clear from the principles given in chapter XII that meditation is one of the highest forms of prayer. It is likewise obvious that the meditation accompanying the mysteries may gradually become simplified, tending towards contemplation. The practice of meditating while saying the *Paters* and *Aves* is very conducive to simplification.

The *Apostles' Creed* and the *Gloria Patri* — certainly excellent prayers — are added only by pious custom, and are not required for the essence of the Rosary.

It is reported that at Fatima Our Lady asked that we add to the end of each decade the following invocation: "O my Jesus, pardon us, and save us from the fire of hell; draw all souls to heaven, especially those in most need." [10] This prayer does not, of course, belong to the essence of the Rosary, but its use is to be encouraged in accordance with Our Lady's request. Some have expressed fear that the insertion of this prayer would nullify the indulgences of the Rosary. The reason for this fear is a provision in Canon Law,[11] according to which indulgences attached to any prayer are lost if there is any addition, subtraction, or interpolation. A decree of the Sacred Penitentiary issued in 1934[12] has made clear, however, that only such additions are forbidden as would alter the substance of the prayer. It hardly seems that the addition of this prayer in any way alters the substance of the Rosary, especially since we are told that it was requested by Our Lady herself.

Since, then, the prayers of the Rosary come from such excellent sources — from Our Lord Himself, from inspired Scripture, and from the Church — it is not surprising that the Rosary is so dear to our Blessed Mother and so powerful with heaven.

If we consider the power of the Rosary as seen in its effects, we find a great abundance of proofs of its wonderful value. Many are the favors granted to private individuals through its devout recitation: there are few devoted users of the Rosary who cannot testify to experiencing its power in their own lives. If we turn to history, we see many great triumphs of the Rosary. Early tradition (the question of its authenticity is, of course, intertwined with the question of St. Dominic's role) attributes the defeat of the Albigensians at the Battle of Muret in 1213 to the Rosary. But even those who do not accept this tradition will admit that St. Pius V attributed the great defeat of the Turkish fleet on the first Sunday of October, 1571, to the fact that at the same time the Rosary confraternities at Rome and elsewhere were holding their processions. Accordingly, he ordered a commemoration of the Rosary to be made on that day. Two years later, Gregory XIII allowed the celebration of a feast of the Rosary in churches having an altar dedicated to the Rosary. In 1671, Clement X extended the feast to all Spain. A second great victory over the Turks, who once, like the Russians, threatened the ruin of Christian civilization, occurred on August 5, 1716, when Prince Eugene defeated them at Peterwardein in Hungary. Thereupon Clement XI extended the feast of the Rosary to the whole Church.

Today, when dangers far greater than those of the ancient Turks threaten not only Christianity but all civilization, we are urged by our Blessed Mother to turn again to the Rosary for help. If men in sufficient numbers do this, and at the same time carry out the other conditions that she has laid down (which we saw in the preceding chapter), we have the greater reason for confidence that we will be delivered from our dangers.

The most difficult problem about the Rosary is not the question of the Prouille apparition: it is the practical question of how to meditate while reciting the *Paters* and *Aves*. The objection is sometimes raised that one cannot do two things at a time: meditate, and continue saying the *Paters* and *Aves*. A moment's reflection is sufficient to show the emptiness of this objection: do we not at times, voluntarily or involuntarily, allow our mind to run on various subjects while reciting vocal prayers? Our very distractions prove the possibility of this meditation.

Actually we are not required to pay attention to the sense of each word in the *Paters* and *Aves,* and, at the same time, keep a meditation going. To give full attention to both would be psychologically impossible. Nor is it required that we keep some consciousness of the words in the background,[13] as it were, while our thoughts are focused on the meditation. As St. Thomas tells us,[14] there are three kinds of attention possible in the recitation of vocal prayers. The first kind of attention is called verbal; in this we take care that we do not omit or mispronounce any of the words. The second is called literal attention, in which we attend to the meaning of the words. Beyond these there is a third, a higher form of attention, called spiritual. In it we leave aside the literal meaning to rise to the thought of some particular mystery or to praise and bless God. This third form may rise even to the point of contemplation, as it did for a certain nun of whom St. Teresa of Avila speaks.[15] Therefore, when we pay attention to thoughts on the mysteries of our salvation while we are reciting the vocal prayers of the Rosary, we are employing a very high form of attention. Speaking of the ordinary level of meditative attention to the Rosary, Garrigou-Lagrange writes:

> The words are a kind of melody which soothes the ear and isolates us from the noise of the world around us, the fingers being occupied meanwhile in allowing one bead after another to slip through. Thus the imagination is kept tranquil and the mind and will are set free to be united to God.[16]

Nor should we forget that, in virtue of our general intention of making a prayer, the very words of the *Paters* and *Aves* really are valid prayers of praise and petition even when we are not paying direct attention to the words.[17]

Many methods have been devised for carrying on the meditation while saying the vocal prayers. Some persons try to visualize the scenes of the mysteries in stages — that is, imagining the action as progressing a step at each bead.[18] Others prefer to use only one mental picture for an entire decade: while keeping it before their mind, they imagine they see Mary, and offer to her sentiments appropriate to the decade. For although material things can be given but once, and no more, spiritual things can be given over and over again. We can, then, offer to Mary over and over again the joy she felt at the Annunciation, adding our congratulations and thanks. In the sorrowful mysteries we can offer our regrets for the pain we caused her Son and her by our sins, which are the cause of those dolorous scenes.

Still others will be able to use a discursive style of meditation, such as was described in chapter XII.

Finally (though we have by no means exhausted the list of possible methods) a very simple form of gaze at Jesus may be employed by those who are more advanced. Garrigou-Lagrange describes it thus:

> A more simple and still more elevated way of reciting the Rosary is, while saying it, to keep the eyes of faith fixed on the living Jesus Who is always making intercession for us, and Who is acting upon us in accordance with the mysteries of His childhood, or His Passion, or His glory. He comes to us to make us like Himself. Let us fix our gaze on Jesus Who is looking at us. His look is more than kind and understanding: it is the look of God, a look which purifies, which sanctifies, which gives peace. It is the look of our Judge and still more the look of our Saviour, our Friend, the Spouse of our souls. A Rosary said in this way, in solitude and silence, is a most fruitful intercourse with Jesus. It is a conversation with Mary too which leads to intimacy with her Son.[19]

The Scapular

Just as the Rosary holds an eminent place among the various forms of prayer to Mary, so also, although there are many different Scapulars, the Brown Scapular of Our Lady of Mount Carmel holds a most special position. The other Scapulars are excellent in various ways, but to none of them are such extraordinary promises attached as to the Brown Scapular, nor have any of them received such outstanding signs of favor from the Holy See. Hence it is that when good Catholic laymen refer simply to "the Scapular" without any further qualification, it is ordinarily this Scapular that they have in mind.

The Brown Scapular has its origin in a vision. In the year A.D. 1251, when the Carmelite Order, newly transplanted to England, was meeting with many difficulties, St. Simon Stock, the Prior

General, prayed earnestly to Mary for help. In an early Carmelite Catalog of the Saints, we find the following account of the apparition:

> The ninth was St. Simon of England, the sixth General of the Order. He constantly begged the most glorious Mother of God to fortify the Carmelite Order, which enjoys the special title of the Virgin, with some privilege. He prayed most devoutly: "Flower of Carmel, Flowering Vine, Splendor of Heaven, Singular Virgin and Mother, Mother Mild, who knew not man, grant privileges to the Carmelites, Star of the Sea." To him did the Blessed Virgin appear with a multitude of angels, holding the Scapular of the Order in her blessed hands, and saying: "This will be a privilege for you and for all Carmelites, that he who dies in this will not suffer eternal fire," that is, he who dies in this will be saved.[20]

The historical evidence for the authenticity of this vision, as shown by the recent researches of Father Xiberta, O.Carm., is impressive indeed: it gives us at least some degree of moral certitude on the fact of this apparition.[21] But we are not forced to depend merely on such studies, for many Popes have shown the highest favor to this Scapular, enriching it with many indulgences, and exhorting us to wear it. Out of the many papal statements on this Scapular, let us quote but one passage from a letter of Pope Pius XII written to the major Superiors of the Carmelites for the celebration of the 700th anniversary of the appearance of Mary to St. Simon Stock:

> There is no one who is not aware how greatly a love for the Blessed Virgin Mother of God contributes to the enlivening of the Catholic faith. . . . In the first rank of the most favored of these devotions that of the Holy Carmelite Scapular must be placed. . . . Therefore it has pleased Us greatly to learn of the decision of our Carmelite Brethren . . . to take all pains to pay homage to the Blessed Virgin Mary in as solemn a manner as possible on the occasion of the Seventh Centenary of the Institution of the Scapular. . . . Prompted therefore by our constant

love for the tender Mother of God, and mindful also of Our own Enrollment from boyhood in the Confraternity of this same Scapular, most willingly do We commend so pious an undertaking. . . . For not with a light or passing matter are we here concerned but with the obtaining of eternal life itself which is the substance of the Promise of the Most Blessed Virgin which has been handed down to us. We are concerned, namely, with that which is of supreme importance to all and with the manner of achieving it safely.[22]

One of the principal problems concerning the Scapular is the question of the proper interpretation of the great promise given through St. Simon Stock. In it our Blessed Mother promises that all Carmelites who die while wearing it "will not suffer eternal fire." It is clear that to gain this promise one must, at least in some way, be affiliated with the Order of Carmel; for most Catholics, this is accomplished through enrollment in the Confraternity of the Scapular. But once enrolled, will a person who dies while wearing this Scapular surely be saved?

In answering this question two extremes are to be avoided. One is that of superstition, by which we would trust that a man who persists in sinning presumptuously would be saved if he wore his Scapular at the moment of death. The opposite extreme is to make such demands, in an effort to avoid the superstitious extreme, that the promise of Our Lady would become meaningless. It is true that the words of the promise seem to demand (in addition to enrollment) nothing other than that one be wearing the Scapular at the moment of death. Pope Benedict XIV, however, points out wisely that Holy Scripture also contains many promises that seem to demand only one condition; e.g., St. Paul in Rom. 3:28 seems to promise salvation for faith alone, while in Rom. 8:24 he says that "we are saved by hope," and Tobias 12:9 states that it is almsgiving that saves a man from eternal death.[23] It is obvious, Benedict XIV says, that other conditions are presupposed. Precisely what, then, is required in order that one may obtain the Scapular Promise? Kilian Lynch, Prior General of the Carmelites of the Ancient Observance, puts it thus:

How much good will is required to gain the promise of the scapular? Eternity alone will answer this question, for we should be careful not to place limits upon the mercy of her who is the refuge of sinners and the Mother of mercy. . . . In this age of measurements, we should beware of attempting to reduce at least our Blessed Mother's love for sinners to fixed formulas.[24]

Pope Pius XII, in the letter from which we have quoted above, supplies this guidance. On the one hand he insists that we have a right to trust greatly in the promise of Mary:

For not with a light or passing matter are we here concerned but with the obtaining of eternal life itself which is the substance of that promise of the Most Blessed Virgin which has been handed down to us. We are concerned, namely, with . . . the manner of achieving it *safely*. For the Holy Scapular, which may be called the Habit or Garment of Mary, is a sign and a pledge of the protection of the Mother of God. [*Emphasis added.*]

But then he continues, adding a warning against presumption:

But not for this reason, however, may they who wear the Scapular think that they can gain eternal salvation while remaining slothful and negligent of spirit, for the Apostle warns us: "In fear and trembling shall you work out your salvation."

It is clear then, on the highest authority, that we should not attempt to draw a hard-and-fast line. Yet we would certainly be staying far from all the borderlines in saying this: he who treats his Scapular as a sign of sincerely meant consecration to Mary, who makes an honest and persevering effort to be a devout servant of Mary — such a one may lean confidently on the Scapular Promise.[25] In speaking of devotion to Mary in general, Pope Pius XI gives us ample warrant for this statement:

. . . nor would he incur eternal death whom the Most Blessed Virgin assists, especially at his last hour. This opinion of the

Doctors of the Church, in harmony with the sentiments of the Christian people, and supported by the experience of all times, depends especially on this reason: the fact that the Sorrowful Virgin shared in the work of the Redemption with Jesus Christ. . . .[26]

Pope Pius XII likewise urges us to treat the Scapular as a sign of consecration:

. . . finally may it be to them a Sign of their Consecration to the Most Sacred Heart of the Immaculate Virgin, which (consecration) in recent times we have so strongly recommended.[27]

Father Lynch himself, in line with the recommendation of the Holy Father, explains beautifully that the ideal form of the Scapular devotion is that it should be the outward sign of a total consecration to Mary, a consecration according to the method explained by the Venerable Carmelite, Michael of St. Augustine, and by St. Louis de Montfort.[28]

Besides the great Scapular promise given through St. Simon Stock, there is another extraordinary favor attached to the Scapular. This favor, which is called the Sabbatine Privilege, was announced by our Blessed Mother in a vision to Pope John XXII on March 3, 1322.[29] The original copy of the Bull in which Pope John XXII proclaimed the privilege has been lost. Several copies of the original were made, but there are certain variations in the wording of these copies. According to one text, Our Lady promised that those who fulfill certain conditions would be freed from Purgatory on the first Saturday after death; the other form of the text merely promised special assistance towards a speedier deliverance.

The fact that the original copy of the Bull is lost, and the fact that there are variations in the text, have caused some Catholics to doubt the authenticity of the Sabbatine Privilege vision. Unfortunately, we do not yet have any complete study of this matter such as Father Xiberta has made of the St. Simon Stock vision. Again, however, the warm approval and recommendation of the

Holy See makes such discussion less necessary. Out of the several papal texts on this matter, we shall be content with one from Pope Pius XII, who, in the letter from which we quoted above, said:

> And certainly this most gentle Mother will not delay to open, as soon as possible, through Her intercession with God, the gates of Heaven for Her children who are expiating their faults in Purgatory — a trust based on that promise known as the Sabbatine Privilege.[30]

We note that the Holy Father does not undertake to decide which of the two forms of the promise is the original. Following his example, we shall leave the matter undecided, although we may justly, and not without reason, hope that the stronger reading is true.

Three conditions are required for gaining the Sabbatine Privilege: one must wear the Scapular, observe chastity according to his state in life, and recite the Office.[31] The observance of chastity means that one must keep the Sixth and Ninth Commandments according as they apply in his state of life. A grave sin against chastity cancels one's claim to this promise. It is, however, common teaching and probable that by regaining the state of grace, the claim is re-established, though repeated failures would probably mean that one would not gain the privilege in its fullest extent. The recitation of the Office is satisfied by saying the Divine Office in the case of those already bound to it. Others must recite (in any language) the Little Office of the Blessed Virgin. Those who are unable to read are allowed to substitute the observance of the fasts of the Church, plus abstinence on Wednesdays and Saturdays. If one who can read wishes this recitation of the Office commuted to something else, he must apply to a priest who has special faculties from the Carmelites for this purpose.[32] The most usual commutation is to a daily Rosary or to seven *Our Fathers, Hail Marys,* and *Glory be to the Fathers.*

Both the Rosary and the Brown Scapular are related in their

origins to private revelations, yet both have great intrinsic value independent of these revelations. The Rosary, as we have seen, does not depend at all on the Prouille vision; its power to please Heaven derives from the very excellence of its nature as a prayer. The Scapular too, if it is worn as a sign of a true interior consecration, gives us an assurance of Mary's protection in our last hour which does not depend entirely on the promise given us through St. Simon Stock. For, as we can see from the words of Pope Pius XI cited above, it is morally impossible for anyone who practices a solid, persevering devotion to Mary ever to be lost.[33] But the Scapular Promise does give us an additional reason for trust: it is a visible, tangible pledge of the care of our Blessed Mother for us, a care which, through the Sabbatine Privilege, extends even into purgatory.

In becoming man in Mary's womb, the Word made flesh showed to us the light of His glory "so that while we know God in visible form, we may be drawn by Him to the love of things unseen."[34] He continues through the visible Church and through the visible signs of the sacraments to lead us to interior union with Himself. Similarly, the beads of the Rosary and the cloth of the Scapular, though they are not sacraments, perform the function of outward signs: if we use them well, they will serve as means to lead us interiorly to an ever closer and higher union with Jesus through Mary.

NOTES

1. For a general survey, see Gabriel M. Roschini, O.S.M., *Mariologia*, IV.
2. In chap. XVI.
3. See C. C. Martindale, S.J., *The Meaning of Fatima* (New York, 1950), p. 75.
4. For a discussion of the evidence, see Appendix V.
5. See *AER*, July, 1950, p. 64.
6. See Garrigou-Lagrange, *The Mother of the Saviour*, p. 255.
7. On this problem see Appendix V.
8. Luke 1:41–42.
9. See Roschini, *Mariologia*, IV, 84–89.
10. This is the most literal translation of the Portuguese text. See both the original and the translation in W. T. Walsh, *Our Lady of Fátima* (New York, 1948), p. 225.

11. Canon 934.2.

12. See Seraphinus de Angelis, *De Indulgentiis,* pp. 192–93.

13. Such a method is suggested in Maisie Ward, *The Splendor of the Rosary* (New York, 1945), pp. 11–12.

14. See *ST,* II–II, q.83, a.13.c.

15. In *Way of Perfection,* XXX. See chap. XII, note 13 above.

16. In *The Mother of the Saviour,* p. 254.

17. See *ST,* II–II, q.83, 13, o.

18. See the pamphlet by Richard L. Rooney, S.J., *Let's Really Pray the Rosary* (St. Louis, 1947).

19. In *The Mother of the Saviour,* pp. 253–54.

20. Translated from B. Xiberta, O. Carm., *De Visione S. Simonis Stock* (Rome, 1950) p. 283 (Old Speculum text. See Appendix VI, A.1, text 3). The precise date of the vision seems to have been July 16.

21. See the summary of his study in Appendix VI, A.

22. See the complete text of the letter in the book: *Your Brown Scapular,* by Kilian Lynch, O.Carm. (Westminster, 1950), pp. vii–ix; or in *AAS,* 42:390–91.

23. In: Benedict XIV, *De Festis Domini Nostri Jesu Christi et Beatae Mariae Virginis,* II, 6, 8 (Prati in typographia Aldina, 1843), IX, 269–70 (written as a private theologian, not as Pope).

24. K. Lynch, O.Carm., *op. cit.,* p. 60. See also H. Esteve, O.Carm., *De Valore Spirituali Devotionis S. Scapularis* (Rome, 1953).

25. For a brief but excellent study of the theology of the great promise, see *Analecta Ordinis Carmelitarum,* XVI (1951), pp. 317–21, and Esteve, *op. cit.*

26. February 2, 1923: *AAS* 15:104. See similar statements by Benedict XV (*AAS* 10.182) and Pius XII (*AAS* 39:584).

27. In the letter quoted in Lynch, *op. cit.,* p. viii.

28. See esp. pp. 54–110 of *Your Brown Scapular,* and also Ven. Michael of St. Augustine, O.Carm., "The Mariform and Marian Life In Mary, For Mary," McGinnis (ed.), *Life with Mary.* On St. Louis de Montfort, see chap. XVIII above.

29. See Appendix VI, B.

30. Quoted in Lynch, *op. cit.,* pp. viii–ix.

31. Some writers group the material differently, and therefore list two or even four conditions.

32. These faculties are readily given to any priest who requests them.

33. See also Xiberta, *op. cit.,* pp. 24–27.

34. From the Preface of the Nativity.

XXIII... *Suggestions for a Marian Rule of Life*

I T IS DESIRABLE that one should formulate, with the help and approval of his director, a daily program, a general rule of life to be followed. This rule makes for perseverance, and tends to prevent us from doing or omitting things merely on the whim of the moment. It is obvious, of course, that such a daily program will vary widely according to the state in life and work of each individual. It is true that sanctity — growth in sanctity — does not consist primarily in a certain set of devotions; holiness consists in perfect love of God. But it would be a mistake to suppose that we can reasonably hope to grow if we do not make use of various spiritual exercises. Hence we shall suggest a sound spiritual program for a normal day. Priests, seminarians, and religious will find that their normal obligations amount to much the same thing as the proposed schedule. Lay persons will be able to approximate this scheme more or less closely. All will do well to remember that the chief difference lies in the amount of love that we devote to what we do. A modest program carried out with persevering, fervent love is worth much more than a packed and elaborate list performed in a perfunctory fashion.

A fixed hour should be chosen for rising. It should be early enough to allow ample time for washing and other natural needs, as well as for the essential spiritual exercises. It is bad for spiritual morale, and a sign of self-indulgent softness, to remain in bed for some time beyond the previously fixed time of rising. Those who live in the same building in which Mass is celebrated will find one hour before the time of Mass to be about the right amount to allow.

Even before actually arising, we ought to say some short prayer containing a brief offering of the day — e.g., the indulgenced prayer: "I am all thine, and all I have is thine, O most loving Jesus, through Mary thy Holy Mother." [1]

Since emerging from bed is for many persons one of the more difficult acts of the day, we try to put more love into it by means of some such short offering.

After dressing, many persons think it well to recite a few private morning prayers, even though they are going to attend community prayers. This is not necessary, if group prayers are to follow, but it is commendable. Whether alone or in a group, however, we should be sure to recite, among other things, a more complete form of morning offering. The one of the Apostleship of Prayer is excellent and widely used; and it is worth noting that if one interprets the words of that offering in the strongest sense, they could mean precisely the same as does the De Montfort consecration. [2]

We should also form the intention of gaining all the indulgences that will be available to us during the day. Most persons are in a position to gain many plenary indulgences on various days, through various titles — e.g., the indulgences of the Scapular, of the Rosary, of various pious associations such as the Propagation of the Faith Society. To keep track of all days on which various indulgences are to be had on these varied titles would be somewhat difficult, but there is a simple way to insure gaining at least the majority of the plenary indulgences available to us (only a little additional care would be needed to gain the others). In addition to the intention of gaining the indulgences, and the state of grace, a set of stipulations known as the "usual conditions" are required for *most* plenary indulgences. It is a simple matter to insure that we are fulfilling these "usual" conditions at all times if we go to confession at least twice a month; [3] receive Holy Communion at least once a week (the Communion required for an indulgence may be received from one day before, up to eight days after, the date on which the indulgence is to be obtained; therefore if one receives Communion at least once each week, he will automatically fill this condition); and make extra "pop-in" visits to the Blessed Sacrament whenever possible, and at each one say once the *Our Father, Hail Mary,* and *Glory* for the intentions of the Holy Father. Thus the third (and fourth) of the "usual conditions" will be assured.

One who is in earnest about his spiritual advancement will try to go to confession at least every two weeks, or better, every week, and will also endeavor to obtain at least some spiritual direction. Although it is not necessary that the same priest be both confessor and director, many advantages are gained thereby. Since direction is a normal and very effective means of spiritual growth, everyone should try to obtain at least occasional direction, according as the need arises.[4] Such help is especially needed in forming a private rule of life, and thereafter, in making any changes in our program of mortification, in difficulties in mental prayer, in the choice of spiritual reading, and, in general, whenever any decision of considerable importance is faced. In order that the director may know us well enough to be able to give helpful advice, we will need to open our soul as completely as possible to him; this means more than a mere impersonal recital of venial sins. If direction is sought in the confessional, it will be necessary to make oneself known to the confessor in some way (not necessarily by name) so as to insure continuity of direction.

Most persons will make their meditation best in the early morning, after their morning prayers. It is not strictly necessary that the morning be chosen for meditation, but there are certain advantages: there are likely to be less distractions in the early hours, and there is great danger of omitting meditation entirely if it is postponed until later in the day. Furthermore, meditation made in the morning serves as a good preparation for Mass. If one finds, however, that he actually does meditate better at another time of the day, *and also* if there is no serious danger of missing meditation by choosing a later period, there is no objection to such a change, unless, of course, one lives in a community where the rule fixes the hour.[5] Everyone should be able to find time for at least fifteen minutes of meditation, and preferably thirty.

By all means, Mass and Holy Communion should be included

in our daily program if at all possible. In order to assist most fruitfully at Mass and Holy Communion, we need to recall the principles explained in chapters XVI and XVII. We ought to try to realize that the Mass is the re-presentation of the sacrifice of Calvary. In the original sacrifice, Mary had an important role of co-operation as the New Eve. Hence she can help us greatly to join in the offering that her Son makes on the altar. We should also spiritually renew this oblation of the Mass many times during the day, thinking not so much of our own trifling gifts as of the priceless merits and sufferings of Jesus and Mary which are ours to offer, with which we "pool" our own infinitesimal offerings.

When Mass is finished, we should remain for some time in thanksgiving. For lay persons, this ought to amount to at least fifteen minutes from the time they actually receive Holy Communion until the time they leave the church. It is lamentable that the pendulum today has swung so far in the direction of laxity towards Holy Communion. Before the time of Saint Pius X, the Jansenistic ideas then widespread exaggerated the dispositions required for frequent or daily Holy Communion. The saintly Pope required only the state of grace and the right intention for daily Communion.[6] But he surely did not envision the neglect of proper thanksgiving which is becoming commonplace. In our thanksgiving, let us not forget the suggestions given in chapter XVII on the way to ask Mary's help in welcoming her Son.

Once we have left the church after Mass, we will go to our daily work. Let us not forget during the day to try to live in the presence of Mary, and in a spirit of union with her and dependence on her so that she may keep us close to her Divine Son. We should remember also that even the ordinary acts of our day provide opportunity for merit. The more love we put into them, and the more we learn to see them as part of God's plan for us, the more valuable they will become. It is possible to grow in holiness by doing merely ordinary things with really great love. Hence we ought to renew the morning offering fervently many times during the day. Even recreations and the pleasure we find in our work can be means of merit. In taking pleasure in any of these lawful things, it should be in this spirit: "O my God, you have placed this pleasure here for me as a part of your plan. I accept it with thanks from your hands. O Mary, help me to use it without attachment, and in such a way that it may be for me a means of serving God better." But we should not forget to practice at least a little mortification every day, especially at meal-time.[7] For, as we noted in chapter XV, some persons who practice mortifications well in other respects, make of eating and drinking a compensation for the sacrifice of other pleasures, though they probably do not realize that they are doing so. Eating and drinking are not inspiring means of recreation for human beings.

At any opportune time in our day, in addition to our brief visits we should try to get in one longer visit, of at least fifteen minutes. It is best not to fill this time, at least not entirely, with prayers from a book. It is good to make it an informal conversation like the colloquy in meditation (it may be mental or vocal prayer). We begin much as at meditation, realizing where we are, before whom we are, thinking of our nothingness and sinfulness. Therefore we should ask Mary to help us to speak to her Son, and to offer her own love and adoration to supply for our deficiencies. But we should also offer our own small love. Then we might tell Him of our daily affairs, both pleasant and unpleasant, and offer the acts of the day to Him through Mary. We should express our sorrow for our defects, ask for needed help, and give thanks for favors received.

We should pause occasionally, not expecting a voice from the tabernacle, but hoping for a response in the form of ordinary actual graces of light and strength (being careful to avoid mere emotional self-deception). If at times we are too dull to converse in this way, we may use vocal prayers, or may use a book to help us, or we may choose a familiar prayer, and say it slowly, pausing to let every phrase sink in. And, of course, we need not go through all these steps on each occasion; sometimes we may spend the entire period on one phase — e.g., on adoration. Something very much like the prayer of simplicity[8] easily develops during visits. At least once a week we should make a complete Holy Hour.

Outside the time of our daily visit, we will be sure to accommodate at least five decades of the Rosary. If time allows, we will recite the complete fifteen decades. While it is desirable to recite it in church, we will find opportunity to manage an extra Rosary now and then — e.g., en route to work.[9]

So far as time permits, we will do some spiritual reading. Some days may permit only five minutes, other days much more. The important thing is to see that over the space of a week we average a respectable amount of good reading. This reading may be done in the presence of the Blessed Sacrament (but should not be counted as our visit) or in any other place. There are many kinds of suitable books for our reading. The rate of speed at which we read and the general attitude to be taken will vary with the book and with ourselves. Obviously, some writings should be read very slowly, so as to apply them to ourselves, to remember all we can of their content. In this class fall especially the more solid works containing much systematic information about the spiritual life — e.g., *The Three Ages of the Interior Life,* by Garrigou-Lagrange, or St. Francis de Sales' *Introduction to the Devout Life.* Books such as these should be read very slowly, no more than a chapter a day, and should be taken as seriously as though the author were speaking personally to us about our own souls. Some other works are not so packed with information, but are useful for providing spiritual stimulation and inspiration; such are the various lives of the saints, or some lives of Christ. According to the character of each, we may read in larger or smaller doses. And of course the most basic spiritual reading is Holy Scripture; one should read at least a chapter of it daily. As souls grow spiritually, their love and appreciation of Sacred Scripture increases.

It is not good to read too many things at once; dissipation of energy might result, and we might not finish anything. Yet it is profitable to read parallel treatments of the same subject at the same time; e.g., while reading the *Introduction to the Devout Life* of St. Francis de Sales, we might read the writings of others on the same subject as the chapter we have just read in the *Introduction*. But this parallel method should not be attempted until one has first carefully covered one general treatment of the area to which this topic belongs, in a standard work. It is good also to vary the diet, remembering that *some books provide inspiration, some provide information — both types are needed;* and we should avoid making one type our exclusive fare for long periods. Our director should be consulted on this matter. All our reading should be prayerful, and done in the presence of Mary, to whom we ought to feel free to comment on the reading. We should not forget to begin with a prayer for light.

Finally, we have our private night prayers, which should include, among other things, thanksgiving for the blessings of the day and a diligent examination of conscience. In this examination, after an opening prayer for light and contrition, it is very beneficial to make not only a general survey, but also what is called a particular examen.[10] In the latter, we concentrate, for many consecutive days or even weeks, on some one special fault of ours, noting carefully whether or not it is becoming more or less frequent and studying the causes and occasions that led us into each instance of it. St. Ignatius of Loyola suggests keeping a written record, by means of check marks on a paper, of the varying frequency of the fault. He would have us make this particular examen both at noon and in the evening. By concentrating on our principal faults, one at a time, over a long period, it will be possible to eliminate our fully deliberate faults, and reduce the faults of frailty and surprise. We should carefully distinguish our fully deliberate faults from faults of frailty and surprise. *For fully deliberate sins, even though slight, are incompatible with perfection, and, if we allow ourselves to commit such sins out of affection for them or habit, they block our progress.*[11]

In particular, we should seek out the one fault called the dominant fault, the one at the root of most or all of our sins. There are many vices that may serve as the dominant fault; it varies with the individual. Some of the more usual dominant faults are sloth, gluttony, sensuality, anger, pride. Some persons, after looking for a time to find their dominant fault, prematurely decide that it is pride. But by the dominant fault we mean something a bit less deep; we might say that pride is, as it were, the sub-basement in all of us; whereas the dominant fault is nearer the surface — it is the basement. In some persons pride may serve on both levels; this is not rare. It is not too difficult to find the dominant fault in beginners; later it may hide under the appearance of virtue. We ought to study every sin we commit — even slight ones, and ask ourselves: What tendency helped lead me into that sin? It will be found that the dominant fault underlies most if not all our sins. We may find clues by asking: What is the thing that most generally motivates me, gives me sadness or joy? where do my thoughts drift when I am free? Our close friends and our director probably know what the fault is, if we ask them. And, of course, we must ask Mary to obtain for us the light and strength of the Holy Spirit, so that we may not only find this fault, but conquer it.[12]

In our general examination of conscience, we will do well to be constantly on guard for the appearance of any signs of the terrible spiritual disease called lukewarmness, of which the Spirit of God says in the Apocalypse:

> I would that thou wert cold or hot. But because thou art luke-warm . . . I will begin to vomit thee out of my mouth. [13]

Lukewarmness is a kind of spiritual languor that lays holds of a soul that once had been making progress. The soul allows itself to fall into sluggishness and a slackening of effort. The performance of spiritual exercises is merely routine: they are overrun with distractions which it makes little if any effort to banish. In time this leads to shortening, and then to suppression of many exercises. The soul no longer makes progress: it moves backwards, and conscience is blinded and the will is weakened. We must carefully distinguish this state from mere dryness, for in lukewarmness the soul is not merely dry, but practically gives up all effort. Lukewarmness is extremely dangerous and hard to cure, for it creeps on gradually, almost insensibly;[14] but if we are loyal to Mary, always trying to serve her well, she will guard us against this, as well as against other dangers.

The best act of contrition we can make should follow upon our examination of conscience. It will help to recall, in a general way, the worst sins of our past life, so that we may use them as a stimulus to greater sorrow and to humility. Of course, this remembrance should be cautious in the case of certain sins, lest we bring on fresh temptations thereby. A firm resolution of amendment, and a prayer for help to carry it out, should be added.

Last of all, we should have an approximately fixed time for retiring. We ought to retire in time to obtain sufficient sleep, considering our hour of rising. The amount of sleep needed varies with the individual and with his age and state of health.

Priests and religious still will have the Office to recite. Not that they should leave it until the last thing. It is far better, for those who do not recite it in common, to divide it into two or three portions, well distributed throughout the day. After the Mass, the Office is one of the most powerful of all prayers; one who is assigned by the Church to recite it does so in the name of the Church, even though he recites it alone. His is a weighty obligation, not to be treated lightly. Furthermore, practically all of the Office is taken from Holy Scripture, and hence is inspired by the Holy Spirit. The psalms, which Mary herself so often said, provide excellent food for meditation, sometimes on the subject of the text, sometimes on other fitting subjects; i.e., we may use them like the *Aves* in the Rosary, and meditate while saying them. Many lay persons today are taking up the Office, either the Little Office of the Blessed Virgin, or the Divine Office. This is to be encouraged.

This list of suggestions may seem formidable at first sight. It is not necessary, however, that everyone adopt every practice suggested: there will certainly be variations according to one's state in life, spiritual attractions, and other individual differences.

But the means suggested are among the most basic and valuable; they include chiefly those exercises that the Church suggests or prescribes for priests and religious. Even persons living in the world, if they sincerely try, will find it possible to carry out a great many of these suggestions. Of course, all these things are but means to growth in the love of God and neighbor; it is love that makes the great difference. But to pretend to wish to grow in love, while neglecting the normal means that are readily available, is to deceive oneself.

Thus we have come to the end of a day with Mary. We have much cause to be thankful for our Faith, for Mary. The words of Our Lord certainly apply in the fullest sense to us: "For I say to you, that many prophets and kings have desired to see the things that you see, and have not seen them; and to hear the things that you hear, and have not heard them." [15] Of all men of all ages and even of those alive today, few have been or are privileged to live so close to Jesus and Mary as we are able to do. Great should be our gratitude, and our sense of unworthiness. Great too and constant should be our joy, a joy that earthly troubles, shallow as they are, cannot destroy. Hence it is that St. Paul, in enumerating the fruits of the Holy Spirit, mentions joy, but not gloom or sadness.[16] Hence it is that the same Paul writes to the Philippians: "Rejoice in the Lord always; again I say, rejoice." [17] Let us respond to the divine generosity by joyfully giving to God all that we can through Mary.

NOTES

1. This is really a short renewal of the De Montfort consecration described in chap. XVIII.

2. See the revised edition of the Statutes of the Apostleship of Prayer, as approved by the Holy See on October 28, 1951.

3. Anyone who receives Holy Communion at least five times a week is exempt from even the twice-monthly confession so long as he stays in the state of grace. A Jubilee indulgence, however, requires an extra confession by all.

4. See also note 6 on chap. X.

5. See the note at the end of chap. XII on the problem of the time of meditation for married persons.

6. That is, the intention of pleasing God, of growing in His love, and of obtaining a divine remedy for our weaknesses and defects.

7. St. Francis de Sales, in his *Introduction to the Devout Life,* III, xxiii, explains this well.

8. See chap. XII.

9. See again chap. XXII on methods of meditating on the mysteries.

10. On the particular examen, see especially the treatment in the *Spiritual Exercises* of St. Ignatius Loyola. See also Tanquerey, *The Spiritual Life,* §§468–76; and L. Beaudenom, *Spiritual Progress* (Baltimore, 1950).

11. On the relation of fully deliberate sins and imperfections to spiritual progress and on the possibility of avoiding all venial sins, see chap. IX. In our examination, we may notice that sometimes we can scarcely find any faults in ourselves. This is ordinarily due to poor spiritual eyesight. We need to pray for light and humility. We need to become conscious even of imperfections, and of the possibilities of sin accidentally occurring in imperfections. On this latter point, see chap. IX, and Garrigou-Lagrange, *Christian Perfection and Contemplation,* pp. 427–34, and, by the same author, *The Love of God and the Cross of Jesus,* I, 318–44.

12. Garrigou-Lagrange, *The Three Ages of the Interior Life,* I, 314–22.

13. Apoc. 3:15–16.

14. On lukewarmness, see Tanquerey, *The Spiritual Life,* §§1270–80 (but note that Tanquerey uses the term "illuminative way" in a considerably different sense from that in which we used it in chap. XIII; see note 29, chap. XIII). See also L. Beaudenom, *Spiritual Progress,* Vol. I.

15. Luke 10:24.

16. Gal. 5.22–23.

17. Phil. 4:4.

APPENDIX I

Selected Passages from the Fathers on the New Eve and Related Ideas

1. *St. Justin Martyr* (c. A.D. 100–165)

... we have understood that He came forth from the Father before all things ... and was made man of the Virgin, so that the disobedience brought on by the serpent might be canceled out in the same manner in which it had begun. For Eve, being untouched and a virgin, conceiving the word from the serpent, brought forth disobedience and death. But Mary the Virgin, having received faith and joy, when the angel Gabriel announced to her that the Spirit of the Lord would come upon her and the power of the Most High would overshadow her so that the Holy One born of her would be the Son of God, answered: "Be it done to me according to your word." *Dialogue with Trypho,* 100.

2. *St. Irenaeus* (c. A.D. 120–202)

Just as she ... being disobedient, became a cause of death for herself and the whole human race, so Mary ... being obedient, became a cause of salvation for herself and the whole human race. ... for in no other way can that which is tied be untied unless the very windings of the knot are gone through in reverse: so that the first joints are loosed through the second, and the second in turn free the first. ... Thus, then, the knot of the disobedience of Eve was untied through the obedience of Mary. *Against Heresies,* III, xxii, 4

Although the one had disobeyed God, the other was persuaded to obey God, so that the Virgin Mary became the advocate of the virgin Eve. And just as the human race was bound over to death through a virgin, so was it saved through a virgin: the scale was balanced — a virgin's disobedience by a virgin's obedience. *Against Heresies,* V, xix, 1

And just as it was through a virgin who disobeyed that man was stricken and fell and died, so, too, it was through the Virgin, who obeyed the word of God, that man resuscitated by life received life ... for Adam had necessarily to be restored in Christ that mortality be absorbed in immortality, and Eve in Mary, that a virgin, become the advocate of a virgin, should undo and destroy virginal disobedience by virginal obedience. *Proof of the Apostolic Preaching*, 33, trans. Joseph P. Smith, S.J., "Ancient Christian Writers" (Westminster, 1952), XVI, 69

3. *Tertullian* (c. A.D. 150–c.240)

Therefore, since we are told that the first Adam was from the earth, God fittingly also made the next, the new Adam, into a life-giving spirit out of the earth — that is, of a flesh not yet used for generation. And yet, lest I miss the opening provided by the name of Adam — why did the Apostle call Him Adam if Christ as man was not of earthly origin? But here reason also helps to show that God, by a rival method, restored His image and likeness which had been captured by the devil. For into Eve when she was yet a virgin had crept the word that established death; likewise, into a virgin was to be brought the Word of God that produced life: so that what had gone to ruin by the one sex might be restored to salvation by the same sex. Eve had believed the serpent, Mary believed Gabriel. What wrong the one did by her belief, the other destroyed by her belief. *On the Flesh of Christ*, 17

4. *St. Cyril of Jerusalem* (A.D. 313–86)

Through the virgin Eve came death. It was necessary that life appear through a virgin, or rather, of a virgin, so that just as the serpent deceived the one, so Gabriel brought the good tidings to the other. *Catechesis*, XII, xv

5. *St. Jerome* (c. A.D. 347–419)

But after the Virgin conceived in her womb and brought forth for us a child for whom "the government is upon his shoulder . . . God the Mighty, the Father of the world to come," the curse was dissolved. Death [came] through Eve: life through Mary. *Epistle*, XXII, xxi (internal quotation, Isa. 9:6).

6. *St. Ambrose* (c. A.D. 333–397)

Through a man and a woman flesh was cast out of paradise; through a virgin it was joined to God. *Epistle LXIII*, xxxiii

From the virgin earth [came] Adam, Christ [came] from a virgin;

the former was made to the image of God, the latter [was] the image of God; the former was exalted above all irrational animals, the latter above all living things. Through a woman [came] folly, through a virgin [came] wisdom. Death [came] through the tree, life through the cross. *On the Gospel of Luke* 4:7

7. *St. Augustine* (A.D. 354–430)

For He received flesh from us and offered it. But whence did He receive it? From the womb of the Virgin Mary, so that He might offer clean flesh for the unclean. *Sermon on Psalm* 149:2
(Note that here St. Augustine presents Mary as being the representative of the whole human race at the Annunciation. *W. M.*)

Here also is a great mystery: since death had come upon us through a woman, life was born for us through a woman, so that the conquered devil was tormented by both sexes, that is, male and female, since he had rejoiced in the ruin of both. His punishment would have been too small if both had been freed and had not been freed through both. *On the Christian Combat* XXII, xxiv
(A very important passage. Note that St. Augustine associates Mary with Christ *in the very act by which we were liberated*. This seems to imply Calvary itself. *W. M.*)

... but certainly she is the Mother of His members, which we are; for she co-operated in love that the faithful be born in the Church. ... *On Holy Virginity*, VI, vi

Since our original fall took place when a woman conceived in her heart the poison of the serpent, it is not surprising that our salvation came when a woman conceived in her womb the flesh of the Almighty. Both sexes had fallen: both had to be restored. Through a woman we were sent to ruin: through a woman salvation was restored to us. *Sermon* 289, ii

8. *Oriental Rite Liturgy of the Second Century*

The following titles appear abundantly since the second century: Effacement of the malediction; Cause of salvation; Bridge to the Creator; Reconciliation of the world; Mediatrix of salvation; Reparatrix of the ages; Salvation of the world; Common salvation of men.

See E. Druwé, S.J., "La Médiation universelle de Marie," H. Du Manoir, S.J. (ed.), *Maria* (Paris, 1949), I, 433.

For a more extensive collection of Patristic New Eve texts in English, see: T. Livius, *The Blessed Virgin in the Fathers of the First Six Centuries* (London, 1893), pp. 47–59. Other Fathers quoted in Livius are: St. Theophilus of Antioch, Origen, St. Gregory Thaumaturgus, St. Gregory of Nyssa, St. Amphilocus, St. Ephrem, St. Epiphanius, St. Maximus, St. John Chrysostom, St. Peter Chrysologus, St. Proclus, St. Eleutherius Tornacensis, and the Epistle to Diognetus.

Still more texts in Latin are contained in Gabriel M. Roschini, O.S.M., *Mariologia* (2nd. ed.; Rome, 1947), II, 300–1, 304–9.

APPENDIX II

Mary's Knowledge of the Divinity of Christ at the Time of the Annunciation

The traditional view, and the view held today by the vast majority of theologians, is that Mary knew of the divinity of Christ at the time of the Annunciation. Since some few have doubted this fact, however, let us examine the evidence.

First of all, Mary certainly knew the Old Testament prophecies about the Messias. Among these, Ps. 109:1 spoke of Him as "Lord" and Isa. 9:6–7 (quoted in chap. II) called Him "God the Mighty." It is clear that the Hebrew *adonai* ("Lord") could be used of creatures, and it seems that *el gibbor* ("God the Mighty") was so used, once, in Ezech. 32:21. Yet, since *el* is one of the normal words for God, and *adonai* similarly is a normal word for Lord in the divine sense, it is hard to suppose that the Holy Spirit, the true author of Scripture, when speaking of the Messias who as a matter of fact *is* God, would mean them in some other sense. Now if the Holy Spirit meant divinity by these words, then, although many Jews did not understand, surely Mary, the Spouse of the Holy Spirit, full of grace and the light of grace, would be unlikely to miss the meaning. St. Paul, in the first twelve verses of the Epistle to the Hebrews, was able to see that the divinity of Christ is spoken of in several other verses of the psalms: how could Mary, with her surpassing grace, fail to see what St. Paul saw? Although St. Paul is great, his grace is incomparably less than that of the Mother of the Messias. Would a fact pertaining so closely to her mission be revealed to an apostle, but withheld from the Queen of the Apostles?

She could have learned of His divinity more easily from the words of Gabriel, for he spoke of Christ as "the Son of the Most High" and said that "he shall reign in the house of Jacob forever" (Luke 1:32) and also called Him "the Son of God" (Luke 1:35). Now the expressions "Son of God" and "Son of the Most High" could, of themselves, stand for an adoptive son, but in the context they obviously mean the true natural Son of God. For vs. 32 states that Christ "shall reign . . . *forever*," and only God can be king forever. In Ps. 88:38 the promise was made that David's *throne*, his line, would endure forever — but here the angel does not say that the

throne of the Messias will endure forever, but that "*He* shall reign
. . . forever."

Furthermore, numerous Fathers of the Church interpret the
"adoration" of the Magi as a recognition of the divinity of Christ.
The liturgy of Epiphany and its octave is full of this thought and of
patristic texts giving this view. Now how could we suppose that
the Magi would know of the divinity of Christ so soon, if Mary
herself could not recognize the clear indications in the Old Testament prophecies and in the words of Gabriel? The Magi had not
had these advantages.

The objection is sometimes raised that Mary did not understand
the words of Christ in the temple at the age of twelve, but it is
not necessary to suppose that every detail was revealed to her. If
she knew His divinity, and the general divine plan of keeping Him
hidden until the age of thirty, she could easily wonder at this de-
parture from the general plan.

Another objection argues that Mary would have to understand
the mystery of the Blessed Trinity (not revealed in the Old Testament) to know the divinity of Christ. But the Three Persons are
clearly mentioned in the words of the Archangel: Christ is said to
be the "*Son* of the *Most High*" — an indication of the first two
Persons. And He is to be conceived when "the *Holy Ghost* shall
come upon thee" — the Third Person.

Finally, it would be surprising indeed if Mary did not know of
her Son's divinity at this time. She would have had to miss or misunderstand so many texts that are clear enough in themselves. After
all, it does not seem that any very extraordinary grace would be
needed to show her their clear meaning — and how could we suppose that such a grace would be withheld from her who was full
of grace?

See also *Marian Studies* (Mariological Society of America, Washington, 1952), III, 122–25, and further references there; and P. F.
Ceuppens, O.P., *De Mariologia Biblica* (2nd ed.; Turin, 1951),
pp. 67–68, 76–77.

APPENDIX III

Mary as Co-redemptrix

A. Theological Terminology

For the sake of precision, theologians today commonly distinguish between the objective and the subjective redemption. The objective redemption is the payment by Christ of the price of our salvation, through His merits and satisfactions, culminating in the sacrifice of Calvary, by which a boundless treasury was set up, to which treasury nothing was to be added in future ages. The subjective redemption is the application to men of the fruits of the objective redemption.

It is clear, then, that the term *merit* will have a somewhat different sense, depending on whether it applies to the objective or the subjective redemption. Only Christ and Mary merited in the objective redemption. When anyone else merits, he does not contribute to this once-for-all acquisition of the treasury; rather, he merely obtains that graces be drawn from that treasury and distributed.

Furthermore, Mary's co-operation in the objective redemption may be called both remote (mediate) and proximate (immediate). Her remote co-operation is the divine motherhood. Her proximate co-operation is her service as the New Eve on Calvary. In chapter III we have shown that Mary co-operated immediately in the objective redemption.

B. Papal Texts

1. Pope Pius IX

Text: Ineffabilis Deus (December 8, 1854)

And therefore just as Christ, the Mediator of God and men, having assumed human nature, blotted out the handwriting of the decree that was against us, and, as a conqueror, fastened it to the cross, so the most holy Virgin, joined with Him in a most close and indissoluble bond, together with Him and through Him, carried on eternal enmity against the poisonous serpent, and, most fully triumphing over him, crushed his head with her immaculate foot.

Comment: We note that Christ and Mary are always associated in an "indissoluble bond"; therefore this bond should not be broken even on Calvary. Mary triumphs "with Him and through Him" in the struggle in which He "as a conqueror" took the decree against us and "fastened it to the cross." In the light of statements of later

Popes, it appears that Pope Pius IX had in mind Mary's immediate co-operation in the objective redemption. But without the help of other texts it would be hard to be entirely sure of that fact from the above passage alone.

2. Pope Leo XIII

Text 1: Iucunda semper (September 8, 1894; *ASS* 27:178)

For when she . . . gave herself to God as a handmaid to be His Mother, or dedicated herself wholly with her Son in the temple, by both these actions she already became a sharer with Him in His laborious expiation for the human race. . . . Furthermore, it was in her presence and sight that the divine sacrifice was to be accomplished, for which she had generously nourished the victim . . . [at the cross] she willingly offered her own Son to the Divine Justice, dying in her heart with Him, pierced with the sword of grief.

Comment: The statement that by her motherhood and dedication she "*already* became a sharer" implies that she remains a sharer later, even on Calvary.

Text 2: Adiutricem populi (September 5, 1895; *ASS* 28:130)

For thereupon, in accord with the divine plan, she began so to watch over the Church . . . so that she who had been the helper (*administra*) in the accomplishment of the mystery of human redemption, should also be the helper (*administra*) in the distribution of the grace coming from it for all time.

Comment: This text distinguishes clearly the objective and subjective redemption, and assigns her a similar role in each. Since there is no doubt of her role as New Eve in the distribution of all graces, by parallelism she must have been the New Eve in the once-for-all acquisition of the divine treasury.

3. Saint Pius X

Text: Ad diem illum (February 2, 1904; *ASS* 36:453–54)

Moreover, we must praise the most holy Mother of God not merely for the fact that she presented "to God the only-Begotten who was to be born of human members the material of her own flesh" (St. Bede, *L.IV, in Luc. XI*) by which He was prepared as a Victim for the salvation of men; but also for her office of guarding and nourishing this same Victim, and even, at the appointed time, of presenting Him at the altar. Hence that never dissociated manner of life and labors of the Son and the Mother, so that the words of the Prophet apply equally to both: "For my life is wasted with grief and my years in sighs" (Ps. 30:11). And when the supreme hour of her Son came, "there stood by the cross of Jesus, his Mother" (John 19:25), not merely occupied in looking at the dreadful sight, but even rejoicing that "her only Son was being offered for the salvation of the human race; and so did she suffer, with Him, that, if it had been possible, she would have much more gladly suffered herself all the torments that her Son underwent" (St. Bonaventure, *I Sent., d.48,* ad Litt. dub.4). Now from this common sharing of will and suffering between Christ and Mary she "merited to become most worthily the Reparatrix of the lost world" (Eadmer, *De Excellentia Virg. Mariae,* c.9) and therefore Dispensatrix of all the gifts which Jesus gained for us by His Death and by His Blood. . . .

But Mary, as St. Bernard fittingly remarks (*De Aquaeductu,* n.4), is the "channel" or, even, the neck, through which the body is joined to the head, and likewise through which the head exerts its power and strength on the body. "For she is the neck of our Head, by which all spiritual gifts are communicated to His Mystical Body" (St. Bernardine of Siena., Quadrag. *de Evangelio aeterno,* Serm. X, a.3, c,3). We are thus, it will be seen, very far from declaring the Mother of God to be the author of supernatural grace, which is the function of God alone: yet, since she surpassed all in holiness and union with Christ, and was associated by Christ with Himself in the work of human redemption, she merited for us congruously, as they say, what Christ merited condignly, and is the principal minister in the distribution of grace *(princeps largiendarum gratiarum ministra).*

Comment: Saint Pius X stresses several times the close and never-broken sharing of Mary with Christ: "never dissociated manner of life and labors," "common sharing of will and suffering," "associated by Christ with Himself in the work of human redemption." If her association and sharing held for the Annunciation and for the distribution of all graces (see chap. V on the latter), but not for Calvary, then Saint Pius could not say *"never* dissociated."

He makes clear that the very reason she is Dispensatrix is that she shared in Calvary: "Reparatrix . . . *and therefore* Dispensatrix. . . ." By the same words he also clearly distinguishes between the objective and the subjective redemption, and makes Mary's role in the subjective redemption depend on her role in the objective redemption.

"She merited for us congruously *(de congruo)*, as they say *(ut aiunt)*, what Christ merited condignly *(de condigno)*. . . ." The verb she *merited* in Latin is *promeret*, a present tense. This is, however, the commonplace historical present, a tense familiar in all Latin authors. We have rendered it by a past, since it refers to the past. Otherwise we would have to suppose either that Mary is still meriting (which is untrue, for merit ceases with death) or we would have to translate *promeret* as "obtains" (by prayer). Now this meaning would be badly out of place in the familiar balanced formula, *de congruo . . . de condigno*. We would have to suppose that Saint Pius X meant to do a thing never done before or since: that he abruptly changed the sense of this old and well-established theological formula, so that we would have, on Mary's part, a prayer *de congruo* (whatever that would be!) balancing a merit *de condigno* on Christ's part. This would be an almost nonsensical combination. A change so violent and unheard of must be proved, not assumed. See also the comments in chap. III, especially note 10 on the phrase "as they say."

In spite of the above reasoning, some Mariologists who admit that later Popes clearly teach Mary's immediate co-operation in the objective redemption maintain that Saint Pius X has not made himself clear beyond doubt.

4. *Pope Benedict XV*
   See chap. III.

5. *Pope Pius XI*
   Text 1: Explorata res (February 2, 1923; *AAS* 15:104)
   . . . nor would he incur eternal death whom the Most Blessed Virgin assists, especially at his last hour. This opinion of the Doctors of the Church, in harmony with the sentiments of the Christian people, and supported by the experience of all times, depends especially on this reason, the fact that the Sorrowful Virgin shared in the work of the redemption with Jesus Christ. . . .
   Comment: Mary is represented as the Mediatrix of all graces, especially of the all-important final grace; her share in the objective redemption is given as the chief reason for her present position.

Text 2: Miserentissimus Redemptor (May 8, 1928; *AAS* 20:178)

May the most gracious Mother of God smile upon and favor these our prayers and undertakings, she, who since she brought forth Jesus the Redeemer for us, nourished Him, and offered Him as a Victim at the cross, is, and is called, the Reparatrix, in virtue of her intimate union with Christ and an altogether singular grace of His.

Comment: Mary is in "intimate union" with Christ not only at the start of His life; but she also "offered Him . . . at the cross." This is an "altogether singular grace" and hence is different from the grace St. John possessed at the cross.

6. *Pope Pius XII*

See two texts in chap. III, the second of which is quoted at greater length in chap. VII; also a very important text on the New Eve in chap. VI, p. 46.

Text 1: In *Osservatore Romano,* December 8, 1937 (quoted in *AER,* November, 1949, p. 360)

After all, the application of the merits of Christ constitutes, together with their acquisition, a single complete work, that of salvation; it was fitting that Mary should co-operate equally in the two phases of the same work: the unity of the divine plan demands it.

Comment: Since this statement was made when he was still Cardinal Pacelli, it does not carry the authority of the Pope, but it does cast light on his later statements — if light be needed. "The unity of the divine plan demands" that "Mary should co-operate *equally* in the two phases of the same work." Now, since there is no doubt (see chap. V) that Mary shares in all stages of the distribution of grace, she ought to share in all stages, remote and immediate, of the acquisition of graces: "the unity of the divine plan demands it." Otherwise she would not co-operate *equally* in both.

Text 2: In *Osservatore Romano,* April 22–23, 1940 (quoted in *AER,* October, 1951, p. 265)

Are not Jesus and Mary the two sublime loves of the Christian people? Are they not the New Adam and the New Eve whom the tree of the Cross unites in sorrow and in love to offer reparation for the guilt of our first parents in Eden?

Comment: This text is from the Pope, not the Cardinal. Note the mention of the New Eve "whom the tree of the Cross," Calvary, "unites in sorrow" with the New Adam, "to offer reparation for the guilt of our first parents" — that is, for original sin: but that reparation was made in the immediate objective redemption.

C. Minimist Theologians

A very small minority of Catholic theologians have tried to argue that Saint Pius X and Pope Benedict XV did not intend to say that Mary shared immediately in the objective redemption, but rather that the Popes referred only to the subjective redemption: the *distribution* of the fruits of the objective redemption. Only about a dozen theologians today hold such a view, in contrast to over two hundred who give the same interpretation, at least substantially, as we have given above. All of the two hundred insist that it is certain that Mary co-operated immediately in the objective redemption, although some are not certain that the text of Saint Pius X is absolutely clear.

In the case of the text of Saint Pius X, the chief argument of the minimists centers about the present tense *promeret,* which we have already shown must refer to past time. In fact, one of the minimists, A. Michel, freely admits that *promeret* really does have past force (*AER,* March, 1950, p. 185, note 4).

The real root of the minimists' attitude, however, is found, not in any lack of clarity in the papal texts, but in a theological objection. Although it is stated in various forms, it can be reduced to the following difficulty: Mary was conceived immaculate by anticipation of the merits of the passion of Christ. How, then, could she share in earning grace when she herself stood in need of it? (see also *AER,* August, 1951, pp. 204–6).

Before giving the direct answer to the problem, we must note that the procedure of the minimists is faulty. Theology is a science based primarily on authority: in other theological questions all theologians look first to see what is contained in Scripture and Tradition, as interpreted by the Popes — and only then deal with speculative considerations. Or, again: a thousand difficulties do not make a doubt. A truth that is well grounded on positive evidence cannot be shaken by having an objection raised against it; otherwise, whenever any objection or doubt against the faith assailed a Catholic, he would be obliged, if he did not know the answer, to doubt his faith — which is absurd.

But to answer the difficulty directly: we freely admit that Mary did not join in earning her own redemption; she had to be redeemed first, and only presupposing that fact could she join in redeeming others. The word *first,* however, need not imply any difference in time (a difference of time would violate the unity of the redemption). For there are two ways of giving a thing first or second place: one in the *order of time,* another in the *order of intention.* In the order of *time,* I may do one thing at 4 P.M., and then, an hour or so later, do the second. But in the order of *intention,* I may decide that one thing ranks first, another second: I need not have any difference of time in the order of intention. Now it is similar in the case of the objective redemption. There are not two objective redemptions: there is only one, but within the one we may distinguish priority of intention, without making any distinction of time. In these two stages of intention (not time) we have, first, a stage in which the redemption is applied to Mary; and, second, the stage in which Mary is associated with Christ in meriting for all. It is obvious that there is no need to suppose any distinction of time. After all, as far as time is concerned, Mary had already been given the fruit of the objective redemption in an anticipated way at her Immaculate Conception — long before Calvary. Hence the problem vanishes. We might also note in passing that a similar difficulty on the Immaculate Conception continued to worry some theologians for centuries after Duns Scotus had correctly solved it.

One of the prominent minimists, Werner Goossens, has admitted that it is this difficulty that leads him to approach the papal texts with a feeling that he must not find the immediate co-redemption in them. See his *De Cooperatione Immediata Matris Redemptoris ad Redemptionem Obiectivam* (Paris, 1939), p. 56:

> Now that we are about to examine the chief arguments given by them [the defenders of the immediate co-operation] we consider it of the greatest importance to repeat that the *difficulties* just explained *forbid us,* in *interpreting the statements of the magisterium of the Church . . . to suppose that the doctrine* subject to these objections *is present unless the text or context express or demand it.* [*Emphasis added.*]

Goossens, on p. 57, cites the words of Fr. Lennerz, S.J., another of the chief minimists, in the same vein. Goossens himself shows his own preoccupation with the "difficulty" by returning to it again and again (pp. 142, 145, 153, 158, after dwelling on it in a long chapter, pp. 29–57). Such a preconceived notion forces the minimists to twist the meaning of the papal texts. It is really straining a point to suppose that all the words of the Popes about Calvary refer not to the *acquisition* of redemption (which was actually taking place then) but to the *distribution* of the fruits of Calvary.

When faced with the text of Pope Benedict XV, Goossens (p. 71) admits that the Pope affirms Mary's co-operation in the objective redemption, but he cannot see that it is an *immediate* co-operation, although the Pope was speaking of Calvary! So far as the present writer knows, no minimist has thus far attempted to explain away the Fatima text (see chap. III) and the Assumption text (see chap. VI) which proves not only the Assumption but the immediate co-operation as well.

Moreover, it is one of the gravest duties of the Holy See to guard against erroneous innovations in doctrine. The doctrine of the Co-redemption is no trifling thing. The minimist Lennerz rightly remarks that this is no mere pious question, but one "about the nature and essence of the very work of our redemption" (*Gregorianum,* XXVIII, 575). Now if so vast a majority of theologians were being led into so serious an error (it would be serious were it an error) by the words of Saint Pius X, surely the succeeding Popes would have an obligation to correct the majority — and at least they should refrain from giving more and more forceful statements to substantiate the "error." But the truth is, *every Pope* since Saint Pius X has given further texts that strongly support the majority view. The texts of Pope Pius XII seem completely inescapable. If this were error, the Holy See itself would be open to an extremely grave charge not only of not hindering error, but of giving it repeated support.

Not only the Popes, but the bishops in large numbers also preach this doctrine of the Co-redemption to their flocks. Juniper Carol, O.F.M., asked about 350 bishops scattered all over the world to approve a prayer containing this doctrine, and to grant indulgences for its recitation. Of the approximately 320 bishops who replied, 317 approved it. See his *De Corredemptione Beatae Virginis Mariae, Disquisitio Positiva* (Vatican Press, 1950), pp. 607 ff.

For further references, see (in addition to Fr. Juniper's work, which is perhaps the most exhaustive in any language): Gabriel M. Roschini, O.S.M., *Mariologia,* II, 251–393, and articles in *AER:* November, 1949, pp. 353–61; June, 1950, pp. 401–15; October, 1951, pp. 255–73. On the mode of Mary's co-operation, see *AER:* July, 1951, pp. 1–6; August, 1951, pp. 120–29; and September, 1951, pp. 196–207.

APPENDIX IV

Mary in the Protoevangelium and Apocalypse

INTRODUCTION: THE SENSES OF SCRIPTURE

In order to discuss the passages in the protoevangelium and Apocalypse 12, we must define some terms used in biblical criticism.

Literal sense: That which is primarily and immediately intended by the author. The author may, within the literal sense, use figurative expressions (e.g., "lamb of God") and may adapt his language to the usual way of speaking at that time (e.g., "the sun rose").

Scholars do not agree on the question whether or not one passage may have more than one literal sense *(plural literal sense)*. Nor do they agree on the existence of a *sensus plenior* (fuller sense), a literal sense determined not only from the words of a given text, but from comparison of many texts, and also, at times, from the teaching of the Church. Hence, the fuller sense may not have been perceived by the human author, though it was intended by God, who is the principal author of Scripture.[1]

Typical sense: In this the writer uses an event, a person, or an action to foreshadow something that is to come later. The original person or thing or event is called the type, and the later person or thing to which it refers is called the antitype. The existence of this typical sense in a given passage can be determined only through revelation, which is interpreted for us by the Church. Thus, for example, Isaac being offered in sacrifice is a type of Christ.

Accommodative sense: This is not really a sense of Scripture at all. A speaker or writer (the Fathers of the Church were fond of this practice) may *apply* a passage in Scripture to something not at all intended by the sacred writer.

A. THE PROTOEVANGELIUM: Genesis 3:15

We give two translations of the text. The Confraternity reflects the Hebrew, the Douay reflects the Latin Vulgate. The Confraternity is the more exact, but the Latin probably manifests an ancient tradition going back to St. Jerome, which expresses Mary's association with the promised Redeemer.

Douay: "I will put enmities between thee and the woman, and thy seed and her seed: she shall crush thy head, and thou shalt lie in wait for her heel."

Confraternity: "I will put enmity between you and the woman, between your seed and her seed; He shall crush your head, and you shall lie in wait for his heel."

State of the Question: The Marian interpretation is traditional. It is found in many Fathers. From patristic times to about the twelfth century many writers, especially those under the influence of St. Augustine, gave a merely allegorical interpretation to the text. But then, under the influence of St. Bernard, St. Bonaventure, and St. Albert the Great, the Marian view came forward strongly. Thereafter, up to modern times, the percentage of writers favoring the Marian view has been heavy. Since 1854, only nine out of 166 authors checked opposed it.[2] A text in the recent constitution *Munificentissimus Deus* (see below) caused some prominent opponents to change.[3]

Objections to the Marian interpretation.

Objection 1. It is a general principle of interpretation that in one and the same context a given word must everywhere have the same sense. Furthermore, a prophecy must be explained according to its context. But the word *woman* elsewhere in this context refers to Eve. Hence it must mean her also in vs. 15. Mary is nowhere mentioned in the context.

Answer: The above principle is incomplete. If *two different speakers*[4] use the same word in the same context, the sense need not necessarily be the same. E.g., in Isa. 28:10–13, compare the words of the drunkards in vs. 10 to those of the Prophet in vs. 13. Or again, in John 2:19–21 the word *temple* is used in one sense by Our Lord, in another by the Jews. But in Gen. 3:15 there are *two speakers:* the human writer, and the words of God Himself to Adam and Eve. As to the context of a prophecy, consider Isa. 42:1 and 19. In vs. 1, the word *servant* refers to the Messias, while in vs. 19 it refers to blind Israel. Now Gen. 3:15 certainly refers to the Messias. Is it out of context to find the Mother of the Messias with Him?

Furthermore, in interpreting Gen. 3:15, we can learn from St. Peter the Apostle himself. On the day of the first Pentecost, Peter gave a sermon in which he quoted the prophecy made in Ps. 15:

> . . . because thou wilt not leave my soul in hell, nor suffer thy Holy One to see corruption.[5]

Now in this Ps. 15 Christ is not even mentioned. The Psalmist speaks in the first person, and so seems undoubtedly to mean himself. Yet St. Peter tells us that he does not mean himself, but Christ. Why? Because the sense of part of the Psalm simply could not fit David:

> Ye men, brethren, let me freely speak to you of the patriarch David; that he died, and was buried; and his sepulchre is with us to this present day . . . he was a prophet . . . he spoke of the resurrection of Christ. For neither was he left in hell, neither did his flesh see corruption.[6]

David's flesh obviously did see corruption; hence he cannot be the one meant in the prophecy. Christ alone fulfilled it, so argues St. Peter. There are many prophecies to which this technique could be applied, and has been applied by the Fathers of the Church.

Similarly in Gen. 3:15, although the prophecy may seem to refer to Eve, yet she surely does not fulfill it, except perhaps in a very imperfect sense. For the enmity spoken of between the woman and the devil implies that the woman is to be sinless. How could we suppose Eve would win so outstanding a victory over the devil now in her weakened state, after the fall, when before the fall, with the help of the gift of integrity and rich graces, she fell so easily? We might admit some enmity between Eve and the devil, but hardly anything so striking as to fill the terms of this prophecy. Only Mary, by her absolute sinlessness and perfect generosity, and her co-operation in the Redemption, really has the enmity for the devil of which the prophecy speaks. Furthermore, if Eve is meant, why is she singled out for such attention by God? After all, it is Adam who is the head of the human race, he alone could ruin us. And the New Adam alone can restore us. It would make a strange conglomerate to see in this verse only Eve without Adam, and only Christ (for it is beyond doubt that He is prophesied here) without His Mother.

Objection 2: In the Hebrew text, the definite article is used with the word *woman.* Hence it points to Eve.

Answer: The definite article can refer not merely to someone in the context, but to some outstanding person, distinct from all others, who is known to the prophet, even though not mentioned by name.[7] Thus in Isa. 7:14 the definite article is used: "Behold *the* virgin shall conceive. . . ." [8] We may add also that there are certainly two passages in the New Testament (perhaps three) in which Mary is referred to merely by the title "woman." One is at Cana, the other at the foot of the Cross. Is our Lord perhaps giving her that title (otherwise rather puzzling) on those occasions to show us that she is the one promised in Gen. 3:15? In support of this idea we may note that He used that title for her precisely at two important points in her life: at Cana, when she first publicly exercised her mediation with Him, and on Calvary, when she was co-operating in the objective redemption as the New Eve. The third passage is in Apoc. 12, which, as we shall see below, certainly alludes to the protoevangelium. The argument given on the use of the article in Hebrew is sufficient, but the relation to the above texts also seems highly probable.

Objection 3: Not all the Fathers give the Marian interpretation. A study by L. Drewniak, O.S.B., *Die Mariologische Deutung von Gen. III.15 in der Väterzeit* (Breslau, 1934), shows that there are many Fathers who hold to other interpretations.

Answer: It is true that not all the Fathers mention Mary here, but many of them, especially under the influence of a passage in St. Augustine, are giving merely *allegorical,* not literal, interpretations. Drewniak failed to see this fact. His procedure is not always perfectly scientific. There are many Fathers, going back to the first century, who do give a Marian interpretation. The Douay reading, reflecting the Vulgate, goes back to St. Jerome, and probably reflects an old tradition. Other studies of the Fathers show that many more than Drewniak found do favor the Marian interpretation.[9] Furthermore, mere lack of support from some Fathers would not *disprove* the Marian interpretation.

Arguments for the Marian interpretation.[10]

1. All admit that the word *He* in vs. 15 refers to Christ. Now, if *He* refers to Christ, the *her seed* also refers to Christ, for a pronoun serves no other purpose than to stand for the same person or thing as its antecedent. Therefore, if *her seed* means Christ, the woman implied in *her* must be the Mother of Christ — Mary.

2. In the bull of definition of the Immaculate Conception, Pope Pius IX wrote as follows:

The Fathers and ecclesiastical writers . . . in commenting on the words: "I shall put the enmity between you and the woman, and your seed and her seed," have taught that by this utterance there was clearly and openly foretold the merciful Redeemer of the human race, that is, the Only-Begotten Son, Jesus Christ, and that His Most Blessed Mother the Virgin Mary was designated, and, at the same time, that the enmity of both against the devil was remarkably expressed.

Pope Pius IX here seems to be giving an official interpretation of the protoevangelium in a Marian sense. The objection has been made that the Holy Father continues his statement, telling us that the Fathers also say Mary was prefigured in the ark of Noe, in the ladder that Jacob saw, etc. Therefore, the objection continues, since it is obvious that these other texts refer to Mary only in an accommodated sense, Pope Pius IX must mean also to interpret the protoevangelium as referring to Mary only in an accommodated sense. It is to be granted that the context written by Pope Pius IX does, at first sight, create a difficulty. Yet we must note that the application of the protoevangelium to Christ is, by admission of all, in the literal sense. Is it easy to suppose then that the Holy Father, in the same sentence, and in stating the close tie between Mary and Christ (see "the enmity of *both*"), meant one in the literal sense, the other only in the accommodative sense (which is no sense of Scripture at all, as we have seen)? Furthermore, the accommodated texts *do not follow immediately* on the passage cited above; several lines, developing the thought of the *consortium* of Christ and Mary, intervene, and only then does the Holy Father cite the accommodated texts. And in citing them, he uses a different word: in speaking of Gen. 3:15, he had said, "The Fathers . . . have *taught* that . . . Mary was *designated*. . . ." But as to the accommodated texts, he says that ". . . the Fathers *saw* (the Immaculate Conception . . . in the ark of Noe, etc.)."

3. Pope Pius XII, in the preliminary part of the Constitution defining the Assumption, wrote as follows:

We must remember especially that, since the second century, the Virgin Mary has been presented by the Holy Fathers as the New Eve, who, although subject to the New Adam, was most closely associated with Him in that struggle against the infernal enemy which, as foretold in the protoevangelium, was to result in that most complete victory over sin and death. . . .[11]

Since we have already studied the context of the passage in chap. VI, a lengthy study will not be needed in order to show the meaning of the statement on the protoevangelium. In brief, we note that the struggle, the cross, was "foretold in the protoevangelium." Now Our Lord was certainly foretold in it in the literal sense, and Mary "was most closely associated with Him in that struggle" which the protoevangelium foretold. How, then, could we suppose that the struggle is meant in the literal sense, that Christ is meant in the literal sense, but that Mary, who is *"most closely associated"* with Him in the struggle, is not meant at all (for the accommodated sense is, as we have said, no sense of Scripture at all)? As a result of this text, many former opponents of the Marian sense have changed their opinion.

4. In the encyclical announcing the Marian Year of 1954, Pope Pius XII wrote, referring to the definition of the Immaculate Conception:

> . . . the foundation of this doctrine is seen in the very Sacred Scripture in which God . . . after the wretched fall of Adam, addressed the . . . serpent in these words, which not a few of the Holy Fathers and Doctors of the Church, and most approved interpreters refer to the Virgin Mother of God: "I will put enmity between you and the woman. . . ."[12]

Now if Gen. 3:15 contains the doctrine of the Immaculate Conception, how can we suppose that Mary is not meant in it?

Some theologians like to say that Mary is meant in the *sensus plenior,* while Eve is meant in the narrower literal sense.[13]

B. Apocalypse 12

The text:

> And a great sign appeared in heaven: a woman clothed with the sun, and the moon under her feet, and on her head a crown of twelve stars. And being with child, she cried travailing in birth, and was in pain to be delivered. And there was seen another sign in heaven: and behold a great red dragon . . . and the dragon stood before the woman who was ready to be delivered; that, when she should be delivered, he might devour her son. And she brought

forth a man child, who was to rule all nations with an iron rod: and her son was taken up to God, and to his throne. And the woman fled into the wilderness, where she had a place prepared by God, that there they should feed her a thousand two hundred sixty days. . . . And when the dragon saw that he was cast unto the earth, he persecuted the woman, who brought forth the man child. And there were given to the woman two wings of a great eagle, that she might fly into the desert unto her place, where she is nourished for a time and times, and half a time, from the face of the serpent. . . . And the dragon was angry against the woman: and went to make war with the rest of her seed. . . .[14]

Who is the woman? Some say it is Mary, some, the Church, others combine both views.

Objections to the Marian view:

Objection 1. The woman is said to be laboring in birth. But the birth of Christ was without pain. Therefore the woman cannot be Mary.

Answer: Pope Pius X, in the encyclical *Ad diem illum,* explains:

"And being with child, she cried travailing in birth and was in pain to be delivered." Therefore John saw the Most Holy Mother of God already enjoying eternal happiness, and yet laboring from some hidden birth. With what birth? Surely, ours, we who, being yet detained in exile, are still to be brought forth to the perfect love of God and eternal happiness.[15]

Objection 2: In the *Munificentissimus Deus* Pope Pius XII made this statement:

We frequently find theologians and preachers who, following the footsteps of the Holy Fathers, use words and events from Sacred Scripture with some freedom to explain their belief in the Assumption.[16]

After citing a number of these free interpretations of the Old Testament, he continued:

And furthermore, the Scholastic doctors have considered the assumption of the Virgin Mother of God as signified not only in the various figures of the Old Testament, but also in that woman clothed with the sun, whom the Apostle John contemplated on the island of Patmos.[17]

Hence it seems that the doctrine of the Assumption cannot be proved from Apoc. 12, and so Mary is not the woman referred to in the text.

Answer: It is one thing to say that the woman is Mary; another to claim the passage as a proof of the Assumption. Even if the woman is Mary, the text would not necessarily prove the Assumption. Some theologians think the Holy Father meant to cite only the Old Testament passages as examples of loose interpretation, making no such comment on the New Testament passages.[18]

Objection 3: How could the flight of the woman be understood of Mary?

Answer: The meaning is obscure. Some have taught it refers to the Assumption.[19] The fact that she was taken up on the "wings of the great eagle" might mean she went up by the power of her Son, while He Himself earlier "was taken up to God and to his throne" — the Ascension. The same interpreters then would make the mysterious 1260 days refer to all the time from the Assumption to the end of the world. Noting that 1260 days equal about 3½ years, they would equate that number to the "time and times and half a time," which would also total 3½. But this entire interpretation, according to some theologians, seems difficult to reconcile with the words of Pope Pius XII quoted above. Others would say the flight refers to the flight into Egypt.

Arguments in favor of the Marian interpretation.

1. Many allusions in this passage fit Mary well. She brings forth a son who is taken up to the throne of God, a son who is to rule all nations with an iron rod (compare Ps. 2:9, which refers to Christ).[20] She is clothed with the sun, that is, with the Sun of Justice, which is Christ. She has the moon under her feet: the moon is a symbol of the changeable things of earth, to which Mary is superior. The twelve stars could represent the twelve Apostles, whose Queen she is. The fact that she is spoken of in this passage as "a sign" recalls Isa. 7:14: "Therefore the Lord Himself shall give you *a sign.* Behold a virgin

shall conceive and bear a son. . . ." The mention of the dragon, the enemy of the woman, seems to be an allusion to the protoevangelium. And the use of the title "woman" may form part of the series suggested above, in the treatment of the protoevangelium (see protoevangelium — Cana — Calvary — Apoc. 12).

2. Saint Pius X, in the *Ad diem illum,* wrote:

> . . . "a great sign appeared in heaven: a woman clothed with the sun. . . ." No one is ignorant of the fact that that woman signifies the Virgin Mary, who, remaining a Virgin, brought forth our Head. "And being with child, she cried out travailing. . . ." Therefore John saw the Most Holy Mother of God already enjoying eternal happiness, and yet laboring from some hidden birth.[21]

Some have thought that the Pope here gave only an accommodated sense of the text, and it is possible that he did so, but not too likely. For we note the strong expressions: "No one is ignorant of the fact: . . . John saw the Most Holy Mother of God already enjoying eternal happiness." Recall that the accommodated sense is really not a sense of Scripture at all; would such strong language fit with what is not really a sense of Scripture?

Arguments for the interpretation of both Mary and the Church.

Those who wish to see the woman as *only* the Church have been greatly moved by the problem of her pain in birth. We have solved this difficulty in the words of Saint Pius X. Yet we must admit that in the context of chapter 12 St. John does seem to have the Church in mind. Now the woman cannot be the Church *alone,* for the Church is in no sense the Mother of Christ. Nor could this last difficulty be solved by saying that the Church continues the Jewish Church, and that the latter would be the Mother of Christ, for the Jewish Church persecuted both Christ and His Mystical Body.

Probably the solution lies in the fact that there was a tendency in patristic times to identify, in a certain sense, Mary and the Church.[22] In that way, we could take the woman of Apoc. 12 to stand for both Mary and the Church at the same time. The fact that the word "son" in this text seems to have a collective as well as an individual sense also favors this view (recall note 20 below).

Now if this double sense is true, then, since the vision seems to refer to the last days of the world, it might indicate that the Church toward the end is to take on a specially Marian character, in an age of Mary, as if Mary were again to bring her Son into the world (though not, of course, by human birth). St. Louis de Montfort prophesied that an age of Mary would precede the end — though he did not pretend to know if its length would be only a few years or some centuries.[23] Our present Holy Father, in a private conversation,[24] is reported to have said to the Director of the General Secretariate of all Sodalities in Rome, that we are now in the age of Mary.[25]

Conclusion.

From all this it seems certain that Mary is the woman of the protoevangelium. It is highly probable that she is meant, along with the Church, in Apoc. 12. But we must wait for clearer guidance from the Holy See before we can be certain of the meaning of the Apocalyptic passage.

NOTES

1. On this sense, see *Catholic Biblical Quarterly* XV (1953), pp. 141–62.

2. See the statistics cited from Gallus and Bertelli by A. Bea, S.J., in the article "Maria SS nel Protovangelo," *Marianum* XV (1953) I, 9–19, esp. p. 16.

3. Especially notable is F. Ceuppens, O.P., formerly a strong opponent. The *Munificentissimus Deus* appeared November 1, 1950. On January 15, 1951, he already had a *Nihil obstat* for a new edition (2nd ed.) of his *Theologia Biblica IV: De Mariologia Biblica* (Turin, 1951). See pp. 1–17, esp. p. 11, note 1.

4. In commenting on the sense of the radio message of Pius XII to Fatima in chap. III, we worked with similar principles — but in chap. III we were not dealing with *two* different speakers, as in Gen. 3:15. Furthermore, Gen. 3:15 is a prophecy, and as such needs special treatment.

5. Acts 2:27, citing Ps. 15:10.

6. Acts 2:29–31.

7. See Ceuppens, *De Mariologia Biblica, loc. cit.,* p. 5.

8. The translations do not carry the definite article, but the original does. See Bea, *op. cit.,* p. 8.

9. For an exhaustive study see Dominic J. Unger, O.F.M.Cap., *The First-Gospel: Genesis 3:15* (St. Bonaventure, N.Y., 1954). See also Bea, *op. cit.,* pp. 9–16; and Ceuppens, *op. cit.,* pp. 9–10, 12–13.

10. In addition to Bea and Ceuppens, see also Francis X. Peirce, S.J., "The Protoevangelium," *Catholic Biblical Quarterly* XIII (1951), pp. 239–52.

11. *AAS* 42:768.

12. *Fulgens corona gloriae* (September 8, 1953), *AAS* 45:579.

13. E.g., Ceuppens, *op. cit.*, p. 17.

14. Apoc. 12:1–6, 13–14, 17.

15. *ASS* 36:458–59.

16. *AAS* 42:762.

17. *AAS* 42:763.

18. See M. Jugie, A.A., "Le dogme de l'Assomption et le chapitre XII de l'Apocalypse," *Marianum* XIV (1952), pp. 74–80.

19. Jugie, in "Assomption de la Sainte Vierge," Du Manoir, *Maria,* I, 629–31.

20. The word "son" is apparently used in a collective sense as well as an individual sense, as shown by vs. 17, which speaks of the rest of her offspring. This double sense is easily understood of Mary, who is the Mother of both the individual Christ and of the Mystical Body of Christ (see chap. II).

21. *ASS* 36:458–59.

22. See G. Montague, S.M., "The Concept of Mary and the Church in the Fathers," *AER* 123 (November, 1950), pp. 331–37. See also Alois Mueller, *Ecclesia-Maria. Einheit Marias und der Kirche* (Fribourg, Switzerland, 1951).

23. St. Louis de Montfort, *True Devotion to the Blessed Virgin Mary,* §§ 51–59 and 158.

24. Reported in *Our Lady's Digest,* August–September, 1951, p. 119.

25. For an excellent defense of the view that the woman is both Mary and the Church, see B. J. Le Frois, S.V.D., "The Woman Clothed with the Sun," *AER* 126 (March, 1952), pp. 161–80. For a detailed study of the evidence of tradition favoring the same view, see Dominic J. Unger, O.F.M. Cap., "Did St. John See the Virgin Mary in Glory?" *Catholic Biblical Quarterly* (July, 1949, to October, 1950): XI, 249–62, 392–405; XII, 75–83, 155–61, 292–300, 405–15.

APPENDIX V

St. Dominic as Author of the Rosary

The problem: Is St. Dominic in any sense to be considered as the author of the Rosary, and, did he receive the Rosary from Our Lady herself in a vision at Prouille in A.D. 1206, as reported by Alan de la Roche (died 1475)?

The opposition. The Bollandists[1] and Herbert Thurston, S.J., have attacked the reliability of Alan, both in the case of this vision, and in general. They have been joined by many other writers, such as G. Roschini, O.S.M.,[2] who flatly states that the account of Alan lacks all historical foundation. Even some Dominicans discard the testimony of Alan. The position of the opposition is rather well summed up by Fr. Thurston in an article in the *Catholic Encyclopedia*,[3] in which he says:

> Alan was a very earnest and devout man, but, as the highest authorities admit, he was full of delusions, and based his revelations on the imaginary testimony of writers that never existed. . . .[4]

The writers referred to by Thurston are Joannes de Monte and Thomas de Templo. In an article published in *The Month,* Thurston adds:

> Never once, so far as I am aware, in Alan's numerous references to St. Dominic and the Rosary, does he profess to have acquired his knowledge from any tradition of the Order.[5]

Instead, according to Thurston, Alan bases his claim on the above-mentioned "imaginary" writers and on private revelations.

Thurston distinguishes three chief stages in the development of the Rosary: 1. Early in the 12th century, the *Aves* began to be popular, especially in multiples of 50. 2. Clauses of meditation were inserted by Dominic of Prussia (a 14th century Carthusian). 3. Establishment of Rosary Confraternities by Alan. Alan had delusions, in Thurston's belief, and, to help promote the work, Alan attributed the Rosary to St. Dominic.

Other evidence cited by the opponents of the Prouille apparition: counting devices of beads were in existence long before St. Dominic;

the custom of reciting many Hail Marys is earlier than St. Dominic; eight or nine early lives of St. Dominic make no mention of the apparition; the witnesses at the canonization of St. Dominic did not mention the apparition; [6] the early constitutions of Dominican provinces likewise are silent. Even some Dominican writers today are diffident. Thus Bede Jarrett, O.P., in his *Life of St. Dominic*, does not even mention the alleged apparition.[7] Having admitted that a practice of saying *Paters* and *Aves* on beads is not due to St. Dominic, Fr. Jarrett continues: [8]

> St. Dominic did not invent these things, though it would seem that he popularized them. To him, however, a papal tradition points as the originator of the division into decades or groups of ten, separated by larger beads called *Paternosters*.

Defense of the claims of St. Dominic:
1. *Papal support:*

For many centuries there has been a strong papal tradition that not only speaks of St. Dominic as the author of the Rosary but also suggests, in very guarded language, that there was heavenly influence on this authorship. The tradition can be traced to Pope Alexander VI, who, on June 13, 1495, wrote:

> Through the merits of the Virgin Mary herself and the intercession of Saint Dominic, [who was] once the excellent preacher of this confraternity of the Rosary, this entire world was preserved.[9]

Pope Leo X, on October 4, 1520, wrote of the Confraternity of the Rosary as being established by St. Dominic, "as we read in the histories." [10] St. Pius V (himself a Dominican) stated that "the blessed Dominic, inspired by the Holy Spirit . . . contrived . . . the Rosary." [11] Many other Popes throughout the centuries, up to our own times, have made similar statements; [12] Gregory XIII, Sixtus V, Clement VIII, Alexander VII, Clement IX, Clement X, Innocent XI, Benedict XIII, Benedict XIV, Clement XIV, Pius VII, Pius IX, Leo XIII, Benedict XV, and Pius XI. Benedict XIII is especially notable because of the fact that he, by a decree of March 26, 1726, extended to the whole Church the new historical lessons for Matins on the Feast of the Rosary. In them we read, among other things, that St. Dominic had begged the help of the Blessed Virgin against the Albigensian heresy, and then:

When he had been advised by her (as the tradition says) that he should preach the Rosary to the people as a singular protection against heresies and vices, he carried out the task enjoined on him with wonderful fervor and success.[13]

Benedict XIV, himself a good scholar, whose work *On the Beatification and Canonization of Servants of God* still enjoys high esteem, wrote in favor of the papal tradition before his election as Pope; [14] and after his elevation, he wrote to the Bollandists: [15]

You ask us if St. Dominic is really the author of the Rosary. You say that you are perplexed and full of doubt on this point. But what do you make of so many utterances of the Sovereign Pontiffs, of Leo X, Pius V, Gregory XIII, Sixtus V, Clement VIII, Alexander VII, Innocent XI, Clement XI, Innocent XIII, Benedict XIII, and still others, all unanimous in attributing the institution of the Rosary to St. Dominic?

Pope Benedict XV claimed that the Queen of Heaven, "used his [St. Dominic's] services to teach the Church . . . the most Holy Rosary . . ."; [16] and Pius XI wrote: " . . . St. Dominic wonderfully promoted it, not without inspiration from the Virgin Mother of God and heavenly admonition. . . ." [17]

There is, then, strong support from the Popes since Alexander VI for the view that St. Dominic was the author of the Rosary. Since this could be true even without the need of any apparition, we cannot safely infer that these statements of themselves endorse the Prouille apparition: references to the apparition are, as we can see, in carefully guarded language. Probably the strongest text on the apparition is that of the historical lessons approved by Benedict XIII. Even there, however, we note that the lessons do not explicitly mention an apparition, but merely say that St. Dominic was "advised" (*monitus*) by Mary. This could refer to a mere interior prompting of grace. On the other hand, the context in which the passage occurs is such as to recall the story of the apparition, and hence contains a suggestion that there was an apparition.

Regarding the force of the papal support, we must distinguish two questions. As to the Prouille apparition, the general principles on private relations apply: even when approval is given, the Church does not give any positive assurance of the reality of such apparitions (see chapter XXI). In the case of Prouille, the Popes have not provided any absolutely clear endorsement. As to the question of St. Dominic's authorship of the Rosary, independently of such an apparition, this is an historical point, outside the domain of public revelation. Many Popes have spoken clearly in favor of this claim of St. Dominic, but, on such matters, it is not considered that the Popes have the intention of binding the consciences of Catholics.[18] Their statements are primarily commemorative. Even so, the texts are deserving of great respect, in view of the position and the scholarship of the Popes.

2. *The testimony of Alan.*

According to Thurston's charge, Alan based his statements *solely* on the testimony of nonexistent writers and on private revelations. Whatever may be said for the disputed writers and for the revelations of Alan, Thurston has missed an important text, in which Alan states that his information comes not only from private revelations, but that he has the same facts ". . . both from tradition, and from the testimony of writers. . . ." [19] Therefore, Alan claims to rely *not only* on the two questionable writers and on revelations, *but also on the tradition of the Order.* It is strange that Thurston overlooked this text, which appears in Alan's *Apology,* the only work of his in which we are practically certain that we possess his authentic thought.[20] Many criticisms advanced by Thurston and others against Alan's revelations and his reliability in general are based on works that are known to have undergone considerable alteration at the hands of others. How can one be confident of conclusions based on works that have been tampered with?

In addition, it is difficult to write off completely all value from the account of a man who was, as even Thurston admits, a very devout person. And we must also keep in mind that, even though we might reject the account of the apparition, we are not forced thereby to reject also the view that St. Dominic in some way, such as the preaching-praying method suggested, could really deserve the title of "author of the Rosary," as so many Popes seem to insist.

3. *Evidence before Alan.*

The opponents charge that there is silence on the role of St. Dominic before the time of Alan. But silence is the weakest of all arguments, particularly when there is a plausible explanation for the silence. If, as we have suggested, St. Dominic introduced the Rosary by the preaching-praying method, then, since this method would easily fuse with already existing devotional elements, contemporaries might easily fail to realize what he had done, and hence, think it unnecessary to mention it.

But there is not complete silence before the time of Alan. First of all, it seems probable that the mysteries of the Rosary were well established in Spain before the time of Dominic the Prussian, whom Thurston credits with first inserting clauses of meditation in the Rosary.[21]

The most impressive evidence prior to the time of Alan has appeared since Thurston wrote. In his work on *the Rosary and its historical antecedents*,[22] M. Gorce, a French Dominican, has made a careful analysis of a set of verses by a French Dominican which seem to be from the early fourteenth century — that is, about a century after the time of St. Dominic. These verses (to sum up the conclusions of Gorce) seem to represent St. Dominic as having a mission from heaven to save the world in preaching a devotion to the *Ave Maria,* which is associated with meditation on some mysteries of our faith. Of course, the mysteries are not precisely the present set of fifteen — they are chiefly the joys of Mary, who is pictured as the Rose. The document is entitled *Rosarius.*

The analysis of Gorce shows that the document *Rosarius* probably reflects the view that the preaching-praying method is due to St. Dominic, with divine support, although whether this support was in the form of an apparition, is not sufficiently clear in the *Rosarius.* As to the name of this document we must note that the term at that age (early 14th century) was not restricted to meaning a set of prayers and meditations, such as our Rosary, but could also refer to a set of sermons.[23] This would fit admirably well with the view that St. Dominic employed a preaching-praying method.

Gorce, in the same book, also brings forth a few other pieces of evidence tending in the same direction. Chief among them are these: 1. A Dominican nun, Bl. Clare Gambacorta (1362–1419), is described in a contemporary biography as being accustomed "to say the rosary or other prayers on bended knee";[24] 2. a set of Latin verses, which were probably written in 1213, after the battle of Muret.[25] These verses represent St. Dominic as bringing roses, and as moving heaven and earth with his preaching. Victory is attributed to Mary:

Jam exultans Gallia dicit	Now exulting France says
Augusta Maria vicit. . . .	the August Mary has conquered. . . .
Dominicus rosas afferre	While Dominic so humbly begins
dum incipit tam humilis	to bring roses
Dominus coronas conferre	the Lord at once prepares
statim apparat agilis. . . .	to confer crowns quickly. . . .
Veritas surgit triumphans	Truth rises triumphant
Quia Dominicus praedicans	because Dominic by his preaching
coelum et terram commovit. . . .	has moved heaven and earth. . . .
Dominicus ab oratione	Dominic by prayer
finem malorum obtinet	obtains the end of evils
et dum pugnat praedicatione	and when he fights by his preaching
sortem justorum sustinet.	he upholds the lot of the just.

Conclusion.

The evidence in favor of a Prouille apparition is somewhat poor. No papal text openly supports such an apparition, even though some may hint at it. But the papal texts do often and clearly refer to St. Dominic as the author of the Rosary. For this latter claim, although not all writers accept it, we do have really respectable evidence. Hence it is preferable to support the traditional view on at least this second point, particularly out of regard for both the authority and the scholarship of the many occupants of the See of Peter who have favored and do favor it.

A note on indulgences

The chief groups of indulgences for the Rosary are:

1. *Rosary indulgences:* They include (among others) especially these: five years for each five decades; plenary for reciting five decades before the Blessed Sacrament (which need not be exposed; but Confession and Communion are required).

2. *Apostolic indulgences:* A different list is issued by each Pope early in his pontificate. The present list includes many plenary indulgences on certain feasts.

3. *Brigittine indulgences:* These include chiefly: 100 days for each

Pater, Ave, or *Credo* (but one must add the Creed at the end of each decade for the Brigittine indulgences).

4. *Crosier indulgences:* 500 days for each *Pater* or *Ave* (it is not necessary to recite the entire Rosary to gain these indulgences: even single *Paters* and *Aves* are indulgenced).

5. *Dominican indulgences:* They include (among others): 100 days for each *Pater* and *Ave* (if at least 5 decades are recited). There are many additional indulgences for members of the Rosary Confraternity.

The Rosary indulgences do not require the use of a blessed Rosary, or of any beads at all. But for the other groups of indulgences, the Rosary must have been blessed by a priest having the various faculties. Meditation on the mysteries is required for the Rosary and Dominican indulgences, but not for the Brigittine or Crosier indulgences. It is possible to gain simultaneously the Apostolic, Crosier, and Dominican indulgences for one recitation, if the Rosary has been blessed for each of these indulgences.

The Rosary must be made of solid material. Cord Rosaries,[26] and Rosaries with plastic beads are sufficient for the indulgences, but the so-called Rosary rings and bracelets are useful only for the Rosary and the Apostolic indulgences. The Rosary indulgences require no beads at all to be used, and the Apostolic indulgences may, if the priest has a sufficiently broad faculty, be applied to any religious object. The rings and bracelets may qualify as religious objects, but not as Rosaries.[27] In view of these principles, it is clear that one should be cautious, and slow to accept any modification whatsoever in the traditional form of the Rosary, lest he thereby endanger the gaining of so many valuable indulgences.

NOTES

1. In *Acta Sanctorum* 35, Augusti Tomus Primus, Die Quarta Augusti (esp. pp. 365ff.), Victor Palme, Parisiis et Romae, 1867. The Bollandists are a very scholarly group, founded in the 17th century by John van Bolland, S.J. They carefully sift the facts in the lives of the saints, to separate truth from legend, and give their results in the *Acta Sanctorum.*

2. G. Roschini, O.S.M., *Mariologia* (2nd ed., Rome, 1948), IV, 107, n. 1.

3. *The Catholic Encyclopedia* (New York, 1912), XIII, 184–87.

4. *Ibid.,* p. 186.

5. *The Month,* XCVII (1901), p. 298.

6. It is sometimes said that three hundred witnesses at the canonization were silent on the Rosary. This is true in a sense, but these three hundred

did not all give separate testimony: most of them merely signed as approving the testimony already given. See P. Denys Mézard, O.P., *Étude sur les origines du Rosaire* (Rhône, 1912), pp. 467–70.

7. Bede Jarrett, O.P., *Life of St. Dominic* (New York, 1924), pp. 110–12.

8. *Ibid.*, p. 110.

9. Cited in Mézard, *op. cit.*, p. 405, quoting from *Acta Sanctae Sedis pro Societate SS. Rosarii* (Lyon, 1888), IV, 1179.

10. Mézard, *op. cit.*, pp. 405–06, citing *Act. S. Sedis pro Soc. SS. Ros*, IV, p. 1117. It is true that Pope Leo X is quoting from a Dominican petition, but he seems to make the thought his own; such, at any rate, is the view of Pope Benedict XIV (see below, note 14).

11. September 17, 1569. Mézard, p. 410: "*Spiritu sancto*, ut pie creditur, afflatus . . . Rosarium . . . excogitavit."

12. See Mézard, *op. cit.*, pp. 411–12, 414–17 for these Popes up to Leo XIII (inclusive). See also Pope Leo XIII in *ASS* 16:114: "[St. Dominic] set out to fight for the Catholic Church . . . relying especially on that prayer which he himself first established under the name of the sacred Rosary . . ." (precatione cónfisus, quam sacri Rosarii nomine ipse primus instituit . . ."). Pope Benedict XV and Pope Pius XI are cited below in the text.

13. The Latin text in the Roman Breviary reads: A qua (ut memoriae proditum est) cum monitus esset ut Rosarium populis praedicaret, velut singulare adversus haereses ac vitia praesidium; mirum est quanto mentis fervore et quam felici successu injunctum sibi munus sit exsecutus.

14. Pope Benedict XIV, *De Festis Domini Nostri Jesu Christi et Beatae Mariae Virginis*, II, 12 (Prati in typographia Aldina, 1843), IX, 294–98.

15. Cited in Mézard, *op. cit.*, pp. 414–15.

16. June 29, 1921; *AAS* 13:334.

17. September 29, 1937; *AAS* 29:376: ". . . quem S. Dominicus mirabiliter provexit, non sine Deiparae Virginis instinctu supernoque admonitu. . . ."

18. See *AER* 123 (July, 1950), p. 64.

19. "Idem tum ex traditione accepimus, tum ex relictis scriptorum monumentis, ut legi" — from the *Apology* of Alan, cited in Mézard, *op. cit.*, p. 296.

20. See *Mézard*, pp. 303–14.

21. See *Enciclopedia Universal Illustrada* (Madrid, 1926), LII, 348–52.

22. M. Gorce, O.P., *Le Rosaire et ses antécédents historiques d'après le manuscrit 12483 fonds français de la Bibliothèque Nationale* (Paris, 1931). For those who might wish to examine the argument of Gorce in detail, the following list of pages and items found in the verses is to be noted: p. 51 — the Dominican order is especially the order of Mary; p. 53 — Mary obtains from Jesus that Dominic shall have great success in his preaching; p. 61 — the five principal joys of Mary on which one should meditate: Annunciation, Nativity, Resurrection, Ascension, and Assumption-Coronation; pp. 63–64 — in meditating on the five wounds of Our Lord, one should say five *Paters* and many *Aves;* p. 65 — comparison to the Psalter, which contains 150 psalms.

23. Gorce, *op. cit.*, pp. 42–43.

24. *Ibid.,* p. 100.

25. At the battle of Muret, Simon de Montfort defeated the Albigensians — with the aid of the Rosary, according to tradition. On pp. 104–6 Gorce gives the Latin verses as part of an excerpt from a work by Benoist, *Suite de l'Histoire des Albigeois* (Toulouse, 1693), p. 85. Benoist says that this set of verses appeared in October, 1213, and that he found them in an old register of a well-known notary who had many ancient documents.

26. This is the opinion of Seraphinus de Angelis, Substitutus pro Indulgentiis, in his *De Indulgentiis* (2nd ed.; Vatican, 1950), p. 163. He points out that cord Rosaries (unless, of course, made of thin string) are more solid than most Rosaries of the usual type.

27. *De Indulgentiis,* pp. 163–65.

APPENDIX VI

The Brown Scapular

A. The Historicity of St. Simon Stock's Vision

At one time the defenders of the vision of St. Simon Stock relied on the Swanyngton fragment, which purports to be a narrative of the vision by the secretary of St. Simon Stock; but it is too dubious to be used. Until recently, one of the chief supports was the Viridarium of John Grossi, who was Carmelite General 1389–1430. But the recent researches of B. Xiberta, O.Carm., have given us far more solid evidence. We shall summarize it below, and add a few additional arguments. The evidence can be considered under four heads: 1. the Catalogs of the Saints; 2. the testimony of William of Sanvico; 3. supplementary historical facts; and 4. statements of saints and theologians.

1. *The Carmelite Catalogs of the Saints:*

These catalogs exist today in six different forms: 1. the long, more common text of the Bamberg and Oxford manuscripts (dating from the 15th century); 2. the long text of the Paris manuscript (dating from the late 14th century); 3. the short text of the old *Speculum* of 1507; 4. the short text as edited by Thomas Bradley-Scrope (in the fifteenth century); 5. the abbreviated text of the Brussels manuscript (of the fifteenth century); 6. the long text of the new *Speculum* of 1680. For convenience, we shall hereafter designate the various forms by their numbers.[1]

The earliest extant copy of the Catalogs which carries a date is the Oxford manuscript (of text 1), composed in 1426. But the Paris manuscript (text 2) is, in the opinion of paleographers, somewhat earlier; it probably comes from the last part of the fourteenth century. These, however, are merely the dates for the *present copies* of these Catalogs. The question is: When was the *original* Catalog composed, from which these are derived? For it seems that all six, though they differ considerably, must go back to some original earlier form. First of all, it is clear that the Catalog must have had a fairly large circulation in the fourteenth century, since it was able to appear in so many different forms at about the end of that century. Therefore, even without further evidence it seems probable that the

original text must come from a time well before the end of the
fourteenth century.

But further evidence is available. One of the manuscripts, the
Brussels manuscript (text 5) gives us reason to suspect that it may
have been written by John of Hildesheim, a German Carmelite, who
died in 1375.[2] Whatever may be the truth about the author of the
Brussels manuscript, no student of the history of the Order could
claim that the form represented by that text could be later than the
fourteenth century, for after the collection of Philip Ribot appeared
(late fourteenth century)[3] no one could any longer neglect the role
of John of Jerusalem as the Brussels manuscript does. Therefore the
Brussels manuscript must have been written sometime *before* the
work of Ribot, that is, at least by about the middle of the fourteenth
century.[4]

Thus there is excellent reason for pushing the date of the first
form of the Catalog back well into the fourteenth century (only
about a century later than the date of the vision, which was 1251).
But there is good reason to think that we can push the date of com-
position back into the first decades of the fourteenth century. If we
compare the entry on Elias the prophet in the old *Speculum* text
(#3) with the same entry in the long common form of the text
(#1), we find this interesting difference: text 1 cites documents of
Popes John XXII (March 13, 1317) and Clement VI (July 19,
1347) in favor of the Order. But the old *Speculum* text seems not to
know these documents, and mentions only a Constitution of Pope
Boniface VIII issued in 1298. Thus it appears that the old *Speculum*
text goes back *at least* to the first few years of the fourteenth century.
We are thus within about fifty years of the date of the vision.

Now, although the original text of the Catalog cannot be traced
clearly any farther than this point, we may yet readily suppose that
the vision narrative existed in independent form before the Catalog
was composed.

2. *The testimony of William of Sanvico.*[5]

About 1291, William of Sanvico, a Carmelite in the Holy Land,
recorded that at the time when the Order was suffering great difficulties in England, the Blessed Virgin, appearing to the Prior, instructed
him to go to Pope Innocent, as he would receive help from him.

Sanvico does not give details of the vision, and this very fact helps to show his independence of the Catalogs. Yet he does agree with the Catalogs in reporting a vision as taking place at precisely the right time and in the right circumstances. The purpose Sanvico had in mind in writing explains why he does not give the details: he proposed simply to describe the fortunes of the Order in relation to its enemies and to authority. The fact that the Catalogs omit the mention of the appeal to Pope Innocent IV, which Sanvico gives, makes it extremely unlikely that Sanvico could be the source for the Catalogs. Hence we have at least two independent, early witnesses, within about fifty years of the vision.

3. *Supplementary historical facts.*

One of the tests of the credibility of any statement on a historical fact is this: How well does it accord with the background and known data of the era in which it lies? Viewed in this light, the account of the vision acquires new support. For Carmelite Constitutions at a very early date show a remarkable esteem for the Scapular.

This esteem is quite clear in the fourteenth century. The Constitutions of 1369 decree *ipso facto* excommunication for a Carmelite who would say Mass without his Scapular.[6] Still earlier, the Constitutions of 1324[7] and the Bordeaux Constitutions of 1294[8] consider it a grave fault to sleep without the Scapular.[9]

The ritual of 1324 prescribes, at a certain point in the ceremony, that the novice be given the "habit." The Constitutions of 1357 and 1369, explaining the word "habit" in the Ritual, add "that is, the Scapular."[10] The Bordeaux Constitutions of 1294 also use the words "Scapular" and "habit" interchangeably,[11] in the ritual of profession.

But the high regard for the Scapular can be traced to an even earlier date. In 1287, only thirty-six years after the date of the vision, the General Chapter of Montpellier declared:

> . . . the outer garment, which is commonly called the mantle, is not essential to the Order, nor is it our special habit. . . .[12]

The outer garment mentioned was the old brown and white barred mantle. It was changed to pure white, and declared nonessential. The same Chapter also ordered that the outer garment be so arranged as to reveal the Scapular and tunic beneath. These facts by themselves alone do not prove the special esteem for the Scapular at that time, nor do they prove that the Scapular was identified with the habit. But we gain further light on the situation from two early editions of the Constitutions (by Peter Raymund in 1357, and John Ballester in 1369). In those editions, a description is given of the Chapter of 1287. Speaking of those present at the Chapter, they say:

> They took a white cape as a sign of their religious profession . . . keeping however, *as before,* the Scapular, which was once called the capuche, for the special habit of the Order.[13] [*Emphasis added.*]

Thus, according to these early editions of the Constitutions, the Chapter of 1287 officially designated the Scapular as the habit. Furthermore, the words "as before" seem to indicate that, in declaring the Scapular the special habit, the Chapter merely confirmed officially an attitude that had already been in existence for some time.

These subsidiary facts do not, of course, constitute independent proofs that the vision of 1251 really took place. But they do provide some confirmation for the more cogent argument from the Catalogs.

We have also the minutes of the meetings of a Carmelite Confraternity for laymen in Florence, Italy. The records extant are from August 22, 1280, to November 1, 1298. In the record for November 1, 1298, we read that certain men who had been deprived of membership for some reason, came, *with capuches,* before the officers of the Confraternity to seek pardon.[14] Now, if we recall that the editions of the Constitutions by Raymund and Ballester (quoted above) spoke of "the Scapular, which was once called the capuche," it seems that this Confraternity was wearing Scapulars. Another part of the minutes of the same Confraternity contains what may be an allusion to the promise of final perseverance. For in it we read that the members met:

> . . . to render glory to God and to His glorious Mother, the Blessed Virgin Mary, that she may grant and give us the *grace* that we may be able *to persevere in good and to come to a truly good end.*[15] [*Emphasis added.*]

We cannot be sure that these two texts of the Florence Confraternity prove that the laymen were then wearing Scapulars as a result of a belief in the vision.[16] And the hope of final perseverance expressed might be founded on the general intercession of Mary,[17] not on a belief in the St. Simon Stock vision. Yet the evidence is of great interest.

The evidence from the early Constitutions, while not absolutely conclusive by itself, is much more impressive than the evidence from the Florence Confraternity. And, of course, it is best to consider both groups of evidence together as providing a historical setting into which to put the more cogent arguments from the Catalogs. In that way the subsidiary facts add something to the proof from the Catalogs, and show how well the narrative of the vision fits in with the history of the period in which it is set.

4. *Statements of saints and theologians.*

Many learned and saintly men have strongly declared their acceptance of the Scapular vision. Blessed Claude de la Colombière, S.J., the confessor of St. Margaret Mary, wrote a great deal on the Scapular. Here are two of his statements:

> I dare to say that of all the practices of piety . . . in honor of the Mother of God, there is none so sure as that of the Scapular, since there is none that has been confirmed by such great, such wonderful, and such authentic miracles as it.

> It is not enough to say that the habit of the Holy Virgin is a mark of predestination as well as the other pious practices that have been devised to honor her. I maintain that there is none that makes our predestination more certain than it, and therefore none to which one should attach himself with more zeal and confidence.[18]

When the Gallican Launoy attacked the Scapular, the learned Daniel Papebroech, S.J., one of the greatest of the Bollandists,[19] considered it a calumny when he was accused of siding with Launoy, and wrote:[20]

> He would be base who would deny that the practice of devoutly wearing the Scapular of Mary has been adorned with many favors and privileges from the Roman Pontiffs, and approved by divine favors.[21]

Pope Benedict XIV (writing as a private theologian, not as Pope) quoted with approval the words of Papebroech, and added in his own words:

> . . . let no one ever dare to reject the devotion to Our Lady of Mount Carmel, which the Roman Pontiffs have enriched with so many and such great indulgences; for, by the intercession of the Blessed Virgin, God has worked many miracles for the advantage of those who practice this devotion. . . .[22]

In our own day St. John Bosco, who died in 1888, was a great lover of the Scapular. He was buried wearing his Scapular. When his body was exhumed in 1929 the Scapular was found intact beneath the rotted garments, though his clothing had decayed.[23]

The Popes have shown their esteem for the Scapular by enriching it with a long list of indulgences.[24] To list all the papal statements would take many pages, but the statement of Pope Pius XII cited in chapter XXII should be sufficient. Additional statements may be found in *Take This Scapular* (Chicago, 1949), pp. 78–82.

Conclusion.

The evidence from the Catalogs, from Sanvico, and from early Carmelite Constitutions and other records shows clearly that we are not dealing with a mere legend; they provide at least some degree of moral certitude concerning the historicity of the Scapular vision. The extraordinarily high favor shown by the Church lends further support, although we must remember that the Church does not give a positive guarantee on matters of private revelation.

B. THE SABBATINE PRIVILEGE VISION

1. *The problem of the lost original Papal Bull.*

Many documents of Pope John XXII have been lost, so that the loss of this document does not militate against its authenticity. But official transcripts of the Bull allow us to trace it to an authenticated copy made in 1421.[25] Similar copies of the original Bull were approved by Popes Clement VII, St. Pius V, Gregory XIII, and others as well.

2. *The problem of the variant readings.*

The question of a number of minor variations in the reading of the text need not detain us: such variants were common in Carmelite documents of that age. Even some books printed before the sixteenth century, which are copies of other printed books, display small variations in wording. But, as to the two large variant readings, the copy of the Bull of Pope Clement VII, dated May 15, 1528, referred to liberation from purgatory, but this copy was never solemnly issued, and is therefore technically invalid. The disturbed state of Rome, after the sack of 1527, might explain the fact that it was never properly issued. Whatever the cause, the same Pope, on August 12, 1530, did formally issue a transcript, containing only a promise of special help, not liberation.

3. *Approval of the Privilege by the Church.*

On January 20, 1613, the Roman Inquisition, in the presence of Paul V, decreed that the Carmelites might lawfully preach the Sabbatine Privilege. The statement of 1613 was quoted with approval in our own day by the Sacred Congregation of Indulgences.[26] Moreover, St. Pius X, in granting permission to substitute the medal for the cloth Scapular, approved a decree of the Holy Office declaring that the medal would suffice for "all the spiritual favors and all the indulgences annexed to the Scapular . . . the privilege . . . called the Sabbatine Privilege not excepted."[27] Pope Pius XI, in a letter of March 18, 1922, commemorating the six hundredth anniversary of the Sabbatine Privilege, urged all Carmelite Orders and Confraternities to strive earnestly for all the indulgences available to them and, "particularly . . . that indulgence which is the principal and greatest of them all, namely, the Sabbatine."[28] A quotation from Pope Pius XII on the same subject is given above in chapter XXII.

C. THE SCAPULAR MEDAL

For many years it was debated whether or not the Scapular medal was a valid substitute for the cloth Scapular in all respects. It was clear that it was valid for most indulgences, and for the Sabbatine Privilege. It was debated whether or not it sufficed for the great Scapular Promise. Today we have an assurance in the form of an official declaration by the Carmelite Order that the medal suffices even for the great Promise.[29] It is still to be noted, however, that one should not make the substitution without good reason. To encourage the use of the cloth, the indulgence for kissing the cloth Scapular is not given for kissing the medal. Furthermore, while only the first cloth Scapular, the one used in enrollment, needs to be blessed,[30] every medal must be blessed by a priest having the proper faculty.

In blessing Scapular medals, the priest must use a separate sign of the cross for each kind of Scapular for which the medal is to substitute (for there are other kinds of Scapulars). And he must not convey any other blessing, such as the Apostolic indulgences, by the same sign of the cross.

A Scapular medal must have on one side the image of Our Lord *showing His Heart,* and on the other side, any type of image of the Blessed Virgin (not necessarily the Mount Carmel type). Some medals today are made with an image of Our Lord, but not showing His Heart: *these do not fill the requirements for a Scapular medal,* and must not be used. See *AAS* 3 (1911), p. 23.

D. A Few Practical Rules on the Scapular

1. According to the best canonists,[31] the faculty often given to priests in the Diocesan Faculties, by virtue of the Bishop's Quinquennial Faculties, to bless and impose the Five Scapulars with one form *presupposes* that the priest already has the faculty to impose each of the five separately. Hence it is necessary to obtain, from the proper Carmelite Superior, or through various Mission Societies, e.g., the *Pia Unio Cleri,* the faculty to impose and bless the Carmelite Scapulars. He who has the faculty to bless and impose also has the faculty to bless Scapular medals. Unless there is an additional dispensation, names of those enrolled must be entered in the register of a canonically erected Scapular Confraternity.

2. Cloth Scapulars must be made of two rectangles (other shapes are not valid) of wool, woven, not matted or felt, of brown or black color, or any shade in between. Cords must be sewed to the wool directly, not directly to the picture itself (if used), and only indirectly to the wool. Pictures are not required. It is permitted to sew one of the four edges of the rectangles (the top edge) to the top edge of another Scapular (e.g., of a Third Order). Then only one set of cords is required, but the cords must be put in between the two Scapulars, so as to be sewed directly to each. Cords (as far as the Carmel Scapular is concerned) may be of any material (even chains) and any color. The Scapular must be worn with one cloth rectangle hanging down in front, one in back. It may be worn inside, outside, or be-

tween other garments. It is not sufficient to carry a cloth Scapular in the pocket, nor to wear it in any way other than that described. The medal may be worn in any decent manner — on a chain, or cord, or pinned to the clothing.

3. It is necessary to be enrolled in the Scapular in order to share in the favors and indulgences. This is usually done on First Communion day, or the day before.

NOTES

1. For a description of these Catalogs, see B.Xiberta, O.Carm., *De Visione Sancti Simonis Stock* (Curia Generalitia, Rome, 1950), pp. 84–93.

2. The Brussels manuscript has certain peculiarities which agree with the known ideas of John of Hildesheim, e.g., both make the mistake of calling Peter of Thomas the Patriarch of Antioch. Again, they have in common certain peculiarities in their view of the history of the Order: both ignore the work of John of Jerusalem, who was said to have adapted the rule of St. Basil for Carmelites. We are not sure, however, that John of Hildesheim is really the author of the text found in the Brussels manuscript, for in a few points (omissions) John differs from our Catalog.

3. Philip Ribot was a Carmelite Provincial in Catalonia in 1379 and author of *De Peculiaribus Gestis Religiosorum Carmelitarum*. His work is merely a collection of earlier Carmelite writings.

4. Similarly, our texts 2 and 4 contain certain additions which are not found in texts 1 and 3. These additions appear to have been made as a result of the work of Ribot. Hence, since Ribot died in 1391, and our texts 1 and 3 are written *before* his work appeared, the original texts of 1 and 3 must have been written (at latest) by about the middle of the fourteenth century.

5. See Xiberta, *op. cit.,* pp. 83–84, 98–99, 212–16, 223.

6. Xiberta, *op. cit.,* p. 148.

7. *Ibid.*

8. See *Analecta Ordinis Carmelitarum XVIII* (1953), p. 140.

9. It is true that the 1324 Constitutions permitted the sick to sleep without the Scapular. But the reference is probably to the large Scapular, which was made in one piece with the capuche, and was bulky, going completely around the body like a dress. It is likely enough that the sick used a smaller Scapular. The Constitutions of 1357 and 1369 do speak of a nocturnal Scapular: see Xiberta, *op. cit.,* p. 149.

10. *Ibid.*

11. See *Analecta Ordinis Carmelitarum XVIII* (1953), pp. 152–53.

12. Xiberta, *op. cit.,* pp. 146–47, 243.

13. *Ibid.,* p. 150.

14. *Ibid.,* p. 152.

15. Quoted in *Analecta Ordinis Carmelitarum Discalceatorum* IV, 3 (January–March, 1930), p. 174.

16. We have evidence for the existence of Carmelite Confraternities at a still earlier date. For there is a Bull of Urban IV, dated May 8, 1262, which mentions permission to hear confessions of *Confratres*.

17. See chap. VIII.

18. Quoted in Xiberta, *op. cit.*, p. 45, n. 1.

19. On the Bollandists, see note 1 on Appendix V.

20. Quoted in Pope Benedict XIV, *De Festis Domini Nostri Jesu Christi et Beatae Mariae Virginis*, II, vi, 10 (Prati in typographia Aldina, 1843), IX, 271.

21. Papebroech did, it is true, disagree with our position on some points: he thought the promise was attached to the old barred mantle, which the Order put aside in 1287 — but he defended the vision. See Xiberta, *op. cit.*, p. 47.

22. Pope Benedict XIV, *De Festis*, II, vi, 10 (IX, 271). This was written as a private theologian, not as Pope.

23. See *Take This Scapular* (Carmelite Third Order Press, Chicago, 1949), p. 67. See also pp. 65–77 for other saints and the Scapular.

24. For a list, see Seraphinus de Angelis, *De Indulgentiis*, pp. 270–72.

25. See Eugenius a S. Joseph, "Dissertatio Historica de Sacro Scapulari Carmelitico," *Analecta Ordinis Carmelitarum Discalceatorum* IV, 3 (January–March, 1930), p. 182.

26. July 4, 1908: *ASS* 41:609–10.

27. *AAS* 3:23.

28. *AAS* 14:274.

29. See *Take This Scapular*, pp. 48–52.

30. This is true only if each candidate has been given his own blessed Scapular during the enrollment. If only *one* Scapular has been used in the enrollment for *all*, then the first one worn will need to be blessed.

31. See Seraphinus de Angelis, *op. cit.*, pp. 234–35.

QUESTIONS FOR DISCUSSION

For private, class, or study-club use

INTRODUCTION

1. Apply the principles given in the Introduction to explain the sixth beatitude: "Blessed are the clean of heart, for they shall see God."

2. Explain the growth of a hardened conscience.

3. What is the relation of external action to love? What is the "heresy of action"?

4. What is the relation of love to emotion?

5. How can one use his knowledge as a means to increase in the love of God?

CHAPTER I

1. How could Pope Pius IX define the Immaculate Conception when some great medieval theologians had denied it?

2. On how many different points can you compare and contrast Mary and Eve?

3. Compare the thoughts of the three witnesses quoted in this chapter.

4. If Mary was in the position of the New Eve even on Calvary, how would her position differ from that of St. John, who was also there?

5. What is your tentative opinion on whether or not Mary really was in the role of the New Eve on Calvary? Why?

6. How can we ever arrive at certitude on the correct interpretation of the patristic texts?

CHAPTER II

1. Did Mary merit to be the Mother of God?

2. Find out what the apocryphal Gospels are and of what value they are.

3. Why did not Mary after the Annunciation run to the Jewish priests and tell all about the visit of the angel, and that she was to become the Mother of Christ?

4. What virtues especially appear in Mary's conduct here?

5. Compare the Annunciation to the fall.

6. Who was Nestorius?

7. What does "full of grace" mean? If Mary was full of grace at the Annunciation, did she grow? How could she?

8. Were the relatives of Christ saints?

9. If Mary had infused knowledge, why did she have to question the angel?

CHAPTER III

1. Compare and contrast the roles of Mary and John on Calvary. What is meant by her official position?

2. Compare Christ and Mary on Calvary to Adam and Eve. Was Mary necessary?

3. Show from the words of Saint Pius X that Mary was the New Eve on Calvary.

4. Does Pope Benedict XV refer to Mary's work in the objective or the subjective redemption?

5. Compare the words of Cardinal Pacelli (in Appendix III B) to those of Pope Pius XII.

6. What is the difference between Mary's merit on Calvary and the sort of merit that any ordinary person can enjoy?

CHAPTER IV

1. What courses were open to God after the fall?

2. By what means was the Redemption made applicable to all mankind?

3. In how many ways did Mary co-operate in the sacrifice of Calvary? Compare her role to that of a layman at Mass.

4. Read and explain Psalm 49.

5. Look up in the Missal the official prayers of preparation for Mass which the priest is urged to say, and find the prayer to Mary. Comment on it in the light of this chapter.

CHAPTER V

1. Show how the doctrine of Mary's universal mediation is contained in the New Eve concept.

2. Explain the various theories on Mary's influence in the distribution of grace. Which do you prefer? Why?

3. If the sacraments cause grace, where is there room for Mary?

4. Those in the time before Christ could be saved only by faith in Christ to come. Therefore did they receive grace through the

merits of Christ? Did they receive grace through **Mary?**

5. How can Mary know the needs of all of us?

6. What did Mary do on Pentecost?

CHAPTER VI

1. Can anyone die of love? How?

2. Did Mary die? Can we prove it?

3. If Mary's initial love was greater than the final love of others who died of love, why did she not die sooner?

4. What is the difference between Mary's death and that of others who died of love?

5. What is to be said of the details of her death?

6. What is the principle of *consortium?* Review briefly the steps in Mary's life to which it applies.

7. Draw an argument for the Assumption from the New Eve concept.

8. Why was it especially fitting that the definition of the Assumption be made in our own times?

CHAPTER VII

1. What is the difference between the metaphorical and the literal use of the word "Queen"?

2. What are the titles by virtue of which Mary is Queen in a metaphorical sense?

3. What is the spiritual meaning of *Israel?*

4. Is Mary Queen of Israel?

5. What are the real titles by which we can call Mary a Queen?

6. Comment on each of the invocations to Mary as Queen in her litany. (For additional help, see R. Garrigou-Lagrange, O.P., *The Mother of the Saviour,* pp. 237–45).

CHAPTER VIII

1. What hint of God's plans for Mary can you find in the scene of the Visitation?

2. Since the merits of Christ alone are superabundant, what need have we of Mary? of the saints?

3. What are the advantages of approaching Jesus through Mary? Does this mean that we would never speak directly to Him at all?

4. What are the differences between the intercession of Mary and the other saints?

5. What is hyperdulia?

6. Why does real devotion to Mary assure a happy death for us?

7. Is devotion to Mary optional?

8. Can a Protestant or a Mohammedan be saved without Mary's help?

CHAPTER IX

1. Review the false ideas of perfection listed in this chapter; add more examples.

2. Does devotion to Mary compete with our love of the sacraments?

3. In what does perfection consist?

4. What are the two kinds of love? How are they related? What is pure, unselfish love?

5. What is imperfection? Is it a venial sin?

6. Apply what has been said of love of God to love of neighbor. If a boy and a girl lead one another into sin, do they have real love?

7. What things are excluded by perfect love of God?

8. Since I ought to make constant progress, how many Rosaries a day should I be saying at the age of eighty, if I reach that age?

CHAPTER X

1. What is meant by consolations? by aridity? Distinguish distractions from aridity.

2. What are the three sources of consolations and aridity?

3. What are the dangers of consolations? How can we avoid the dangers?

4. What are the advantages of consolations?

5. What are the ways in which Mary is present to a devout soul? to any soul?

6. How should we behave when in aridity?

CHAPTER XI

1. What is the greatest virtue? What is the relation of humility to it?

2. Imagine a few concrete situations in which pride could counter-

feit various virtues. Can extreme pride make one act humbly to get credit for humility?

3. Find instances in the Gospels in which Jesus or Mary showed humility.

4. Show how every sin implicitly contains pride (if you need help, see *Summa Theologica,* II–II, q. 162).

5. For what things do we need the help of God even in the natural order?

6. In what sense did some of the saints insist that they were less than nothing?

7. How can one honestly consider all others better than himself?

CHAPTER XII

1. What is the importance of meditation?

2. What are the chief qualities a method of meditation should possess?

3. What are the two essential parts of meditation? Which is the more important of the two?

4. What is the direction toward which the simplification of meditation should gradually tend?

5. What elements are usually contained in the introduction to a meditation?

6. Describe how to make the two principal parts of a meditation. What is the use of a book? What are take-off points?

7. What are the optional acts in the conclusion of the meditation? What should never be omitted at the conclusion?

8. What are the general characteristics of our lives which will facilitate meditation?

9. What are the three forms of meditation found in the purgative way?

10. What is Mary's role in meditation? Show her place in the various steps in all three types of meditation.

CHAPTER XIII

1. What are the three ways?

2. What is infused contemplation? How is it related to "acquired contemplation"?

3. What are the two nights? In what respect do they have a passive element?

4. What are the signs of the first passive night? Does St. John of the Cross always give the same three signs?

5. Compare and contrast the prayer of simplicity with initial arid infused contemplation and with prayer of quiet.

6. What is ligature? How should one behave toward it?

7. How should a soul conduct itself when it first receives infused contemplation? Is it totally passive?

8. Did all the saints have infused contemplation? All in sweet forms?

9. Did Mary have infused contemplation in the arid or the sweet form?

10. What service can Mary do a soul in regard to infused contemplation?

CHAPTER XIV

1. What is the relation of mortification to love? to humility?

2. What are the four reasons for mortification? How can we reduce them all to love?

3. Do indulgences make mortification unnecessary?

4. What are the two passive purifications? Are they common?

5. We all have much to do to make up for our own sins. Does this mean that we may not at the same time offer reparation to the Sacred Heart for the sins of others?

6. What factors measure the value of any given act of mortification?

7. What is Mary's role in reparation? Is reparation due to Mary herself?

8. How does Mary make our mortifications more valuable?

CHAPTER XV

1. What is providential mortification?

2. What other kinds of mortification are there? Compare their relative values.

3. What factors govern the extent of our mortification?

4. What are attachments?

5. Which desires are to be mortified? Why?

6. What is the purpose of the vow of poverty?

7. What are the rules for care of health relative to mortification?

8. What are the rules for the right use of pleasures and recreation?

9. Is the practice of detachment a danger to mental health?

CHAPTER XVI

1. What does Mary have to do with each Mass? How can we prove this?

2. How can Mary co-operate in the Mass when she is not physically present?

3. What indications does the liturgy give of Mary's association with the Mass?

4. Is it wrong to say the Rosary during Mass? Why?

5. Show the relation of Mary and the Mass to the Assumption.

CHAPTER XVII

1. What is a remiss meritorious action?

2. Does a remiss act merit an increase of grace? Does the increase come at once?

3. What factors largely control the increase in grace we may earn or receive from good actions?

4. Is the case of the sacraments parallel to that of ordinary good actions?

5. What is to be said of a man who receives Holy Communion daily for years, but does not seem to make much progress spiritually?

6. How can Mary help us to grow more from our Holy Communions?

CHAPTER XVIII

1. What is the precise meaning of the word consecration? What do people commonly have in mind when they recite an act of consecration?

2. What are the two phases of this consecration?

3. What are the spiritual gifts one has to give?

4. What is the effect of this consecration on our temporal property? on our bodies?

5. What does it mean to live in a spirit of dependence on Mary?

6. What does it mean to pray through Mary?

7. How can we know what Mary wants us to do in general? in a particular case?

8. What are the chief marks of a genuine inspiration?

9. Sister X has already promised to give all her merits and satisfac-

tions every Wednesday for a certain missionary priest. How does that accord with this consecration?

10. Sum up and explain in one sentence both phases of this consecration.

CHAPTER XIX

1. What are the three levels on which we may act?

2. In what sense are the activities of a man in the state of grace supernaturalized?

3. In what would such a man be lacking without the Gifts?

4. What is meant by the superhuman manner of acting? What does it do for the will? How does it affect the intellect? Is the intellect decommissioned?

5. In what way are the Gifts beyond reason?

6. Look up the special activities that belong to each Gift, and compare them to the following virtues: faith, hope, love, prudence, justice, religion, temperance, fortitude.

7. How do the inspirations of the Gifts harmonize with obedience to superiors?

8. How do the Gifts affect the clearness of motivation?

9. Do all souls have the Gifts?

10. What is the latent form of operation of the Gifts?

11. What is the relation of Mary to the Gifts?

CHAPTER XX

1. What answer would you give to a friend who said, "This is all very good, but I don't want my life to be Mary-centered — I want to be Christ-centered"?

2. Find out what attention is paid to the Blessed Sacrament at Lourdes.

3. Did devotion to the Immaculate Heart of Mary originate with Fatima?

4. What are the two chief elements in devotion to the Sacred Heart of Jesus and the Immaculate Heart of Mary? How can they be reduced to one?

5. Where do the nine First Fridays and the five First Saturdays fit in?

6. Sketch the life of St. Margaret Mary. Find in her *Autobiography* all the references to her devotion to Mary.

7. It is often said that Sister Josefa Menéndez' *Way of Divine Love* is a kind of continuation in our own day of the revelations to St. Margaret Mary. Find out the place of Mary in it (see especially the introduction and pages 194, 360, 367, 410, and 418).

8. Is the term "slave" opposed to the "liberty of the sons of God"?

9. What is the theological reason that we cannot outgrow our need of Mary?

10. What is the relation of confidence to these devotions? What is sentimentality?

CHAPTER XXI

1. What is the difference between public and private revelation?

2. If you hear of a man who works miracles, are you justified in concluding that he is a saint?

3. Is it permissible to desire to be the recipient of private revelations? Give reasons.

4. Is a saint who receives a revelation infallible in interpreting it?

5. Mrs. X. says: "I *just know* this apparition is genuine. You ought to have more faith." Comment please.

6. What force does the approbation of the Church have in private revelations? Compare the binding force of statements in encyclicals (on public revelation see chap. III) with the force of ecclesiastical approbation of a private revelation.

7. Which are the most valuable kinds of private revelations?

8. Show the relation of the message of Lourdes and Fatima to solid Marian devotion.

CHAPTER XXII

1. Is St. Dominic really the author of the Rosary? Did Our Lady appear to him?

2. Show why the Rosary is so powerful a prayer.

3. How is it possible to do two things at the same time — meditate and recite vocal prayers?

4. Describe the various methods of meditating on the mysteries. Can you add some additional methods to those given above?

5. Have you personally known of any remarkable favors granted through the Rosary?

6. Can we prove that Mary really appeared to St. Simon Stock? Does the value of the Scapular depend entirely on this vision?

7. What is the correct interpretation of the great Scapular Promise?

8. Show the relation of the Scapular to St. Louis de Montfort.

9. What conditions are required for the Sabbatine Privilege?

10. Is the medal sufficient even for the great Promise?

11. Describe the proper method of making a cloth Scapular. How may one unite two different Scapulars correctly?

CHAPTER XXIII

1. What is the advantage of a private rule?

2. How can one avoid bookkeeping in gaining most of the plenary indulgences that are available to him?

3. What is to be thought of meditation in the evening instead of the morning?

4. How can one offer Mass in union with Mary?

5. What is to be said of using the Rosary at Mass?

6. Find out something of the history of Jansenism.

7. What are the particular values of various kinds of spiritual reading? What is the most profitable way to read? Discuss the best way to read some of your favorite spiritual books.

8. What is the particular examen?

9. Mary was the Mother of Sorrows. Was she always sad?

INDEX OF TOPICS

INDEX OF NAMES

317